Front cover: The stele with the names of the hoplites from the Erectheïs tribe, who dies at the Battle of Marathon. Before the list of the names, there is the following epigram:

Φέμις ἆρ' hos κιχ[αν'] αίει εὐφαοῦς ‖ ἔσσχατα γαίες
Τῶνδ' ἀνδρῶν ἀρετέν πεύσεται hos ἔθανον
[μ]αρνάμενοι Μέδοισι
και ἐσστεφάνοσαν Ἀθένα[s]
[π]αυρότεροι πολλῶν δεχσάμενοι πόλεμον.

[The good reput – the eucleia spreading to the ends of the bright earth
Will be informed about the virtue of these men – how they died
And how they won glory for Athens, fighting the Medes,
And although far fewer, faced many in the battle]

After the empigram, the names of the hoplites come as follows:
Δρακοντίδες, Αφσεφής, Χσένον, Γλαυκράτες, Τιμόχσενος, Θέογνις, Διόδορος, Ευχσίας, Ευφρονιάδες, Ευκτέμον, Καλλίας, Αραιθίδες, Αντίας, Τόλμις, Θοκύδιδες, Δίος, Αμυνόμαχος, Λεπτίνες, Αισχραίος, Πέρον, Φαι[δ][ρίας.
Dracontides, Apsephes, Xenon, Glaucrates, Timoxenos, Theognis, Diororus, Euxias, Euphroniades, Euctemon, Kallias, Araethides, Antias, Tolmes, Thucydides, Dio, Amynomachus, Leptines, Aschraeus, Peron, Phaedrias.

The stele was found in Herodes Atticus' epavlis, at Eva Kynourias.

Athens, May 16, 2011

WITHOUT
CAVALRY

Dear   Mark

With

   Compliments

  H.A.G.S.

[signature]

Lt Gen Frogoulis FRAGOS

Original Title - WITHOUT CAVALRY. BATTLE OF MARATHON (490 BC) 2500 YEARS
Author: Fragoulis Fragos

Copyright STRATEGIC PUBLICATIONS

6, Londou str. | 10681 | Athens | Greece
Contact:
Tel. +30.210.3800374 | Fax +30.210.3823370
info@strategicpublications.gr

Translation: Stylianos F. Fragos, Alexis N. Papaconstantinou
Cover & Graphic design: Anna Bougka

ISBN 978-960-8094-66-6

9 789608 094666

FRAGOULIS FRAGOS, Ph.D.

WITHOUT
CAVALRY

BATTLE OF MARATHON (490 BC)
2500 YEARS

Translation
Stylianos F. Fragos
Alexis N. Papaconstantinou

Strategic
publications

Table of Contents

Timeline

547 BC	Cyros II conquers the kingdom of Lydia. Ionan and Aeolian cities surrender to the Persian empire.
546 BC	Peisistratus lands with his mercenaries at Marathon and becomes the tyrant of Athens for the third time.
527 BC power.	Peisistratus dies. The Peisistratides, Hippias and Hipparchus seize
525/524 BC	Cleisthenes elected magistrate.
524/523/BC	Miltiades elected magistrate.
522 BC	Accession of Darius to the throne.
517 BC	Submission of Samos, Lesbos and Chios to the Persians.
516 BC	Miltiades abandons Athens and heads for Chersonisos, where he becomes tyrant of the city.
514 BC	Assassination of Hipparchus by Harmodius and Aristogeiton.
513 BC	Darius campaigns in Thrace and Scythia.
512 BC	Submission of Macedonia. Alexandros I, son of king Amyntas, executes the Persian ambassadors.
510 BC	Spartan intervention in Athens: persecution of tyrant Hippias.
508 BC	Cleisthenes introduces his reforms in Athens.
507 BC	Athenians ward off new Spartan invasion. Alliance pursued with Persia.
506 BC	Athenians defeat Boeotians and Chalkideans.
501 BC	Implementation of Cleisthenes' reforms begins.
499-494 BC	Ionian revolution, supported by Athens and Eretria.
499 BC	Persians attack Naxos.
498 BC	Ionians and their allies burn Sardis.
497 BC	Clashes in Cyprus and its territorial waters.
497-496 BC	Persian ground attacks on Asia Minor. Darius in Egypt.
496 BC	Submission of Cyprus to Persian rule. Hipparchus, leader of tyrannophiles, elected magistrate in Athens.
494 BC	Persians defeat Ionian fleet in the Lade naval battle. Argives defeated by the Spartans at the battle of Sepeia.
493 BC	Consolidation of Persian domination of the Aegean.

	Themistocles elected magistrate in Athens. Miltiades leaves Chersonisos and returns to Athens.
492 BC	Persian campaign in Thrace and Macedonia. Mardonius replaces tyrannies with democracies in the Ionian cities and consolidates Persian rule in the European satrapy. Miltiades stands trial in Athens.
491 BC	Submission of Thasos to the Persians. Darius demands submission from the Greek city-states. Hostilities between Athens and Aegina.
490 BC	March: Athenian fleet defeated by Aegina. Midsummer: Persian campaign against Eretria and Athens. Submission of the Cyclades, destruction of Naxos. September: Capture of Eretria, Battle of Marathon.
489 BC	Aristides elected magistrate. Miltiades is convicted after his unsuccessful campaign against the island of Paros. Cleomenis, king of Sparta, dies.
487 BC	Implementation of ostracism for the first time (Hipparchus)
487/486 BC	Drawing of lots for the selection of magistrates introduced
486 BC	Ostracism of Megacles. Egypt revolts against the Persians. Darius dies. Accession of Xerxes to the throne.
485 BC	New hostilities between Athens and Aegina. Submission of Egypt o the Persians.
484 BC	Ostracism of Xanthippus. Revolt in Babylonia (?)
483/482 BC.	Ostracism of Aristides. The assembly approves Themistocles' naval project and the construction of 200 triremes.
481 BC	September: Athens decides to allow all Athenian citizens to become crew members of the fleet. October: Xerxes arrives in Sardis and decides to send ambassadors to Greece. The Greek Alliance established. November: Athens and Aegina conclude peace.
480 BC	Xerxes' campaign. September: naval battle of Artemisium, battle of Thermopylae. Late September: naval battle of Salamis. Xerxes returns to Asia.
479 BC	Battle of Plataea. Naval battle and battle of Mycale. Island city-states join Greek Alliance.
479-478 BC	Siege of Sestos.

The Battle of Issus. Mosaic found in Pompeii (National Archaeological Museum of Naples)

Foreword

In 1846, the British philosopher John Stuart Mill began his critique of George Grote's *History of Greece* as follows:

> The interest of Grecian history is inexhaustible. As a mere story, hardly any other portion of authentic history can compete with its characters, its situations, the very march of its incidents, are epic. It is an heroic poem, of which the personages are peoples. It is also, of all histories of which we know so much, the most abounding in consequences to us who now live . The true ancestors of the European nations (it has been well said) are not those from whose blood they are sprung, but those from whom they derive the richest portion of their inheritance. The battle of Marathon, even as an event in English history, is more important than the battle of Hastings. If the issue of that day had been different, the Britons and the Saxons may still have been wandering in the woods (Mill 1846: 343)

As a philosopher, Mill was well aware that his counter-factual conditional could have been complemented by any suggestion – the Hastings battle might never have taken place, King Harold may have triumphed instead of William the Conqueror, the Normans and Saxons may not have even existed. This is how he uses an exaggerated ascertainment and chooses to complete it by advocating probability, not that the English nation would not have been created; but it may not have encountered the inception of civilization otherwise. What Mill ultimately concludes is that without the battle of Marathon, all those notions and achievements which comprised the essence of Hellenism and the basis of Western civilization – philosophical, political, social and artistic -may not have existed or been formulated as a consequence. What clashed in Marathon was not civilization with barbarity. The characterization of Persians as barbarians is, on the one hand, ahistorical and on the other, it undermines the significance of victory for the Athenians and Plataeans implying that they fought against unworthy opponents. On the battlefield, in the surrounding lands of present day Burial Mount, two completely different worlds, which were defined not only by their political models, but also by their different ways of thinking, stood in opposition. On the one hand, the Persians, with their great empire – the largest at the time – were the first to pursue expansion into Europe by organizing subjugated nations and tribes into satrapies which paid tax on both animate and inanimate material; with an exceptionally complex administrative and

tax collection system; with an enormous infantry and cavalry; and with the Great King who ruled by "divine right", whose will was the only correct one, without doubt or question. On the other hand, the Athenians and the Plataeans represented the Hellenic world: city-states, free even when they participated in alliances; with collective bodies (the magistrates, the council of elders/Senate, the Ecclesia of the demos) fought with small numbers of hoplites. The Greek world had the the ability to act rationally, to doubt and to debated instead of obeying unequivocally. This is the world which was defended by the hoplites at the battle of Marathon.

One could argue that it is a mistake to equate the Persian empire with Eastern despotism since, after the Ionian revolution, Mardonius abolished the tyrannies in the cities of the Aegean and of Asia Minor and established a democratic political systemp. However, this occurred for reasons of political expediency in order to prevent the Ionians from revolting again. This was not the case in Athens. In 490 BC, Datis and Artaphernis intended to impose a tyranny on the city, reinstating the Peisistratides Hippias to power. In any case, there exists a substantial difference between a "democracy" imposed by a totalitarian monarch and that which emanates from the collective will of a body of free citizens.

Over the course of history, a multitude of opinions about the battle of Marathon have been formulated. Many historians believe that its importance has been overstated particularly given that the outcome of the battle did not eliminate the Persian threat. Nevertheless, the bibliography of studies alluding to it has been extensive. As pointed out by N. Whatley (1964: 31), it is the battle for which the most interpretations and the most ambivalent ones have been formulated. In line with the above, however, it is also the first chapter of pure military history because it provides a great deal of information concerning rival armies, their weaponry, tactics, the battle location, positions before clashing, etc. Our main source is Herodotus and potentially the source of skepticism of scholars. Although Herodotus is considered the "father of History", his narrative style is substantially different from the typical historical narration which was established by Thucydides. The history of Herodotus as suggested by J.S. Mills is probably best described as a "heroic poem". This does not however, imply that it is fabricated or imagined. Despite the use of exaggerated prose on occasion, the information provided is not outside the realm of possibility or reality.

The present study attempts to recreate the conditions and the events of the battle of Marathon based on the work of Herodotus and later historians. The aim is to provide, to the extent that a broader picture of both Hellenic and Persian worlds during the Archaic Age by presenting the historical, political, social and military attributes of each. The actual battle is almost exclusively narrated

from a military standpoint, focusing on issues which are not always examined by historical studies. In addition, the mythical importance attributed to the battle of Marathon by both ancient Greeks and modern Europeans has also been studied in depth. Within this framework, the interlacing between Persian and Trojan wars proves to be particularly interesting as well as exceptionally powerful, ideologically speaking. It is of no concern that this intertwining is based on the theme of "revenge" which has no place in the chain of cause and effect during the historical narration. We know that neither the Trojan War nor the Persian wars occurred solely to seek revenge. However, the repetition of this pattern by both opponents, is a manifestation of their aim to emphasize, if not attribute, the continuity of their history so that the reality of the outbreak can be augmented. For the Persians, this continuity revolves around Memnon and the Phoenician origin of Perses from his mother Io. For the Greeks, this centers around Achilles and Hercules, the crowning ancestors of Alexander the Great. The confrontation between the ancient Greek world and the Persian empire ended with Alexander the Great's expedition to Asia, at a time when the Great King of Persia was another Darius. This expedition concluded the cycle which began with the Athenian victory in Marathon, a cycle which was to transform radically the world and further enrich the Hellenic heritage of European civilization.

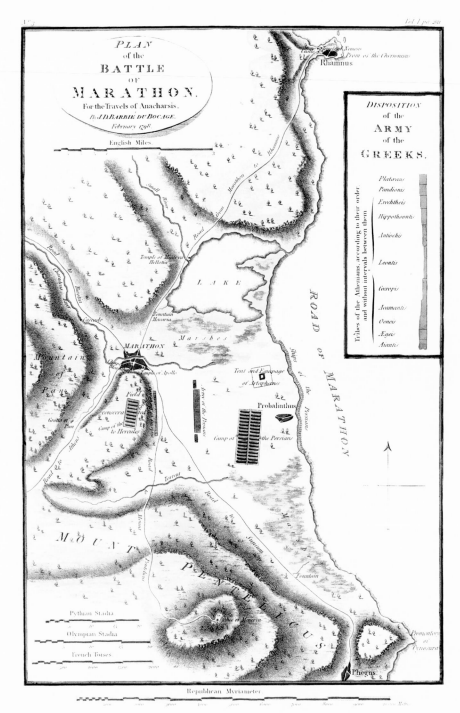

Graphic representation of the Battle of Marathon, according to French military officer J. D. Barbie du Bocage (1798).

The Marathon of myths

In ancient times, Marathon was one of the four demes comprising the so-called "Tetrapolis" (including Marathon, Oenoe, Trikorythos, Probalinthos)[1]. According to Pausanias, it was as far from Athens as it was from Karystos (Pausanias, I, 32.3). Regarding the origin of the name, one explanation given is that it was derived from the fragrant plant "marathos" (fennel), which was found in abundance in the area. Even this seemingly simple linguistic etymology of the origin of the name "Marathon" is not devoid of mythical insinuations since according to tradition, Prometheus carried fire from mount Olympus hiding it in a shoot of fennel. Of course, it is also said that this specific area was named after a hero, Marathon, son of the king of Sicyon Epopeus (who, according to Pausanias, was son of Aloeus and the grandson of Helius). In order to avoid his father's brute and unfair treatment, he abandoned the Peloponnese and settled in Attica where he passed his first laws. After Epopeus' death, he returned to the Peloponnese and ruled the cities of Sicyon and Corinth, which he later divided for his two sons, Sicyon[2] and Corinthus (Grimal 1991: 426). Plutarch, however, believed that Marathon got its name from Marathos, head of the Arcadian allies who took part in the Dioscuri campaign against Attica as a means of getting Helen of Troy back (Plutarch, Theseus, 32.4; Graves 1990a: 366-367; Grimal 1991: 425).

---

1 With the reforms of Cleisthenes, the "Tetrapolis" is divided since Marathon, Oenoe and Trikorythus comprise a third of the Aiantis tribe while Probalinthus is attributed to the Pandionis tribe. This may be due to the fact that the area was under the influence of the Peisistratides (de Ste. Croix 2004: 157).

2 Sicyon is also referred to as the son of Erechtheus or Pelops, quite possibly since the genealogies of heroes are blurred (Graves 1990a: 321).

Panoramic view of the Marathon plain. The Burial Mount can be discerned in the centre

Beyond the various accounts as to the origin of the name "Marathon", myths link the area to some of the most important heroes of the archaic period, as well as Greek founders. In particular, Xuthus, grandson of Deucalion and Pyrrha, and son of Hellen fled to Attica when his siblings, Dorus and Aeolus drove him out of Thessaly. There, he married Creusa (daughter of king Erechtheus) who gave him two sons, Achaeus and Ion.[3] Following Erechtheus' death, Xuthus suggested his wife's older brother Cecrops II be the legitimate successor to the throne; but this decision did not please the citizens, who exiled him from Attica. He settled in the land of Aegialos (Achaea) where he lived until his death. Achaeus, one of his sons, returned to Thessaly whilst Ion became king of Aegialos and was summoned to help the Athenians in the battle against Eleusis (Zimmerman 1966: 21; Grimal 1991: 333-334).

---

3 In his tragedy *Ion*, Euripides claims that the hero was the son of Apollo and not Xuthus; according to Graves, this was intended to demonstrate the superiority of the Ionians over the Dorians and the Achaeans, therefore, confirming their claim of divine origin (Graves 1990a: 160-161).

On the other hand, Strabo provides us with a different version of the myth, according to which Xuthus was the first settler of Tetrapolis. Achaeus was forced to flee to Lacedaemon due to the fact that he committed manslaughter while Ion victoriously fought against the Thracians. The victory prompted the Athenians to proclaim him as their king (besides, his descent from Erechtheus made him a legitimate heir to the throne). Ion is given credit for the division of the people into four tribes (Aegikoreis, Argadeis, Geleontes, and Hopletes) and subsequently into four occupational classes: the farmers, the creators (technicians), the clergy (priests) and the guardians (warriors) (Strabo, *Geographica*, viii 7.1).

As witnessed by Pausanias, the first hero worshipped as a god by the Marathonians was Hercules (Pausanias, ii, 15.3) It is quite possible that his worship was introduced in the area by the so-called "descent of the Heraclids", meaning the Doric invasion from the Peloponnese, which is said to have taken place around 1100 BC (Pausanias, iv 3.3; Thucydides, I, 12.3). This seems to be implied by the legend relating to the exile of Hercules' descendants from Eurystheus. After the hero's death, his children were found in Tiryns, Thebes and Trachis of the Phthiotida prefecture. As Eurystheus became fearful of the threat they posed to his power when they were to come of age, he decided to banish them from Greece. The Herakleids, then, fled to Attica where they were placed under the protection of Theseus, who helped them settle in Trikorythus. When Eurystheus demanded that Hercules' children surrender (including Hercules' friend Iolaus), Theseus refused , leading to the outbreak of war breaking between the Athenians and the Peloponnesians. The battle took place in the Marathon plain. The Athenians and the Herakleids were led by Theseus (or according to others, by his son Demophon), Hylas and Iolaus. Macaria, Hercules' only daughter, took her own life near a spring in the Marathon plain which was then named after her after a prophecy proclaimed that the Athenians would win should a Heraclid be sacrificed. Indeed, it was such a crushing defeat for the Peloponnesian troops that Eurystheus was pursued by Hylas (or Iolaus) up to the Scironian Rocks where he was arrested and put to his death by decapitation - his head buried in a hill in the area (Graves 1990b: 206-212).

A number of adventures took place in Marathon involving the other great hero from Attica, Theseus. In fact, Pausanias claims that it was here that Aegeus' young son was brought up and not in Troezen (I, 15.3). Whichever the case, when the 16-year-old boy arrived at the Athenian palace and was recognized by his father, he took it upon himself to save the Marathonians from the catastrophic raids of the fierce Cretan Taurus, whom Hercules

himself had brought from Crete during his seventh labor[4]. According to one interpretation, this mission was Medea's idea, in hopes that it would lead to Theseus' extermination, paving the way for her son to be heir to the Athenian throne. Theseus managed to catch the Taurus and sacrificed him to Apollo or Athena[5].

Many years later, during Theseus reign as king, Theseus will meet Lapith Peirithous, king of the Magnetes, at Marathon. Peirithous, son of Ixion (or of Zeus) and Dias, had heard great stories of Theseus' power and feats and wanted to ascertain whether they were true. Therefore, he invaded Attica and banished the king's flock from Marathon. Theseus was about to confront him, when the two men standing face-to-face, and in admiration of each other's bravery, decided to become friends instead (Graves 1990a: 360). Later, they both invaded Lacedaemon and kidnapped teenage Helen of Troy. Since they had both previously agreed to wed her, they decided to resolve the issue by drawing lots. The lot fell to Theseus, who settled the young lady in Aphidnae and assigned his mother Aethra to be her guardian.

While Theseus and Peirithus were held captive by Pluto in Hades, Castor and Polydeuces marched with their allies against Attica to free their sister. The residents of Deceleia revealed Helen's location in Aphidnae either because they wanted to escape the brothers' vindictive fury or because they did not agree with the deed of Theseus. The Dioscuri flattened the area and installed Menestheus, son of Peteos, descendant of Erechtheus, in the throne. Menestheus was the Athenian leader during the Trojan war, and after his death in Troy, Athenian power was taken over once again by Theseus' sons, Demophon and Acamas (Graves 1990a: 363-370).

Through these narrations, the mythical and therefore symbolic significance of Marathon gains recognition from antiquity long before the war. Firstly, it is noteworthy that the conflicts which according to myth took place in the Marathon plain seem to include seminal narrations of the Trojans (the Dioscuri invasion in

---

4 In various legendary traditions, the taurus of Marathonas is considered the culprit for the murder of Androgeus, son of Minos; as a result, Minos imposed on the Athenians the annual tax by which seven young boys and girls would be sacrificed to the Minotaur (Graves 1990a: 336-337; Zimmerman 1966: 160). Graves considers that the name "Probalinthos" comes from the Cretan word "volinthos" meaning wild taurus (Graves 1990a: 345).

5 As a rule, legends of heroes attribute the foundation of temples or ceremonies to a certain hero after the successful completion of his mission. More specifically, Theseus is regarded as the founder of the temple of Zeus Hecaleius and the celebrations in his honor. According to the myth, on his way to Marathon, the hero sought shelter due to bad weather in the hut of an old woman called Hecale or Hecalene. Hecale tended to his needs and promised to sacrifice a goat in honor of Zeus should he return safely. When Theseus exterminated the taurus, he tried to find Hecale but she had died in the meanwhile. Thus, he built the temple of Zeus and named the area after her (Graves 1990a: 337).

order to free Helen of Troy) and to provide a (mythical) framework for the eternal rivalry between the Athenians and the Peloponnesians (conflict of Athenians and Eurystheus). Of course, it is no mere coincidence that these legendary conflicts were linked to the persona of Theseus. According to Graves, there must have been at least three legendary personalities named Theseus: one from Troezen, one from Marathon, and one from the Lapiths region. Around the 6th century BC, these three personalities were merged when the Boutades, a Lapith tribe which was considered an important influence on Athenian aristocracy and also took on hieratic duties worshipping Erechtheus, projected the persona of Theseus as the answer to the Dorian Hercules (Graves 1990a: 326). This hypothesis, which is also supported by George Thomson, seems to be reinforced by the significance Theseus had in subsequent times; thus, the perception that the federalization of Attica, which comprised the first democratic reform and formed the basis for later Athenian prosperity, is owed to this hero in particular, probably dates back to the period of Cleisthenes. In this way, a heroic-mythical past was created in support of Cleisthenes' own reforms (Graves 1990a: 349-351). It, therefore, becomes apparent that prior to the battle of Marathon, the holiness and mythical significance of the area had already been established and this provides an additional rationale by which Miltiades was prompted to select Marathon as the location of the battle against the Persians (Kargakos 2004: 212). By the same token, legend has it that the person in charge of the Athenian troops at the battle of Marathon was this hero, Theseus. Finally, it is interesting to note that after the Peloponnesian wars, Theseus rose to prominence as the leading local hero of Athens. In 475 BC, during a campaign on the island of Scyros, Cimon, son of Miltiades, found the hero's tomb and carried his bones to Athens for

Shard of a dark-figured bearer (6th c. BC) depicting the greatest hero of Athens, Theseus

burial. The Theseion sanctuary was built on the location where the bones were buried. In his honor, the Athenians founded the Theseia celebrated on the 8th of October (Pyanepsion), which also coincided with the hero's return from Crete. Moreover, the 8th day of each consecutive month was consensually dedicated to Theseus and Poseidon.

The geopolitics of Hellenism

The narrations of Theseus directly or indirectly cast him relevant to the Argonautic Expedition and the Trojan war[6], two important operations, which underneath their mythical outer shell, may be considered as early manifestations of the geopolitics of Hellenism.The historicity of both these operations continues to be a bone of contention. However, even those who advocate the narrations' mythological dimension accept that at their very core, there exists some objective basis for Greek activity in the area of the Black Sea.

Indeed, beyond their given religious and attitudinal functions, the heroic myths (Hercules' feats, the Argonautic Expedition, the Trojan war) are references to the Greek trade invasion in the Black Sea, during the mid second millennium BC. Moreover, it seems that through these myths, ancient cities attempted to legalize their trade rights in the Bosporus, the Euxenus Pontus and the Black Sea.

Thus, the action of a local hero (Theseus, Jason, etc.) in the Crimea, for example Colchis, functioned as a basis for the claim that, the corresponding Greek city had more rights than another, if the local hero of the latter had little opportunity to act bravely in these remote areas. The Argonaut expedition, the first amphibious commando reconnaissance operation is regarded as the "first colonization" in the Black Sea by the Greeks. This is potentially due to the fact that some of the Argonauts were regarded as founders of temples on the islands and along the coastlines which Jason's Argo sailed.

---

6 According to one of the Argonauts ship catalogues, Theseus was among Jason's mates who began looking for the golden fleece in Colchis. In other catalogues, Athens is represented by Butes, "the master of bees", and Falerus, the Athenian archer. The existence of many different catalogues is due to the fact that subsequently, there were a good deal of cities added; mainly by wandering rhapsodists, who most certainly would not have any objections to satisfying the high expectations of their elite audience. Besides, this can also be observed in the "Catalogue of Ships" of Homer's Iliad. In both instances, the participation of Greek cities in the operations substantiated their right to establish colonies along the coastline of the Black Sea (Graves 1990b: 217-218, 223, 287). At this point Plutarch's additional information must be noted stating that Theseus and Minos had consensually sworn that no ship whose crew exceeded five crewmembers would be permitted to sail in the Aegean waters; from this agreement, Jason's "Argo", which was in charge of clearing the seas of pirates, was ruled out (Plutarch, Theseus, 19.4).

The campaign of the Achaeans against Troy

However, beyond the myths, a large number of historians have claimed that the Greeks arrived at the Black Sea during the Iron Age, in pursuit of the iron ore deposits in the area.

The Trojan war, the first large scale amphibious landing operation, seems to serve as a means of gratifying similar pursuits. On a mythical level, the men in charge of Agamemnon's allies were descendants of the Argonauts; a fact that on the one hand reveals the firm conviction over the cities' "hereditary" rights in the important area of the Hellespont, and on the other hand, demonstrates the stability of the geopolitics of Hellenism in relation to the Aegean.

In light of this, one of the greatest scholars of ancient mythology Robert Grave expressed his position in 1955, characteristically saying that:

> The Trojan war is historic, and whatever the immediate cause may have been, it was a trade war. Troy controlled the valuable Black Sea trade in gold, silver, iron, cinnabar, ship's timber [...]. Once Troy had fallen, the Greeks were able to plant colonies all along the east trade route, which grew as rich as much as those in Asia Minor and Sicily. In the end, Athens, as the leading maritime power, profited most from the Black Sea trade, especially from its cheap grain. It was the loss of its fleet guarding the entrance to the Hellespont that ruined Athens at Aigosopotami in 405 BC, and ended the long Peloponnesian wars. Perhaps, therefore, the constant negotiations between Agamemnon and Priam did not concern the return of Helen so much as the restoration of the Greek rights to enter the Hellespont (Graves 1990b: 302).

Graves integrates the Trojan war into a wider framework placing at its core the competition by the inhabitants of the Eastern Mediterranean to attain supremacy at sea, which manifested itself after the decline of Cnossus (around 1400 BC) and the end of the Minoan thalassocracy. Through this prism, many Cretan raids in Phoenicia that preceded Helen's abduction[7] can be viewed; this also includes Paris' raid in Sidon, which Apollodorus refers to (*Library*, III, 4-5). In this case, the Trojan alliance with other tribes in the region would have aimed at preventing the spread of Greek tribes beyond the Aegean and thus, satisfying their commercial pursuits (Graves 1990b: 287).

Reinforcing Grave's interpretation and apart from legendary narrations, Herodotus compares the expedition of Xerxes to an earlier operation of the Trojans, which helped secure the control of Thrace, Macedonia, and possibly, of the northern and central parts of the Aegean (*Hist.*, VII, 20.2). It is reasonable to say that the Achaeans must have reacted dynamically to the Trojan attempts to expand towards the west along with their intentions of turning the Aegean into a "closed" sea under their control, thus, entrenching their naval power. The myths of Hercules' raids in Troy may undoubtedly entail at their historical core Achaean counter sea operations against the Trojans. In fact, in one of those raids, Hercules was accompanied by Telamon (father of Ajax and brother of Peleus), who abducted Hesione, sister of Priam; upon bringing her to Salamis, he had his second son with her, Teucrus, half-brother of Ajax the Great and one of the finest Achaean archers during the siege of Troy (Graves 1990b: 171). Similarly, Paris' journey to Sparta and Helen's abduction could have mythologically been all about Trojan sea raids. It is,

---

7 Herodotus begins his history with these consecutive raids and hostilities (*The Histories*, I, 1-4; cf. Malalas, *Chr.*. L, II, 19 ff., mentions the Cretan raid in Tyrus; among the prisoners of the looted city was Europe).

therefore, evident that the conflict between the Achaeans and the Trojans outside the Ilion walls was one of the warfare operations, which took place within the framework of long-term competition for the control of sea routes and trade.

All these raids, conflicts, sea and land operations seem to be following a unified theme with respect to the Aegean. The movement of Greek tribes, even in the form of colonial expansion (8th-6th cent. BC) is notably eastwards; targeting chiefly theconsolidation of their dominant positions on both sides of the Aegean, meaning the conversion of the archipelago into a closed sea as opposed to penetrating deep into the Asian mainland. This pursuit had already been made clear from the time of the Minoan thalassocracy and of course was more than relevant to the power of Minoan Crete. In a similar manner, classical Athens conceived and realized her own power (it is sufficient to consider the geographic dimension of the Athenian alliance) as Alexander the Great did. Prior to embarking on his glorious expedition into the depths of Asia, he ensured dominance on both the eastern and the western sides of the Aegean.

Hephaestus gives Thetis Achilles' weapons. Shield, helmet and greaves can be discerned. Representation from a 5th c. BC red-figured kylix

In a similar fashion, there is movement from the legendary (or not) Asian rivals to the Greeks: primarily the Trojans and later the Persians but this time in the opposite direction. The answer to the question why the Persians decided to invade Greece is much simpler than the rationale provided by Herodotus in his *Histories*. According to Herodotus, the powerful empire of the Achaemenids, like all empires, sought expansion in order to acquire control of more land and marine trading routes, while gaining further access to raw materials.

Having made it to the land of the Scythians and the Hindis from the east, the Persians quite naturally chose to extend their domination towards the west as well; besides, they controlled the south and the western parts of the Asia minor

coast. The conversion of the Aegean into a closed sea under Persian control was about to be realized. The Ionian revolution (498-494 BC) must have served as the catalyst for the acceleration of a process which appeared pre-determined; as a result, not only was the danger of Persian control manifest on the coast of Asia minor, but also the possibility that the "people beyond the sea" would evolve into powerful competitors over Aegean dominance was highlighted. Mardonius' expedition in 492 BC set off an act of diplomatic significance, the restoration of democratic political systems in Ionian cities aimed at ensuring and securing the rear for the Persians. This is exactly what Alexander the Great will act upon almost half a century later. Through the prism of geopolitics in a diachronic perspective, the battle of Marathon is indeed a turning point: it constitutes the first substantial obstacle to the realization of the geopolitical aspirations of the Persian empire; and simultaneously, it signals the rebirth

Alexander the Great fighting the Persians in the battle of Granicus River. A bas-relief representation from the "sarcophagus" of Alexander the Great (Archaeological Museum of Constantinople)

of the geopolitics of Hellenism which will be realized by the Athenians at first following the Persian wars, and will ultimately be fulfilled by Alexander the Great.

In relation to the geopolitical parameter, the historical basis of the legendary narrations of the Argonautic expedition and the Trojan war are not of vital importance. Equally interesting as the the interpretation of facts in a chain of historical continuity is the integration of history into a mythological past, something which amplifies its power in the present. It is typical of Herodotus to trace the causes of the Persian wars to the eternal rivalry between Europe and Asia, which had previously culminated in the Trojan war. For the Greeks during the Persian wars, Xerxes was the descendant of Memnon[8], who ar-

---

8 Memnon was son of the king of Assyria Tithonus (brother of Priam) and of Eos. The Romans and later Greek authors, such as Diodorus Siculus, thought that they had come from Ethiopia in Africa. However, Greek

rived in Troy with a grand army consisting of Ethiopians and Hindis following Hector's death; Xerxes proclaimed himself punisher of the Trojans (Georges 1994: 58-66). The pattern of revenge and punishment, which was used as an ideological argument on behalf of the Persians, will be put to use in a similar fashion by Alexander the Great on his expedition into Asia. Finally, to complete the mythical circle, Alexander the Great will proclaim himself a member of the Aeacids on his mother's side, proclaiming his descent from Achilles' son, Neoptolemus, founder of the Molossoi.

authors of a previous time believed that there existed an Ethiopia in Asia, which was identified with Kissia (Kissovatni, Kissovandi or Kizouvatna –what is today called Houjestan in northwestern Iran); in fact, it was said that its capital, Susa, had been founded by either Tithonus or Memnon himself (thus, it got its name as "city of Memnon"). Memnon (like Hector) is regarded as the counterpart of Achilles: he was dark-skinned, handsome like Achilles and his shield had also been made by Hephaestus (Graves 1990b:313-314).

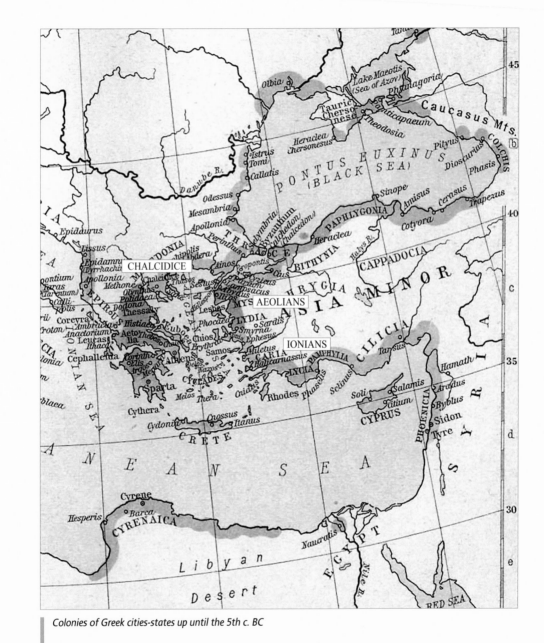

Colonies of Greek cities-states up until the 5th c. BC

Chapter 1

The Greek world at the beginning of the 5th century BC

During the Archaic Age (750-500 BC), a stable evolutionary course emerges, in which the Hellenic world displays the key characteristics, with which it will proceed historically until the period of the Roman conquest. Overall, these characteristics included the dynamic expansion towards the East and the West by means of colonialism; the formation of cities and of confederacies ("koina"); the gradual advancement of political systems from monarchy to more democratic forms of government; the systematic formation of cultural identity with the mythical past serving as the core; the rise of local heroes and gods assigned as protectors of cities; and at the same time, the assembly and union of all Greeks around common institutions, celebrations and Panhellenic temples and oracles (Olympic Games, Isthmia, the Delphic Oracle, Dodona, the Eleusinian mysteries etc.).

Without a doubt progress in certain areas engender broader consequences: the establishment of colonies favored the development of trade; access to raw materials, mainly minerals, contributes to the differentiation of weaponry. This, in turn, had an impact on warfare tactics leading to the formation of the phalanx, significantly reducing the military importance of the nobles. As a result, the hoplites, realizing their ever-increasing role in the defense of the city, sought greater participation in political life.

Simultaneously, within Greece, wars continued to break out due to territorial expansion, involving not only those cities with a direct interest but also their allies. And while the Greek world appeared to be fragmented, the threat coming from the East – beginning with the expansion of the Lydians

and subsequently with the rise of the Persian empire –imposed *de facto* the need for a collective response. For the first time in history, the Greek world, on both sides of the Aegean, is headed towards a new union.

1.1. The enlargement of "boundaries": the completion of colonialism

The basic motive for the establishment of any colony was the search for land. Population increases or economic crises, stemming from factors such as extended periods of drought or interruption of existing commercial exchange due to raids, put pressure on the cities' inner core, with the usual demand for land redistribution. The best solution was decreasing the population, in order for resources to suffice for the remaining population. Naturally, several colonies were established to satisfy specific trade aspirations, functioning primarily as trading stations. Examples include Al Mina in southern Syria, Cumae in Italy, Naucrates in the Nile Delta and Emporion on the eastern coast of Spain; these colonies were called "trades" (*emporiai*), in order distinguishing them from the proper colonies (*apoikiai*) (de Ste. Croix 2004: 349-367).

It was the mother-city (*metropolis*) which was exclusively in charge of the establishment of the colony and not the inquisitive or opportunistic spirit of any single citizen. The mother-city made decisions concerning the location for establishing the colony (frequently seeking prophecy from an oracle); appointed who would be the "settler", meaning the person leading the expedition (the colony was named after this particular person who was also honored after death); and which inhabitants would be chosen to follow the "settler". This settler, who ensured the transfer of customs and laws to the colony, would bring along with him soil and fire from the mother-city. He was also in charge of the military operations that would be necessary for conquering new land. When the conquest was achieved, he allocated and distributed the land, provided he had previously designated the space that was to be taken up by temples and other public buildings (Graham 1964).

The second Greek settlement period (8th-6th c. BC) completed and mostly finalized the Greek tribal movements, which dated back to about 1125 BC. In the 8th century, the Greeks set out westwards, establishing colonies in southern Italy and in Sicily. Around the same time, groups of Greeks from the islands, the mainland and Asia Minor moved towards Africa and Cyrenaica, heading for the northern coast of the western Mediterranean and mostly, to the Bosporus and the Euxenus Pontus. Miletus of Asia Minor - the pioneer in the colonization of the Propontis and the Euxenus Pontus – maintained good

relations with the local population living in the inland since 1000 BC in order to have access to supplies of mineral resources. The cessation of trade with the eastern Mediterranean, due to the invasion of the Cimmerians (8th c. BC), obliged Miletus – as well as other Ionian cities of Asia Minor – to turn to the establishment of colonies; this in turn was aimed at reducing the population and alleviating an unforeseen economic crisis. Therefore, before 700 BC and within approximately one century, the Miletians founded Cyzicus, Artake, Proconnesus, Abydus and Kios in the Propontis. Around the same time, their example was followed by the inhabitants of Aeolis who established Sestus, the Megarians who established Selymbria, Calchedon, Byzantium and Astacus, and the Phokaeis who established Lampsacus.

With the exception of Heracleia and Mesambria, which were built by the Megarians, almost all of the remaining colonies within the Euxenus Pontus were Miletian. The oldest of these was Sinope, home of the Cynic philosopher Diogenes. Its establishment dates back to the mid 8th c. BC and its strategic position allowed for unimpeded communication with the inland of Phrygia whilst facing the ocean. Sinope soon became an important trading centre and further established Trapezous (Trebizond), Kerasounta (Giresun; anc. Gr. Choerades or Pharmakia), Cotyora, Pterion, Cytorus and Cromna. In addition to these, Amisos also prospered and together with Trapezous and became the transit centre for iron ore and steel from Armenia to the Aegean. Until the end of the 6th c. BC, the Miletian colonies were built along the western coast of the Euxenus Pontus; extending as far as the northern regions of the Danube estuaries (Histria, Apollonia, Odessa, Tomoi, Krounoi, Olbia, Tyras, Borysthenes), the region of the Crimea and the Sea of Azov (Pantikapaion, Theodosia, Tyritake, Myrmecion, Cercine, Hermonassa) and the coast of Colchis (Dioskourada, Phases – where the silver mines were located) (Rostovtzeff 1963: 49-71; Sakellariou 1971a: 43-44, 57-60).

In all of these colonies, a new aristocracy was formed. The first settlers, including both nobles and common people, divided the conquered land. This is a matter of great importance since it objectively disconnects land ownership from lineage. However, with the passage of time and the population increase caused by the influx of new settlers, this aristocracy became solidified and more exclusive, refusing to continue with land redistribution. As a result, internal pressures for various reforms within the colonies gradually built up, as was the case in the mother-city. One noteworthy exception was Heracleia, which had been democratic since its establishment due to the fact that at that time the democratic political system had prevailed in its metropolis in Megara (Stasinopoulos 1971b: 211, 229).

By the time the second Greek colonization wave ended, the Greek world and civilization had expanded its boundaries in every direction in the Mediterranean basin. During this expansion, trade[9] and industry developed significantly through broadening and securing land and sea communications. In the Mediterranean basin, a network of trading routes was established from the Aegean to Cyprus, Cilicia, Syria, the Palestine and Mesopotamia, Egypt, the Greek colonies of Italy and Sicily, the Etruscans and the Carthaginians, Lydia, Phrygia, the Propontis and Euxenus Pontus. From 700 BC, the cities that rose to prominence as trading and industrial powers were Corinth, Athens, Chalkis, Eretria, Samos, Miletus, Rhodes and Phocaea; Sparta, Sicyon, Megara, Aegina, Paros, Naxos, Chios and Thasos followed suit. However, with the passage of time, various reclassifications took place. For example, Chalkis and Eretria lost their preeminence in trading exchange around the early 7th century due to the long-term war between them. Corinth maintained its power for several years owing to its geographical position and the port of Kenchreai in the Saronikos Bay - thus, its contacts weree facilitated with both Italy and Sicily as well as the Aegean in the East – but also because Corinthian pottery was in great demand. However, from the first half of the 6th century, the quality of Corinthian ceramics deteriorated to meet the high demand, and as a result, the city gradually lost its comparative advantage in the

One of the most ancient Greek coins, made of amber

market and Athens moved in quickly to replace Corinth. Rhodes, another city that produced pottery although of lower quality compared to that of Corinth, developed trading relations with Egypt and the East, making use of the colonies it had established along the southern coasts of Asia Minor. In the meantime, Samos, Chios and Miletus (the most powerful trading station of the 6th century) all stood to benefit from the trade between the Aegean and the inland of Asia Minor (Stasinopoulos 1971b: 204-208, 228).

One of the most important repercussions of trade activity was coin minting (meaning the sealing of one piece of precious metal with the emblem of a single state). The oldest Ionian and Lydian series of coins date back

---

9 Here, de Ste. Croix's pertinent observation should be noted that, during ancient times in particular, trade was restricted to the import of goods. Cities could of course export the surplus of goods they produced; this was, however, circumstantial and did not determine productivity (de Ste. Croix 2004: 352-358).

to post 650 BC whilst the oldest Hellenic coin is that of Aegina (late 7th c. BC), followed by the Corinthian and Athenian coins around 600 BC. Clearly, the emergence of the "mongers" ("*kapeloi*") around the 6th century BC is of particular importance to trade history. Up until that point , merchants who were also ship owners, used to transport and sell their products themselves. The "mongers" collected the imported goods from various places, placed them in shops and sold them to retail customers. As a result, there was an increase in the volume and variety of goods sold as well as meeting demand consistently since storage became feasible (White 1961; Stasinopoulos 1971b: 205-206).

1.2. Heading towards democracy: Social developments and change

By the end of the 6th c. BC, most Greek states had been through the stage of tribal nations and had developed into city-states, while the creation of con-federacies ("koina") was also noted; namely federations of city-states with limited sovereignty rights (e.g., the "confederacy of Boeotia" was established in the 7th c. BC). The constant rise of the nobles as an economic and political factor contributed to the abolishment of monarchy and the establishment of republican aristocratic political systems with the exception of Sparta, Macedonia, Epirus, Cyprus and Cyrene.

The nobles continued to be defined by two basic characteristics: lineage and land ownership. The development of trade affected them in such a way that influenced city life as a whole. The nobles rarely dealt with trade, typically when the resources of their land were not enough and they had opted not to create a colony. Naturally, nobles did benefit from the economic growth of the city generated by commercial and industrial activity, leading to increased demand for farming goods in local markets and price hikes. This led to the intensive exploitation of land, while simultaneously creating the need for additional arable land. The ones who did not benefit from the economic growth were the lower classes and in particular farmers who saw their profits depleted by both nobles and merchants. The adoption of tax through farming loans from 700 BC onwards, would lead to land redistribution for the benefit of the wealthier classes. The debtors would lose their property and would be sold as slaves due to indebtness.

The oppression of the weaker groups, however, was propagated by the noble's control of local government and justice. The lack of written and codified law coupled with the fact that the nobles governed and exercised

justice without any checks and balances, allowed the nobles' to commit various transgressions, crimes and injustices. Hesiod provides testimony of such unjust decisions by nobles who had been bribed (Works and Days, l. 33-39, 248-252). Hence, the request for written law was common since it was accompanied by the hope that injustice would be terminated.

The power of the nobles was evident on the one hand, through the containment or outright abolition of monarchy, and on the other hand, the restriction of "citizenship" only to nobility or to part of it. Internal competition was inevitable: the nobles that shared common interests and pursuits formed "societies" (hetaireies) through which they attempted to gain more power and to eliminate their rivals.

Within the structure of aristocratic political systems, the pre-existing institutions of authority, namely, the assembly (ekklesia tou demou) and the senate were maintained, while one or more magistrates (archons) replaced the king. The magistrates were elected by the senate or the assembly and the term of their service was pre-determined (typically lasting a year). A common feature of the first aristocratic city-states was the small number of magistrates and the long term of their service (e.g., in Athens it was a 10-year service until 683-682 BC). As time passed however, the trend reversed, as experience demonstrated that a longer term in power, cultivated the ambitions of any magistrate to become a tyrant. During that time, the institution of "Polemarch" (the magistrate of war) was created, as many magistrates were deemed inefficient as military leaders.

The assembly, in which only active citizens (by rule, the nobles) had the right to participate, had limited jurisdiction. Although the assembly convened at regular intervals, it wascalled upon merely to approve significant matters (declaration of war or conclusion of peace, formation or break-up of alliance, etc.), without however any debate and lacking the power to amend the proposals put forth by the senate and the magistrates. The senate or council of elders had life-long members and an undefined and unrestricted jurisdiction, making it practically uncontrollable.

The judicial power was exercised by the senate and the magistrate, whilst what prevailed over some time was to revert to the assembly of the people, in order to reconsider their decisions. With the introduction of a codified law and the introduction of new laws, the creation of new bodies was required in order to deliver justice.

In its pure form, the aristocratic political system was ephemeral. To be exact, it only survived in Crete. In the rest of Greece, either more democratic principles emerged without however progressing towards pure democratic

states or the aristocracy completely collapsed. In certain cities (e.g., in Megara 640-645 BC), the aristocratic regime was overturned by a tyrant. Elsewhere (e.g., Corinth or Athens), the evolution from aristocracy to tyranny was not linear since a timocratic political systems emerged. In any case, the decline of aristocratic rule wass accompanied by severe upheaval, instability and internal pressures: the nobles excluded from power so far, demanded participation in common interests, just like other classes serving as hoplites, whereas the indebted farmers sought exemption from their debts and the landless demanded the redistribution of land. In order to avoid unstable situations (such as insurgencies or tyrannies), the ruling parties would choose one person who was awarded with powers of a supreme ruler - usually for a specific amount of time - entrusted with the mission to introduce reforms varying in scope; these persons were referred to as "legislators", or "mediator" (*diallaktes*) or "elective princes" (*aisumnetes*) (provided they were for life). Solon took on this role in Athens and so did Pheido in Corinth before 660 BC, the latter ensuring the stabilization of the number of active citizens, without however proceeding to land redistribution. The "mediators" proceeded with a core set of reforms, dealing with the extension of political rights to classes other than the nobles, based on income criteria. Hence, a new oligarchy, in which wealthy individuals also participated, was formed, replacing the old aristocracy of nobles and landowners. This political system was called "timocracy" because it was based on the "timema", the estimated value of citizens' property (*telos*), on the basis of which each citizen was taxed; the most distinctive example was the so-called "Solon's constitution", which will be described below.

Figurine of the Geometric Age depicting a warrior (National Archaeological Museum, Athens)

Under timocracy, the assembly was maintained and functioned under the same jurisdiction as before. The small yet powerful senate and a small number of magistrates, who were typically elected by the assembly, also remained. It is certainly true that the expansion of political rights and the limited enlargement of the body of citizens were important developments. Moreover, the timocracy – at least theoretically - appeared to be more solid than the aristocracy, due to its inherent flexibility: the possibility of readjustment and continuous enlargement of the body of citizens, as

long as they fulfilled the criteria of the "timema", did not alter the nature of the political system, making it neither more nor less democratic.

Irrespective of all this, timocracies only temporarily delayed the danger of tyranny. In most Greek city-states (Corinth, Samos, Miletus, Athens, etc.) the oligarchy was overthrown by tyrants, who had seized power guilefully, deceitfully, or forcefully. The tyrants came from the noble class and in certain cases had served as magistrates or had led a successful war campaign. Most of the tyrants dealt with the nobles harshly but differentiated their behavior towards other classes (e.g., some took preventative measures in favor of weaker classes). Furthermore, despite tyranny being already negatively perceived since ancient times[10], some tyrants were assessed positively. In fact, so much so that certain tyrants were to be included in the list of the "seven wise men" (Periander of Corinth, Pittacus of Mytilene, and Cleobulus of Rhodes).

Although there were many differences in the types of tyrannies imposed on various city-states, some common conditions can be detected which seem to have favored their imposition. Tyrannies were not imposed on tribal nations or confederacies, but rather on city-states with an economy not dependent exclusively on agriculture and experiencing political and/or social instability (aristocracies on the verge of collapse or relatively nascent oligarchies). The common characteristic of all the tyrannies, irrespective of specific conditions, was their tendency to limit drastically the number of active citizens and their associated political rights. This is why Aristotle characterizes tyranny as "monarchy exerting despotic power over the political community", "ruling in the interest of the monarch" (*Politics* 1279b 4-5, 16).

The tyrannies were not always short-lived. For example, the Cypselides ruled Corinth for almost 40 years, from 620-584/3 BC. In addition, it became customary to reinstate an oligarchy or an aristocratic regime once a tyranny was overthrown, however that was not always the rule; the case of the reforms of Cleisthenes in Athens is not representative.

In any case examining the Archaic Age overall, we can ascertain the gradual evolution towards political systems with more collective participation. If the reasonable course, even theoretically, of this development evolves from monarchy to oligarchy (aristocracy or timocracy) and eventually to democracy, then tyranny would justifiably be considered a step backwards. However, all this seems sensible only as an abstract notion and such a linear evolution only rarely corresponds to history. Nevertheless, it can be stated with conviction that from the second half of the 6th c. BC onwards, the

---

10 Tyranny was considered to have roots in the Asian way of life whose main characteristic is luxury; for a more thorough analysis of the connection of tyranny and asiatism, see Georges 1994: 13-46.

indicators that signal the development of a democratic city-state became increasingly frequent: the moderate democracies of Megara and Chios, some democratic elements that were adopted in Sparta and of course the reforms of Solon and Cleisthenes in Athens. However, prior to the completion of this evolutionary path, the Greek world was forced to encounter the Persians (Stasinopoulos 1971b: 208-220; Parliament of Greece 2010: 34-36; Kanellopoulos 1982; Kordatos 1956; Mossé 1988; Mossé 1989; Mosé &Scnanpp-Courbeillon 1966; Osborne 2000).

1.3 "having put foot next to foot and leant one shield against another": the creation of the phalanx formation and war practices

The verse by Tyrtaeus, the poet who encouraged the Spartans during the second Messenian war (685-668 BC), is considered one of the earliest literary references to the famous phalanx of the hoplites (Lorimer 1947; Salmon 1977: 91). Around the same time, another poet named Archilochus spoke of the "famed for the spear lords of Euboea" and his reference to the Lelantine war (between 710 and 650 BC) has been linked with a new form of war, which was gradually imposed due to the adoption of the hoplite phalanx (Forrest 1957: 163-164; Donlan 1970). About two centuries later, in the last quarter of the 5th c. BC, Euripides, in his tragedy *Hercules* (between 425 and 415 BC), differentiated between two different forms of war. The tyrant Lycus mocked Hercules for never holding a shield nor ever being close to a spear (l. 159-160: *who never buckled shield to arm / nor faced the spear N.B. need to use the ancient Greek text instead*) but rather used the bow (l. 161: *that coward's weapon N.B. need to use the ancient Greek text instead*), which allowed him to leave the battlefield at any time; in Lycus' view, a truly brave man is he who holds the line and dares to face the fatal blow of a spear (l. 163-164: *who keeps his post in the ranks and steadily faces / the swift wound the spear may plough N.B. need to use the ancient Greek text instead*). To these derogatory remarks, Amphitryon states that the hoplite is the slave of his weapons and his life is in danger, if he fights in a line next to cowardly soldiers (l. 190-192: *a man who fights in line is a slave to his weapons / and if his fellow-comrades want for courage / he is slain himself through the cowardice of his neighbors N.B. need to use the ancient Greek text instead*). If Tyrtaeus' verse describes the new practice of war introduced by the hoplite phalanx, the excerpt from Euripides reveals that this form of war, even if not yet abandoned, had lost the splendor it once had.

Many theories have been formed pertaining to the date of adoption of the phalanx, the rationale underlying this "revolutionary reform" and the role the hoplites played in the political affairs of the Archaic Age, particularly in establishing tyrannies (Snodgrass 1965; Holladay 1982; Salmon 1977; Cartledge 1977; Ferrill 1985: 145: Morris 1987: 196-205; Snodgrass 1993; van Wees 1994; Ober 1996: 60-61). Based on archaeological findings, mainly early Corinthian pottery dating back to the first half of the 7th

Duel between Hector and Achilles. Representation on pottery dating back to the 5th c. BC (Vatican Museum)

c., most scholars agree that the phalanx was a development of the Archaic Age, possibly between 675 and 650 BC (Salmon 1977: 90-93; van Wees 1994; Sage 1996: xvi-xix, 25-28).[11] The adoption of this new trend is possibly related - though not in a strict causality– to economic, social, and military factors.

---

11 Cartledge (1977: 19-20) sets the *terminus post quem* at the end of the 8th c. BC, advocating that since 725 BC and thereafter, the basic elements of hoplite armament (the bell-shaped cuirass, the Corinthian helmet and the shield with its distinctive arm and hand straps called *porpax* and *antilabe*). There are also suggestions of an earlier date; for instance, Latacz (1977: 68-95, 116-212) advocates that the fighters of the *Iliad* fight aligned according to the hoplite phalanx. Latacz's theory is refuted by van Wees (1994: 1-14) who, nevertheless, accepts that the *Iliad* is not descriptive in a detailed manner of the individual confrontations between eminent Achaeans and eminent Trojans, but supplies us with adequate illustrations of collective battles where soldiers line up in a type of open battle array. It would be absurd to dispute the contribution of the multitude (according to the "Catalogue of the Ships") of troops in the Trojan war; yet, the poet's point of view rests with the "prowess of the heroes": over and beyond the troops movement the reader sees Achilles, Diomedes, Ajax fight against Hector, Aeneas, Sarpedon (Beye 1964; Sage 1996: 1-7; Finley 1964: 133). This focus is widely explained for the most part by the socio-political reality of the Mycenaean era rendering its prevailing attitude. The entire army, whether fighting lined up in an open battle array or lined up according to the hoplite phalanx, has not yet achieved its symbolic dimension as a carrier of city-state unity (Runciman 1998: 732-733). Finally, Krentz's (2002: 35-37) fairly recent view should also be noted, which states that, during the Archaic Age there was weaponry improvement despite the prevalence of Homeric form of war (army in loose line-up and personal confrontation of aristocrats/leaders); and that the hoplite phalanx was used for the first time in the battle of Marathon battle since the Athenians felt it was prudent that this was the most contributing way of dealing with the Persians - whose war tactics had been witnessed during the Ionian revolution (499-494 BC). Krentz believes that dating the phalanx in the Archaic Age is due to idealization of the hoplites by Herodotus and he completely overlooks the archaeological data and (the however minimal) poetic allusions. Additionally, Krentz fails to respond to the plausible query about how in a matter of just a few years a warfare tactic managed to change which according to him, was put into effect for three entire centuries; cf. van Wees (1994: 143), who poses that the date 650 BC signifies the end for the use of the Homeric warfare tactics.

The introduction of mineral resources via the colonies contributed to the construction of improved and more solid defensive weaponry, which necessitated the change of warfare tactics to guarantee effectiveness.[12] In particular, the shield was reinforced with added layers of metal and in order to facilitate its transport and use, it was reduced in size and equipped with two handles. Due to the changes, the shield covered only the left side of the warrior's body, leaving the left side of the shield unutilized. Within the tight phalanx formation, the unutilized left section of the shield would protect the right side of the body of the warrior fighting next to the holder of the shield. The drawback was that the adjacent warrior would not be able to use his sword effectively, which was bypassed by using long spears (dorata). In order to keep the line-up intact, the soldiers were placed in more lines creating a solid mobile "wall".

The rationale behind the implementation of the hoplite phalanx has been questioned, since the country's terrain is mountainous or semi-mountainous making it impossible to deploy soldiers in a phalanx formation (Gomme 1945: 10; Adcock 1957: 40; Anderson 1970: 111; Cartledge 1977: 18). The view that it was simply introduced to the Greek world by Greeks who had in turn picked it up from their Carian comrades whilst serving under Pharao Psammetichus I (Snodgrass 1965: 114-115), fails to substantially answer the question and has been also rejected in favor of the argument that the phalanx was indeed a Greek invention (Cartledge 1977: 18). It seems more logical to attribute the gradual emergence of the phalanx to the "arms race" taking place amongst the city-states. It is widely known that during the Archaic Age, conflicts for land expansion emerged particularly when colonization subsided. It would have sufficed for a city-state to adopt the improved weaponry and the new warfare tactics to force its opponents to emulate it, in an attempt to ensure their domination in future confrontations (Salmon 1977: 96). It is estimated that the defeat of the Spartans by the Argives in the battle of Hysiae (669 BC) wass due to the fact that the latter fought "in a phalanx"[13] (Salmon 1977: 93; Cartledge 1977: 25; Holladay 1982: 99); on the contrary, in the later war with Argos (545 BC) the Spartans won since they had mastered the new tactics (Cartledge 1977: 12)[14].

12 Snodgrass (1965) regards the total prevalence of improved defensive weaponry (shield, helmet, cuirass) as one of the necessary conditions for the creation of the phalanx.

13 Because of this, the speculation is formulated that Pheido used the hoplites to become tyrant of Argos (Salmon 1977: 96-99).

14 The agreement made between Chalkis and Eretria, dealing with the prohibition of missiles in the Lelantine war, possibly sheds light on the intention for restricting the role of slingers, archers and other light-armed warriors to ensure hoplite activity (Donlan 1970; Connor 1988: 20). Further information about this agree-

As a rule, the hoplite phalanx is connected with the admission of non-nobles into the army who had the financial ability to afford the necessary fighting gear. However, it is most likely that in the beginning innovation was adopted by the aristocrats and the wealthy members who were not of noble descent and were called upon (or obliged) to become hoplites, when it was already clear that the new way of war required more men. This explanation would also explain the reason why on early Corinthian pottery there are depictions of hoplites holding two spears or a long sword and not just one spear and one short sword as used by the hoplites of the Classical period. Clearly, there must have also been a transitional period during which the old and new forms of war co-existed and gradually through experimentation in the battlefield, the latter gained its final form (Snodgrass 1965: 110-113, 120; Salmon 1977: 91-92; van Wees 1994: 142-143).[15] According to van Wees (1994: 147), it took nearly two centuries to crystallize the form and tactics of the hoplite phalanx. Van Wees notes that from 700 BC onwards the spear replaces the sword as the weapon of choice for close quarters combat, while war-chariots were removed from the battlefield around the same time. Gradually, the hoplites become visibly distinguishable from the light-armed troops (psiloi) whose previous significance lessens. By the end of the 6th c. BC, the hoplites fighting gear was finalized and included a shield[16], a cuirass, a helmet, a spear and a sword.

It is accepted common historical assumption that the hoplite phalanx was a decisive factor in shaping the political reality of the Archaic Age. Even the scholars who are skeptical of hoplite involvement in establishing tyrannies, either through active participation or through a passive stance (Snodgrass 1965: 122; van Wees 1994: 148), have reached consensus that the enlargement of the military body in city-states led to the gradual enlargement of the citizen body. The reforms responsible for transforming aristocracies into timocracies were the result of pressure from the non-aristocrats who took part in the wars as hoplites. Fighting side-by-side with the aristocrats, the social groups who were up to that time excluded from public affairs began to realize the significance their presence and actions played in the preservation

---

ment, which is considered a turning point in world history of international relations and is usually juxtaposed with the Geneva Convention, can be found in Wheeler (1987) along with the relevant discussion about the historical significance of the event.

15 Cartledge (1977: 20) rejects Snodgrass' view that the phalanx was a product of a long and gradual process, objecting that the adoption of the new type shield required that the hoplites should find as soon as possible a way to cover the exposed half of their body.

16 Let it be noted that Connor's observation (1988: 25) concerning the ancient Greek warfare is organically linked with the shield as well as with the hoplite class.

Hoplitic phalanx. Attican dark-figured amphora (c. 560 BC)

and well-being of the city-state. They were gaining the right to express their dissatisfaction and opposition to the governing aristocracy. As far as the aristocrats were concerned, the adoption of new weapons and the subsequent prevalence of the new form of warfare - based on collective action and not on individual prowess - undermined their previous status (van Wees 1994: 148; Salmon 1977: 95-96). As a result, aristocrats had to succumb to the pressures of the hoplites and to abandon the monopoly of political power. Characteristic examples include Solon's reform and the provision of political rights to the zeugites[17]. The zeugites, who by many are associated with the hoplite class, had already become a distinct group and had gained access to political power as bestowed upon them by the Solon city-state (Snodgrass 1965: 122). Similarly, in Sparta the body of hoplites became synonymous

---

17 In contrast to the dominant view that attributes to the term 'zeugites' a mainly agricultural or economical content (the person who owns a pair of oxen, in other words the small land owner) -where military content becomes only secondary-, David Whitehead (1981: 286) considers that the term indicates the person who serves along the hoplite lines. The words 'ζυγός' and 'ζυγόν' also mean the phalanx front (as opposed to the phalanx depth) as well as the middle line of the rowing seats in a trireme.

with the body of citizens. Paradoxically, the Greek word for citizen (*polites*) is an anagram of the word 'hoplites'. It is also possible that the famous "decree" (*rhetra*) of the Spartan city-state had been brought about by the pressure of the body (*damos*) of the hoplites (Salmon 1977: 97). Within this framework, the term '*homoioi*' used for Spartan citizens has military origins, referring to the homogeneity of their fighting armament and training and not to the equality of their material wealth, nor to their common way of life (Cartledge 1977:27).

However, the hoplite phalanx was something more than just a tactical formation. In reality, it represented a way of life, a code of bravery and ethics, the acceptance and the application of a system of rules, values and beliefs (Ferrill 1985: 145). It was inconceivable for a citizen to try to avoid serving in the military. This was true not only for Sparta, but also for Athens, where the laws against objection to serving are traced back to the time of Solon or at the latest Cleisthenes (Runciman 1998: 737; Ridley 1979). The citizen-hoplites fought to defend their vested rights and were opposed to anything that threatened their independence. They also fought to gain control of any region that could be of vital importance to their city-state. One of their most fundamental duties was to obey the laws (*thesmia*) as much in politics as in their military life: to pay tribute to the dead, to respect a truce, to devote the spoils of war to the gods of the Panhellenic temples (Runciman 1998: 738-739, 747).

Studying the funeral oration of ancient Athenians to their dead , Nicole Loreaux (1986: 98) noted that on a certain level, the virtue of the citizen was overshadowed by the virtue of the hoplite. Nevertheless, the hoplite virtue was not projected autonomously from its political context, but worked as a frame within which military action is offered as an exemplar of political action. The democratic essence of the phalanx was based as much on the fact that its tactical effectiveness was dependent on everyone's coopera-tion, as well as on the fact that those excelling on the field of battle were no longer individuals but entire armies. Hence the leader was no longer the sole source of intimidation for his opponents, but the entire force – the Spartans, the Athenians, the Argives (Runciman 1998: 732-733). Finally, the hoplite phalanx both empowers and symbolizes the urban unity of the city-states, depicting their structure and their social system (Connor 1998: 24).[18] Perhaps

---

18 Within this framework it can be easily understood that the "psiloi" did not play as central a role in the battles during the archaic and classical periods although the features of Greek land favoured their utiliza-tion; whatever the upgrade of their role would gradually lead to their demands on more participation in the public affairs. As a consequence, the radical democracy of Athens is related to the fact that, in the course of time, the city, as a marine power, was supported mainly by the rowers and the shipbuilders coming from the

its most significant contribution to the military attitudes of antiquity was that it replaced the egotism of heroic honor with pride of the city-state; or as M.I. Finley (1964: 133) puts it, the laurel wreath took the place of gold, silver, and captured women as the victor's prize.

1.3.1 Armour: Hoplites, Light-armed, and Cavalrymen

Hoplites were named after their shield (*hoplon*) and as we saw previously, the shift in the technology and the construction of the shield had an effect on the development of military affairs during the Archaic period. From the archaeological data available, it can be ascertained that the small cyclical shield of the late Mycenaean period must have been maintained up to the Geometric Age (1100-1800 BC). This type of shield was made of leather and bore one or more bronze discs of about 1.5cm diameter with an arched centre (*omphalion*), which could be adjusted at the centre of the outer side and sometimes had an extended point (Giarenis 2008α: 198-205). The new shield, which emerged after 800 BC, called "*argoliki*" (from Argos) – quite possibly due to its origin - was more curved with a diameter of .90-1.00m[19] and had two handles (grips), the *porpax* and the *antilabe*. The central handle was called the *porpax*, a sheet most often made of metal, which gripped the hoplite's left forearm; the second handle (*antilabe*) was usually made of leather and could be found on the inner side of the shield's edge. In this way, the weight of the shield (7-8 kgs approximately) was no longer concentrated at the end of the hand or the hoplite's wrist but was distributed along the left arm (Hanson 2003: 103).

Wood was the basic material out of which the shield was made and it was applied in layers, in order to achieve greater endurance. The outer curved side was covered in bronze sheets and adorned in the middle with a drawn or carved representation of the hoplite's emblem. With the passing of time, and as the hoplite phalanx was established, personal emblems were replaced by the city-state's emblem[20].

---

class of the thites primarily and only secondary the hoplites (Holliday 1982: 103; Connor 1998: 27-29).

19 Archaeological excavation sites have revealed a unique sample of a shield about 1.20m in diameter. It is, thus, quite possible that the shield dimensions varied depending on the height and physical strength of each hoplite (Snodgrass 2003: 98-99).

20 From the classical period onwards, the Spartan shield bore the L (= Lacedaemonean), the Messenians the M, the Syceans the S, the Arcadians the AR, the Thebes the club (the symbol of Hercules, patron of Thebe), the Euboeans an oxen head etc. (Kampouris 2000: 36).

On the periphery of the shield, there was a solid bronze ring (*stephane*) with an increased tilt pointing outwards, which allowed the hoplite to support the shield with his shoulder, thereby reducing the burden on his arm (Giarenis 2008b; Georgis 1995: 22; Cartledge 1977: 12-13).

The shield's key drawback was that it provided protection to only one side of the body. However, this was counter-balanced by the phalanx formation[21]: each hoplite protected the left side of his body and the right side of the body of the hoplite next to them in the line. In a frontal attack, they would try to bring their left shoulders forward, and at the same time, pull back their right sides; or more frequently, they would try to stay as close as possible to the hoplites on the right, so as to remain protected by their shield. In doing so, a solid wall of shields was formed, which would slightly shift to the right due to the reflexive hoplite movement[22].

In pottery depictions from the Persian wars, hoplites wear a type of cuirass (*thorax*) made of linen layers (*linothorax*) or leather (*spolas*) usually with bronze fittings. This type of armor was established in the early 5th c. BC, to replace the older brass-plated bell-shaped cuirass, which was part of the hoplites' armor from previous centuries. The bell-shaped cuirass weighed about 15-18kgs[23], was 5-6mm thick, and the breast-plate was modeled to imitate the musculature of the torso. It covered both chest and back while it was frequently accompanied by protective shoulder epaulets (shoulder flashes or *epomides*). It slightly curved outward above the hip socket, creating a kind of arch – giving it its characteristic bell shape and protecting the hoplite's abdomen without obstructing his movement. Despite the fact that the bronze bell-shaped cuirass maximized protection [24], its weight and lack of ventilation were the main drivers behind its gradual replacement by the much lighter

---

21 The hoplite shield was suitable exclusively for this specific type of battle. Its use in any other battle was deemed dangerous (Cartledge 1977: 20).

22 Hoplites in the last line of the right flank of the phalanx were completely unprotected. Thus, a flank attack on the right led to catastrophic consequences for the phalanx (see Xenophon, *Hellenica*, IV 2.22 and IV 5.13).

23 This means that the hoplite could not wear his cuirass unassisted (Donlan & Thompson 1976: 34). Nevertheless, despite the gradual decrease of the armor's weight, it seems heavier armor continued to be constructed and left to the warrior's preference. According to Plutarch, the cuirass of king Demetrius of Macedonia weighed 20kgs (Plutarch, *Demetrius*, 21); while as witnessed by Diodorus Siculus, the Syracuse tyrant Agathocles had, from the start, won everyone's admiration because no one could lift his heavy armor (Diodoros Sic., *Hist. Bibl.*, 19.3a).

24 This bronze cuirass could sustain many successive blows. Plutarch characteristically says that during the battle at Cynos Cephales in 364 BC, Pelopidas later succumbed to the multiple enemy blows, which had totally destroyed his cuirass in the end (Plutarch, *Pelopidas*, 32.6-7).

Hoplite with sword, where in the central armband of the shield, the porpax and the antilabe can be discerned (work by Stelios Nigdi-opoulos)

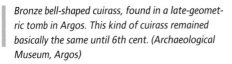

Bronze bell-shaped cuirass, found in a late-geometric tomb in Argos. This kind of cuirass remained basically the same until 6th cent. (Archaeological Museum, Argos)

The back section of the cuirass (Archaeological Museum of Olympia). The greave on the left was found in Olympia and is stored at the Archaeological museum, while the one on the left comes from the Acropolis and it is on display at the National Archaeological Museum (Athens)

one made of linen – although of less endurance compared to the metal one[25] (Giarenis 2008α: 198-205; Steinhauer 2000: 48-50; Cartledge 1977: 14).

The hoplites' defensive armor[26] included a helmet, which was particularly known as the Corinthian helmet, illustrated on pottery in the early 7th c. BC (Snodgrass 1967: 20). It was made from a unified bronze sheet and it covered the entire head and neck, with only a T-shaped opening in the eye, nose, and mouth areas. Its disadvantage was that it obstructed hearing and peripheral vision; but it proved suited to the specific type of battle where maintaining a tight formation was of decisive importance. Improvements were gradually made with the addition of openings in the ear areas and grooves in the neck area (Kormallis 2010: 33-38; Giarenis 2008α: 198-205; Georgis 1995: 55; Cartledge 1977: 14).[27]

The main offensive weapon of the warriors in the phalanx was the spear (*dory*). It was made from ash wood or wild-cherry tree wood, 1.5 to 2cm in diameter, 2.5m in length and weighed approximately 3kgs. The spearhead, which was made out of steel beginning in the 7th c. BC (had previously been

25 In the first half of the 5th c. BC, an improved version of the bell-shaped cuirass appears covering the area of the groin where a series of special flaps are attached for increased protection. This is the type of cuirass usually encountered on Roman statues.

26 Only the greaves remained from the older defensive armour of warriors. The pieces that protected the thighs (*perimeridia*), the ankles (*perisphyridia*) and the arms (*psellia*) were abandoned in an attempt to free the warrior from excess weight (Giarenis 2008a: 198-205; Cartledge 1977: 14).

27 In tandem with the Corinthian helmet, in the early 7th c. BC, the so-called "Illyric" helmet was introduced, mainly in the western parts of Greece which allowed for less facial coverage. A variation of the Corinthian helmet was the "Chalcidic" one with rounded instead of pointed cheekpieces (*paragnathides*) which sometimes had the shape of a goat-like head, and with special openings on the sides so as not to obstruct hearing (Giarenis 2008a: 198-205).

made out of bronze), was leaf-shaped with a central vein and a socket to be fixed on the wooden pole (*xyston*). On its other end, the spear bore a metallic (usually brass) butt, the *sauroter*[28] (or *styrax*) in the shape of a pyramid, 20cm in length. The *sauroter* balanced out the weight of the spearhead and allowed the spear to be placed in an upright position when not in use. During the battle, it extended the spear's fatal potential since vertical wounds could be achieved – even if the spear had been broken. This practice was widespread, as evidenced by the square holes in the cuirasses found in ancient Olympia (Kormallis 2010: 33-38; Giarenis 2008a: 198-205; Giarenis 2008b; Georgis 1995: 52; Cartledge 1977: 15; Snodgrass 1967: 56, 80).

The sword was the warrior's secondary offensive weapon and could be used in close quarters combat, which ensued once the phalanx broke up. Made of iron, with a length ranging from 45cm to 65cm, it was double-edged or with only one curved leaf-shaped edge (*kopis*). It was carried in a case (*koleos*), which hung from the hoplite's shoulder and attached to a leather belt (*telamon*). Apart from the sword, the hoplites also used various kinds of daggers – the laconic one being the most well known(Giarenis 2008b; Georgis 1995: 53; Cartledge 1977: 15).

Hoplites, during archaic and classic times, were obliged to buy and maintain their military armor. At the end of the 6th c. BC, a complete hoplite armor cost at least 30 drachmas in Athens (which was the equivalent of six healthy oxen); while in Thasos in the 4th c. BC, the cost could reach as much as 300 drachmas (Jackson 1999:229; Gregoropoulos 2009: 46). Therefore, it goes without saying that the financial capability of providing weapons was limited to the wealthy citizens, be they nobles or not (the *pentakosiomedimnoi*, the *hippeis* and the *zeugites*, during Solon's period). The *thetes* offered their services to the light-armed infantrymen, who took part in expeditions, but whose role in battle was not central[29].

Depending on their weaponry, the light-armed infantrymen were divided into *peltasts*, *psiloi* and *slingers*[30]. Like the hoplites, the *peltasts* were named

---

28 As indicated by the historian Polybius, the problem with the Romans during their first clashes with the Greeks was that their spears did not have a sauroter; hence, after being damaged they were useless (Polybius, *Hist.*, 6.25.9).

29 Their active involvement was limited to throwing javelins arrows and stones at the enemy phalanx, with the aim of causing confusion and disorder in enemy lines. As concluded by Thucydides, the non-coordinated use of the light-armed infantrymen explains the fact that up until 424 BC, their weaponry had not yet been standardized. Nevertheless, the light-armed forces played a vital role in the Peloponnesian war, when the battles did not take place only in open plains. From the early 4th c. BC, the light-armed infantrymen received a strategic upgrade. Linked to this were the peltasts forces by Iphicrates, who combined characteristics of the phalanx and the usual active involvement of the light-armed units (Georgis 1995: 47-48).

30 Slingers did not have any defensive weapons, other than slings with which they threw rocks or special

The oldest Greek helmet found in a post-geometric period tomb in Argos (left). In the middle, an Illyric helmet, which appeared in the Peloponnese in the 7th c. BC. On the right, a Boeotian helmet

after their shield, the *pelte* (a small light crescent-shaped shield). Though primarily used by Thracian warriors initially from 550 BC onwards, its use became more prevalent throughout Greece[31]. The *pelte* was made from tightly-knitted branches of the chaste tree and reinforced with goat or sheep-skin. The peltasts' weaponry also included three javelins[32] (Giarenis 2008a: 198-205; Georgis 1995: 53; Sekunda 1986: 12-13; Adcock 1957: 21).

The *psiloi* bore no defensive protection and used javelins and arrows (Giarenis 2008a: 198-205; Georgis 1995: 53-54). Despite Hercules being one of the greatest legendary heroes – an excellent archer whose arrows, according to tradition, had to reach the Achaeans camp, so that Troy would fall – the Greeks during the archaic and classical periods viewed the bow/arrow with contempt. One possible explanation is that close quarters fighting either in the form of personal confrontation among aristocrats or in the form of the hoplite phalanx was the dominant mode of warfare at the time. It may have been the case that the arrow got its non-heroic reputation due to the fact that Achilles was cunningly killed by the arrow of Paris. The extensive use of this specific weapon by the Persian troops may have reinforced the Greeks' condescending attitude. This is exactly what is implied by the Spartan Di-

---

shells at enemy groups (Giarenis 2008a: 198-205; Georgis 1995: 54). The sling was one of the most ancient weapons, since there are indications of its usage in the 7th millennium, and its widespread use coincides with the spread of the Neolithic life style. It must be noted that the construction of lead shells at the end of the Bronze Age is considered a type of technological breakthrough in the development of warfare tactics. These new shells, whose caliber was greater than the ones made of stone, were also smaller in volume allowing for their transfer in greater quantities (Bouturopoulos 1996: 64-68).

31 It is possible that the dissemination of the pelte could be linked to the Paeones mercenaries recruited by Peisistratus (Snodgrass 2000: 138, 145; Depastas 1999: 349).

32 The length of the javelin was 1,70-1,80m, its point was smaller than that of the spear and it is possible that its caliber was about 15-20m (Georgis 1995: 53).

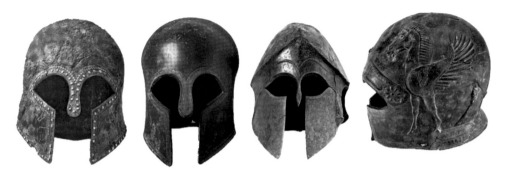

Different types of Corinthian helmets. A variation was found in the 7th c. BC in Axos, Crete (last on the right)

enekes' proud response "we'll fight in the shade" to the news that the arrows of the Persians in the Thermopylae would be so numerous that they would hide the sun (Herod., *Histories*, VII, 226.1-2). Either way, the insufficiency of Persian archers against the heavy hoplite phalanx had been proven in the battle of Marathon. A few years after the end of the Persian wars, Aeschylus would reinforce the dominant mentality regarding the inferiority of the archer contrasting the arch to the triumphant spear (*Persians*, l. 147-149: πότερον τόξου ῥῦμα τὸ νικῶν ἢ δορικράνου λόγχης ἰσχὺς κεκράτηκεν) and forcing the messenger to announce the defeat in Salamis with the confession that the archers were found to be useless (l. 278: οὐδὲν γὰρ ἤρκει τόξα). While it could be that Euripides, through Amphitryon's word, was projecting the military significance of the archers in the tragedy *Heracles*, at that same time the Spartans at the island of Sphacteria (424 BC) preferred to surrender rather than be defeated by coward archers[33].

Up until the 7th c. BC, only Thessaly and to a lesser extent Boeotia and its neighboring cities used the cavalry as an important component of their military power. Of course, Athens and other cities had forces of cavalrymen (*hippeis*) but these did not gain prominence as primary tools of military power, largely due to the terrain in Greece. Furthermore, obtaining and maintaining a horse was very costly. As a result, the number of cavalry was limited and could not have constituted the basic military power of any city. Moreover, the majority of military campaigns and wars occurred in the spring and summer, which made procuring food and water for horses even more problematic.

With the creation of the hoplite phalanx, the cavalry could be put to effec-

---

33 This incident is mentioned by Thucydides (*Histories*, IV, 40). The Spartan prisoners reported that archers did not distinguish the brave from the cowards and they characterized them as "spindles" (*atraktous*), implying that the archers were cowards since the spindles are typical female tools.

tive use only in reconnaissance operations and in pursuit of the enemy army; a practice, however, which was not widely implemented during the Archaic period. However, the flanks and the rear sections of the phalanx were vulnerable to a cavalry attack and there are examples of this occurring, with the brilliant Thessalian cavalrymen as the leading protagonists. A thousand Thessalian cavalrymen, allies of Peisistratides Hippias, crushed a small contingent of Spartan infantry under Anchimolius, in the plain behind the Faleron bay (Herod. *Hist.*, V, 63). Also, after the battle of Plataea, the cavalry of the Thessalians and the Boeotians, which both fought with the Persians, delayed the triumphant advance of the united Greek powers (Herod., *Hist.*, IX, 68) (Adcock 1957: 47-49).

The cavalrymen were derived from the wealthiest classes[34] due to the cost of obtaining and maintaining a horse. For practical reasons, their armor was basic[35], including a cuirass, a helmet (Attic, Boeotian, Phrygian or Thracian type)[36] and a spear[37]. Their uniform was equally simple and limited to a short tunic (*chitoniskos*) since the eastern trousers (*anaxyris*) and leg-bands (*periskelis*) were not adopted by the Greeks. Their special leather shoes (*embades*) had thick soles, which may have reached up to the shins and were tied around the leg with straps. Lastly, instead of a saddle[38] they used a cloth, the *ephippion*, which was secured by belts around the horses' chest and haunches. The horse was also protected primarily from arrow strikes by metal covers on its sides (*parapleuridia*) and its forehead (*prometopidia*) (Gregoropoulos 2009: 44-50; Ray 2009: 18-19; Georgis 1995: 50).

---

34 With Solon's reform, the *"hippeis"* are called triakosiomedimnoi, a fact which perhaps reveals the identification of the military forces and social class just as in the case of the *zeugites*; yet, this does not rule out the *pentakosiomedimnoi* from the forces of cavalry.

35 Although the armor of cavalrymen cost less than that of the hoplites in the early the 4th c. BC, mercenary cavalrymen in serving the tyrant of Syracuse Dionysius the Elder, were equipped through state expense. Likewise, at the beginning of the 3rd c. BC, Athenian cavalrymen received their armor by the state. However, these were isolated incidents, since the *hippeis* could afford to cover such expenses (Gregoropoulos 2009: 46).

36 The use of the Attic helmet by Athenian cavalrymen is witnessed in the 5th c. BC without it being known whether they bore it in battle or only in public, mainly religious, social events. The Boeotian, Phrygian and Thracian helmets may have had a crest at the top. Other known head covers for cavalrymen were the *petasos*, a felt or straw broad-rounded brim, and the *causia* which resemble today's beret and was used by the Macedonians (Gregoropoulos 2009: 50).

37 The cavalrymen's spear extended about 2m having two points, a short iron one on one end and a bronze one on the other, comparable to the *sauroter*. The *hippeis* would use it in order to strike successfully the infantry of the enemy army (Gregoropoulos 2009: 46)

38 Since the saddle or stirrups were missing, the horse-rider would jump on the horse, held by the animal's mane or by using the spear's support (Gregoropoulos 2009: 57).

Hoplite wearing linothorax, holding shield and sword. His broken spear is supported in the ground by the sauroteras. (A work by Stelios Nigdiopoulos)

The shields of the hoplites bore various representations or the emblem of cities-states. This shield depicts the frightening head of the Medusa (A work by Stelios Nigdiopoulos)

1.3.2 The "customs", the ethos of warfare and the battle in phalanxes

Having studied the history and practice of warfare in ancient Greece, V. D. Hanson (2005: 30-35) identified eight general characteristics which flow from a network of social, economic and technological conditions and which were in effect for about four centuries (700-300 BC). These characteristics, which the Greeks bequeathed to western civilization can be summarized as follows:

1. Advanced technology: inventions and improvements such as the *sauroter* or the second grip of the shield make weapons more effective and superior paving the way for innovations in warfare tactics.

2. Exceptional discipline: the successful advance of the phalanx was a direct function of hoplite discipline. This, however, was a product of free will and validation of group consensus, which, was in turn, integrated into the framework of citizen-state relationships.

3. Inventiveness in reactions to unforeseen circumstances: possibly the most important characteristic of the Greek spirit, which did not consider it improper to adopt, apply and amend military practices of other people. Because of this attitude, the Greeks found a way to deal with elephants and later integrate them in their army as well as receive maximum use of the functionality of siege engines[39].

Depiction of hoplitic phalanx accompanied by the piper on Corinthian pottery dated back to 640 BC

4. Creation of a widely-shared military perception in the majority of the population: the practice of cities constituting their armies from their citizens and not from mercenaries was their comparative advantage over the Persians. As for the citizens, it was not fear of being penalized for "disgrace" which compelled them to offer their services to the military, but the self-explanatory obligation to defend the prosperity and the ideals of the city-state within a framework of the ideological link between being a citizen and being a hoplite.

5. Choice of decisive participation: the face-to-face confrontation with the enemy, the close quarters combat and bringing the fight to an end by maxi-

---

39 The example used by the philosopher Stephen Toulmin is interesting, in that it attempts to explain the difference between the rational and the reasonable way of thought and action. Toulmin links rationality with "the focusing narrowly on matters of content" and reasonableness with "a feeling for the dozen ways in which a situation may modify both the content and the style of arguments". Then he explains the difference between the two by saying that the Romans used to set up their camps without deviation following the existing rules in every place (rational), while the Greeks were setting up their camps making use of and benefitting from the terrestrial and geographic conditions of each area (reasonable) (Toulmin 2001: 21-22, 36-37).

mizing speed and determination, were not merely elements of Greek battle tactics, but stemmed from the fact that the conduct of battle was the final military expression of the will of the majority of citizens.

6. Dominance of the infantry: conquering and ultimate victory was a result of hoplite advance according to the tactics imposed by the phalanx formation.

7. Systematic use of capital for military purposes: the engagement in long-term wars, but also the success of operations, was in part a result of the city-states ability to gather material and human capital (money, supplies and men) which they then allocated to military aims. The economic policy of the Athenians (tax collection, tariffs, lending etc.) are a characteristic example. Similarly, Alexander the Great managed to complete his expedition to the East because his treasury staff knew how to tax and collect, in order to enable the funding of a specialized body of attendants (for each day of marching, Alexander's army required over 1,000 tons of food, water and animal feed).

8. Moral opposition to militarism: in ancient Greece war was coded by a system of "laws" (*thesmia)* and "customs" (*nomima)* which aimed to maintain a moral foundation. Despite this, particularly in classical Athens, doubts and criticism of warfare behavior and attitudes could still be found and were expressed by artistic, political and religious groups who obstructed the imprudent use of military power. Remembering Eyripides' tragedy *Trojan Women,* where behind the mythical façade the poet is scathing about the slaughter of the Melians by the Athenians in 415 BC.

These characteristics were prevalent from the Archaic period until the end of the Classical period, coinciding broadly with the cycle of the city-state and the dominance of the hoplite phalanx. Since then, and in tandem with political and social changes, a shift in the form and the manners of war occurs. The first "cracks" were incurred by the Peloponnesian war, but their effects do not manifest themselves fully until the Hellenistic years.

Returning to the period when the hoplites were at their peak, it appears that except for differentiation in the form of war, the hoplite phalanx was also linked to the establishment, the standardization or the systematization of the rules which dealt with the conduct and ritual of war. These rules, called "customs" (*nomima)* or "laws" (*thesmia)* manifested themselves from the second half of the 7th c. BC until the 4th c. BC. Some of these rules which are primarily religious in nature dated back to Homer's time while others are the result of the prevailing practice and common sense of the time and do not necessarily have a religious foundation (Hanson 2005: 88-91, Krentz 2002).

1. Formal declaration of war and explicit lifting of the existing truces and treaties: before the mid 5th c. BC, very few undeclared wars and surprise infantry attacks were carried out. The established practice, which was not always adhered to, was the ceremonial announcement of the beginning of hostilities (mission of messengers) and the formal declaration of those involved, through their leaders, that the war was just, legal and noble.

2. Ceremonial preparations for the battle and the frontal attack of the phalanx: the ceremony prior to the battle comprised the formal announcement of the battle, the performance of a public sacrifice in front of the phalanx, and the delivery of a brief speech by the leader .

3. Battles were held in summer and in spring and restricted only during the day: although it could be attributed to religious reasons, this rule came about from the dominant practice, which was in turn imposed mainly by objective and practical factors. The autumn months were devoted to agricultural activities, so the hoplites could return to their properties; at the same time, the expeditions in spring and summer would allow for the destruction of the cultivated lands of the rival city-state.

4. Termination of murderous acts: the persecution of the defeated stopped at dusk and the defeated could seek shelter in the mountains. Usually, the winners would not execute the wounded or the prisoners of war, who were either released, as a result of a treaty, or via payment of ransom to avoid slavery. This practice was witnessed, with some exceptions, until the 5th c. BC in wars between Greek cities.

5. Restrictions of war: the civilian population and messengers were usually respected by the combatants. Similarly, attacks and seizure of both local and Panhellenic sanctuaries and temples were prohibited. Finally, truces that were valid during the Olympic Games and other religious and/or athletic events were not violated.

6. Restrictions of weapon use: the battle organization with the hoplite phalanx serving as the central force also determined the use of offensive weaponry (spears, shields, swords). The cavalry and the light-armed infantry saw limited action before and after battle, while the slingers and stone-throwers were rarely used, but always on the brink of battle.

7. Posthumous homage to the dead: the plundering and looting of the dead (*skuleusis*) was an abhorrent act. After a cease-fire or a truce, the defeated would normally ask for the return of their dead, an act which was tantamount to accepting defeat. The winners would put up a trophy on the battlefield, which was regarded as sacred and its desecration was prohibited. Paying homage to the fallen in battle was of vital importance to the life of the city-

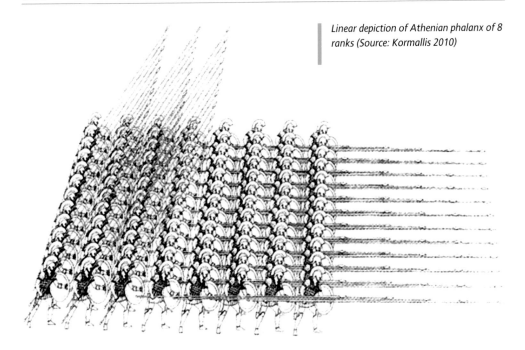

Linear depiction of Athenian phalanx of 8 ranks (Source: Kormallis 2010)

state and functioned as the backbone of their ideological identity. The burial of the dead was conducted with every formality and often their names were inscribed in commemoratory steles. The warriors' heroism and the value of his sacrifice were associated it with the ideal of political virtue and were lauded by funeral orations, perhaps the most exceptional samples of the epideictic genre of rhetoric, battle representations on friezes and pottery as well as the elegies of the poets (Hanson 2005: 69-70, 88, 91).

Around the 6th c. BC, the army of the Greek city-states comprised hoplites, light-armed infantry, peltasts, and cavalrymen. The phalanx was the primary tactical unit of the army made up of 4,000 hoplites, deployed in 8 or sometimes even 12 ranks (zygos) (the Macedonian phalanx had 16 ranks) with the best fighters placed in the first or last lines. The peltasts were deployed at a short distance behind the hoplites, of equal front but at half the depth (4 or 6 ranks). The light-armed infantry had no pre-determined position. Depending on particular battle conditions, they could be placed either at the front or at the back of the lines, or small groups of them could be placed in the gaps between the units of the infantry. Finally, the cavalry (troops of 64 cavalrymen deployed in 4 ranks) covered both flanks of the formation (Connor 1988: 12-13; Panagiotidis 1927:2-3).

The hoplites did not arrive at the battlefield in their full armor, since the armor's heavy weight would not allow for it. Each hoplite was accompanied

by a personal servant (who may have been a slave or a free but poor citizen) who tended to the transport of weaponry and helped his master prepare before the battle commenced (Pritchett 1975: 49-51). For the same reason, namely the weight of the armor, the battles did not last more than a couple of hours and always took place in an open plain; more often than not, it was the combatants who determined the location of the battlefield and when the clash would begin (Pritcett 1975: 147; Georgis 1995: 47-48).

Deployed in phalanx formation (*phallangedon*)[40], the hoplites essentially looked like a mobile wall of shields through which their spears projected. The successive ranks guaranteed the formation's cohesion even if the frontline had broken up. As the battle began, the hoplites speedily proceeded side-by-side maintaining a tight formation under the audible directive of the flutist (Giarenis 2008b; Lorimer 1947: 81-82, 94-95)[41].

The minute the two rival formations clashed, an intense struggle of pushing began (*othismos*: Ray 2009: 11-12; Pritchet 1985: 65; Gregoriadis 1951: 18, 30)[42]. Each hoplite would put the weight of his shield on his left shoulder and push the hoplites in front of him; the concave shape of the shield along with its inclined arch was helpful in this movement.[43] Each phalanx aimed to break up the opposing phalanx while remaining intact. The hoplites' strength and their ability to remain in line were key factors in determining the outcome of the confrontation (Giarenis 2008b; Connor 1998: 14). The phalanx which succumbed to the opposing pressure (*othismos*) retreated and broke up (referred to as the trope[44]). The *trope* signaled not only the opponents' retreat, but also the change in the mode of fighting since what followed were individual con-

---

40 The Generals were not mere spectators of the battle, but fought along with the combatants (in the front line of the phalanx) and in the case of defeat, they were among the first to fall; we mention as examples Leonidas at Thermopylae, the Athenian Callias in Potidaea, the Spartans Eurylochus and Macarius in Olpes, the Corinthian Lycophron in Solygeia etc. For this reason, the hoplites surrounded their leaders with utmost respect (Giarenis 2008a: 427).

41 The flutist is already depicted in pottery of the second half of the 7th c. BC (Salmon 1977: 89-91; Cartledge 1977: 16). During the battle, the sounds heard were usually the paean accompanied by the flute (Thucydides V 70.1; Plutarch, *Lycurgus,* 21); the Spartans even sang to the lyrics of Tyrtaeus (Connor 1988: 13) and the war cries against the enemy (Thucydides VII.44; Xenophon, Anab., 1.8-18, *Hellenica,* 2.4.31) while the commands for advancing or retreating were given with trumpet calls (Thucydides VI 69.2; Xenophon, *Anab.,* 4.4.22).

42 Gradually other maneuvers were incited such as the "laconic movement" (*exeligmos*), which was used for the first time in the battle of Mantineia between the Spartans and the Argives (418 BC) (Cartledge 1977: 16).

43 By the end of the 4th c. BC, infantrymen hung their smaller-sized shields from their neck (whose diameter was 60 cm), so that they could maneuver the heavier Macedonian spear called "sarisa". As a result, the shields no longer had a concave shape or inclined arch.

44 From the word *trope* the word *tropaeon* (trophy) is derived, the memorial put up by the victorious in the battlefield. The etymology of the word reveals that it reminded chiefly the defeat of the opponents.

frontations with swords. The battle ended with the pursuit of the defeated, usually by the cavalry. This pursuit did not aim to annihilate the opposing hoplites[45], but to force them to withdraw quickly, causing them to shed their armament. The abandoned weapons by the defeated were the spoils of war. The winners dedicated a part of these to the gods and kept the remainder as a form of personal reward (Hanson 2005: 69-70).

The maintenance of cohesion was, therefore, of vital importance to both achieving victory and to the hoplites' lives. The result of this interdependence is in part the absolute equality of the hoplites in the lines of the phalanx, since no one is more important than the other during battle (Steinhauer 2000: 65). The meaning of the phrase "comrade in arms" must have been coined in reference to this period as trust and solidarity were necessary ingredients in the transformation of a group of people into a collective whole, with an internal cohesion, discipline and coordinated action.

1.3.3 Addendum: The Navy

If the changes witnessed during the Archaic period in the infantry warriors' equipment and in the form of land warfare are considered significant, the developments dealing with naval matters were of no lesser importance. Up until the 6th c. BC, the warships used in naval operations were biremes which had 2 series of oars and a ram (*embolon*); the penteconters belonged to this type with 25 oars in every row. However, between 538 and 522 BC, the tyrant of Samos Polycrates, who had a powerful fleet with 100 penteconters, used 40 triremes[46], a new type of ship that was faster and more powerful (Herod., *Hist.*, III, 39.44). This ship was to be recognized as the main factor behind the Athenian victory at Salamis, which laid the foundation of its naval power and subsequent maritime hegemony (Steinhauer 2000: 250-259; Sakellariou 1971b: 258).

According to tradition, while the first trireme was built around 704 BC by the Corinthian Ameinocles (Thucydides, *Hist.* i, 13), it did not appear before 530 BC. It is a long, fast, lightly constructed wooden ship, with a shallow hull, a ram and a total of 170 oars in three successive rows. Its dimensions

---

45 As a rule, the basic intention of wars during the classical period was the acquisition or the redistribution of land. The extermination of a rival city-state with raids and sweeping operations were deemed a waste of time and money all at the same time as it contradicted the "customs" (Hanson 2005: 69-70).

46 The term 'trimeme' is mentioned for the first time by Hipponax the Ephesian around 550 BC (Fields 2007: 4).

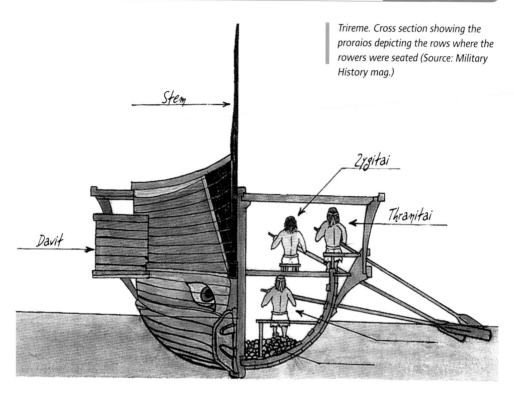

Trireme. Cross section showing the proraios depicting the rows where the rowers were seated (Source: Military History mag.)

Stem

Zygitai

Thranitai

Davit

are estimated to be 33-37m in length, 3.50-4.50m in height above waves level(plus 1m ship's bottom). The anchor was made of either iron or wood with a stone counterweight similar to the ones used today. It is speculated that the stony truncated pyramids with a perforated opening at the top, found at the Zea dockyard, were used as stable anchors for mooring ships (Steinhauer 2000: 250-259).

The Athenian trireme had a crew of 200 people. The170 rowers (eretai) were distributed in three rows as follows: 62 (31+31) thranitai (seated in the upper row, operated the longest oars and usually received additional pay); 32 (16+16) zugioi or zugitai (seated in the middle row); and 22 (11+11) thalami-tai (seated in the bottom row, they operated the smaller oars and therefore got paid the least). Command of the ship belonged to the trierarch followed by 10 fighting men (epivatai)– Athenian hoplites whose place was on deck. The seven officers who served the trierarch were: the steersman (kybernetes; also known as archos, naukleros or oiakostrophos), the officer in command at the bow (prorates), the signalman who directed the rowers (keleustes), the pentekontarch (the quartermaster who, at an earlier time, was in charge of the crew, but who on the trireme performed the duties of treasurer), the ship-wright in charge of repairs (naupegos) and the piper (auletes) who set the

rowing rhythm. The crew also included the trierarch's bodyguards (4 archers located at the stern) and ten sailors in charge of handling the masts and sails (Steinhauer 2000: 250-259; Fields 2007: 13-17; Hunt 2008: 124-125).

With the exception of the Athenian ships, the Greek fleet, which took part in the naval battle of Lade in 494 BC, consisted exclusively of triremes. However, Athens would soon compensate for falling behind, primarily due to the political initiative and astuteness of Themistocles, who built 200 triremes, which would subsequently obliterate the Persians at Salamis. This victory served as a springboard for the growing Athenian naval power (Steinhauer 2000: 250-259)[47].

1.4. Sparta, the powerful city-state of continental Greece

The archaic was a time of decisive importance for Sparta although not devoid of turmoil. The city tried to solve its shortage of agricultural land through a series of wars with its neighbors. Subsequently, Sparta amended its political system so as to ensure the much-desired and rather utopic (for other cities-states) political stability. And, towards the end of the archaic period – when it established itself as the most powerful city-state in all of Greece – Sparta strengthened the Peloponnesian alliance and attempted to interfere with the internal affairs of other city-states.

The Spartan fighting adventures of this period began with a defeat: they were defeated by the Argives in the area of Hysiae (669 BC)., According to some this was due to the fact that the Spartans had not yet adopted the hoplite phalanx. The defeat of the Spartans gave the Messenians the opportunity to revolt, leading to the second Messenian war, which lasted for twelve years (657 BC). According to information provided Pausanias, which should be considered with a degree of skepticism, the first years were dominated by raids. Soon, however, the war stopped being bipartite since Messene was joined by Arcadia, Ileia, Pisa, Sicyon and Argos, while Corinthos, Samos and Lepreos aligned themselves with Sparta. While the Spartans initially lost control of Stenyclaros, by 659 BC they had managed (possibly under the sound of Tyrtaeus' paeans[48]) to repossess portions of Messenian territory as well as the

---

47 We do not know where triremes were built since the shipyards of Piraeus have not yet been detected. It is likely that ship construction took place in Northern Greece where Athens was supplied with lumber. This hypothesis is reinforced by the fact that, the ash grey volcanic rock used for anchors and found at the naval dockyard of Zea, is of North Greek origin (Steinhauer 2000: 250-259).

48 As a rule, when the Spartans were on an expedition, they would be summoned to the king's tent and

Arcadian city Phigaleia. The last bastion of Messenian resistance to fall was Eira two years later.

Around the end of the 7th c. BC, another Messenian uprising erupted, but it was suppressed leaving the Spartans controlling more land, including Pylos which was given to the perioeci and to refugees from Nafplion, who had been persecuted by the Argives. A series of unsuccessful wars against Arcadian cities ensured as well as a failed expedition against Tegea (575 BC). During this time - the exact date is not known – the Phigaleans repossessed their city with the aid of 100 Oresthasians, all of who were killed in battle. According to tradition, the Phigaleans built the temple of Apollo Epicurean in honor of the god who had helped them.

Another confrontation with the Tegeans in 560 BC ended in a Spartan victory, although the Spartans withdrew without taking control of the Tegean plain. This event has been linked to the Spartan defeat in Orchomenos by a united force of Arcadians, Argives and Orchomenians, though the exact timing remains unknown. As a result, the Spartans are forced to abandon Arcadian territory and soon after, possibly led by the wise Chilo of Sparta during his tenure as an *ephor* (556 BC), formed an alliance with Tegea (Sakellariou 1971b: 221-223).

The conflict between Sparta and Argos continued until the second half of the 6th c. BC[49]. Exploiting the weakened statusof the Argives, who were no longer allied with Tegea, the Spartans seized Cythera, Cynuria and Thyreatis. Around 546/545 BC, they will decisively defeat the Argives. This was a confrontation of historical significance because it is in this context that "the battle of the 300" took place. Under mutual agreement, the Argives and the Spartans decided that their entire armies would not participate in the battle. Instead only 300 handpicked warriors would fight to the bitter end. Indeed, the rivals clashed and continued the fight until nightfall at which time two Argives were left standing. After what turned out to be a cursory search for survivors in the battlefield, the Argives rushed to inform their fellow citizens of their victory. However, not all Spartan warriors had been killed: the hoplite Orthryades, who had been wounded, made it back to Sparta where he announced that he was the last man to abandon the battlefield and could therefore technically claim victory; in the end, he committed suicide to leave no room for doubts

---

they would listen to Tyrtaeus' poems being recited, which served to reinforce morale and love patriotic sentiment (Lyc., *Against Leocrates*, 109).

49 It is interesting to note that at this time the Spartans project their city as Agamemnon's (not Menelaus') headquarters, demanding in this way the legendary heritage of Argos (Sakellariou 1971b: 253). This ideological choice may be combined, in part, with their claim to lead Greek ally forces in the battle of Plataea; besides, Agamemnon had been commander-in-chief of the Achaeans in the Trojan war.

that he had not been killed by an Argive sword. Two days later, the Spartans and Argives met at the battlefield, both claiming victory. They ended up clashing again but this time, victory Spartan victory was undisputable(Cartledge 2003a: 87-88; Cartledge 1977: 12; Sakellariou 1971b: 253).

At the end of the 6th c. BC, Sparta was the most powerful city-state in Greece. It controlled a large part of the Peloponnese (about 8,500 sq. km), its political reforms created a stable political system without having to go through the stage of tyranny, and it had forged the Peloponnesian alliance , the most formidable political and military power of the time, which also included cities outside the Peloponnese (Megara, Aegina) (Parliament of Greece 2010: 40). It is noteworthy that when the Greeks of Asia Minor became wary of the Persian threat, they turned to Sparta who responded by sending a message to the king of the Persians, stating that it would not remain passive in the event of an attack against the cities of Asia Minor. Sparta's power was also demonstrated by the fact that it offered assistance to the oligarchs of other Greek city-states, who tried to overturn their tyrannies; thus, Sparta did not refuse to help the oligarchs of Samos when they moved to overthrow Polycrates. This same policy was followed in the case of Athens in the last year of Peisistrides Hippias' tyranny. From that point on, the intertwined history of these two great (and symbolically opposite) Greek city-states began.

Spartans attributed their intervention in Athenian internal affairs to the persistent counsels of the Delphic Oracle, which in this case was favorably predisposed towards the Alcmeonids, great benefactors of the Oracle, to mobilize against Hippias. A more convincing justification was, however, provided by Hippias' friendly relations with Argos; his distancing from Athens surely further weakened the traditional Spartan rival. Therefore, in 512 BC, the Spartans sent an expedition against Hippias, headed by Anchimolus, which landed in the Phaleron plain; but it was decimated by 1,000 Thessalian cavalrymen, allies of the tyrant. Sparta subsequently dispatched a larger force, headed by king Cleomenes. After defeating the Thessalians, the Spartans and the Athenian citizens blockaded Hippias and his mercenaries at the Acropolis. As the siege was dragging on for days, Cleomenes was contemplating the possibility of withdrawal. However, the younger members of Hippias' family, who had been secretly smuggled out of the Acropolis, were unexpectedly captured by the Spartan king. Holding his family members as hostages, the besiegers forced Hippias to withdraw under treaty and abandon Attica (511/510BC) (Cartledge 2002; 125-130; Sakellariou 1971b: 266).

The second Spartan interference in Athenian affairs came at the invitation of the leader of the oligarchs, Isagoras, who aspired to weaken Cleisthenes.

Threatened with an armed invasion, Cleomenes compelled the Athenians to push out the Alcmeonids because they had been "tainted" by the Cylonean Affair (508 BC). Even with the Alcmeonids in exile, Isagoras failed to gain control of Athens. So, Cleomenes, invaded Athens with a Spartan force, driving out 700 families of democrats. Subsequently, Cleomenes attempted to dismantle the Council and to replace it with a senatorial body consisting of 300 members, friends and followers of Isagoras. However, this proved to be a difficult undertaking as both the Council and the Athenian people fought back, forcing Cleomenes, Isagoras and the Spartan army to seize the Acropolis. Two days later, Cleomenes withdrew under the auspices of a treaty.

The ensuing acts after this initial confrontation between Sparta and Athens were about to become more dramatic. Dissappointed with his failure and unwilling to accept the collapse of the oligarchs' power in Athens, Cleomenes gathered his Peloponnesian allies and invaded Attica without revealing his true intentions. The two armies were deployed in Eleusis, but before the battle began, it became known to the allies that Cleomenes intended to re-instate Isagoras to power. The other king of Sparta, Demaratus, questioned Cleomenes' judgement while the Corinthian leader stated that he was not about to be an accomplice to such injustice and withdrew; he was followed shortly thereafter by the rest of the allies[50]. Nevertheless, soon afterwards Cleomenes tried again backing the exiled Hippias who was in Sigeion rather than Isagoras. Though he made his plans known to the allies this time, the Corinthians again refused to support ^the restoration of tyranny in a city-state which had adopted an "isocratic political system". The allies agreed with Corinth's views, forcing Cleomenes to resign from the operation (Grote 2002: 100-104; Sakellariou 1971b: 267-268).

In the first few years of the 5th c. BC, Sparta was once again involved in a war with Argos (possibly in 494 BC). The brilliant Spartan victory was attributed to Cleomenes' planning which deceived the Argives with a diversionary raid in Thyreatis and instead unexpectedly attacked Sepeia. The Argives' casualties were great, spurring internal disputes which weakened Argos for a long time. The Spartans had repossessed Tyrins, Mycenes and established themselves as the only power in the Peloponnese.

Cleomenes' final military operation had various political ramifications in Sparta. In 491 BC, just before Datis and Artaphernes began their expedition in Greece, the Athenians asked for the Spartan king's help to exterminate Aegina, a city which competed with Athens and was favorably disposed

---

50 According to Herodotus, as a result of this discord, the Spartans decided not to send both of their kings on expedition together again (V.75.2).

towards the Persians. Indeed, Cleomenes arrived in Aegina with the intention to arrest its most important leaders and then to hand them over to the Athenians. His plan failed however because Demaratus had warned the Aeginites, possibly aiming to weaken his co-leader and to damage his reputation in Sparta. Upon his return, Cleomenes succeeded in dethroning Demaratus, compelling his successor Leotychides to condemn him under oath to the Ephors as an illegitimate child. The Delphic Oracle, where the Ephors sought refuge, confirmed the accusation, according to Herodotus (VI.65-66), after being bribed by Cleomenes, (*his enemies shamelessly bribed the oracle*, as the Greek poet C.P. Cavafy stated in the poem "Demaratos"). Following the Oracle's prophecy, the Ephors exiled him and installed Leotychides on the throne. Demaratus fled to the king Darius's and his court, offering his services both to Darius and to his successor, Xerxes. With the cooperation of the new king, Cleomenes returned to Aegina, took 10 magistrates as hostages and surrendered them to Athens. His actions later proved wise as Aegina remained neutral when the Persians landed in Marathon.

Hoplite in full armour (work by Stelios Nigdi-opoulos)

However, after his successful operation in Aegina, Cleomenes himself was accused by the Ephors of bribing the Delphic Oracle in the Demaratus case. So, he fled to Arcadia, where he tried to incite the Arcadians to rise against Sparta - a fact which forced the Ephors to allow him to return to the city ,"forgiving" his previous transgression. The circumstances surrounding his death (around 491 BC or according to others in 489/488 BC) remained unclear. Herodotus (VI.75) mentioned that he was lost his mind, forcing his relatives to arrest him and put him in jail, where he took his own life; yet, it is more likely that the Ephors themselves imprisoned and killed him (Cartledge 2002: 127-132; Jeffery 1988: 356-357; Pelekidis 1971: 289-290; Smith 1870: 1/792-793, 958-959).

The conflict between Cleomenes and Demaratus was mainly political in nature and it concerned matters of both internal and foreign affairs. With the information we have at our disposal, we can conclude that Cleomenes –through his implementation of an expansive policy, pursued a more prominent role for Sparta in Greek affairs. Demaratus' objections during the invasion to Attica, as well as his position on the Aegina matter, reveal that he leaned towards more conservative political choices, perhaps fearful that increased exposure or expansion of Sparta would further weaken Sparta internally and possibly spur another Messenian revolt. The kings' divergent political views regarding Spartan policy in the case of Persian attack should be viewed in this context. Cleomenes was in favor of aligning with the Athenians and participating in the war against the Persians whilst Demaratos was in support of neutrality. The fact that Demaratus fled to Darius' court does not necessarily prove his friendly predisposition towards the Persians suggesting that he supported that the Spartans should side with the Persians. In fact, it can probably be ascribed to his bitterness over his unjust exile. The involvement of the Ephors in the disputes was also politically motivated because Cleomenes, through his remarkable military achievements, threatened to restrict their power, while reinforcing that of the kings'. In the case of Demaratus, the situation resolved itself when he sought refuge in the Persian court. However, Cleomenes had proven he was dangerous as long as he was alive. While his death may have been beneficial for The Spartan political system, at least as perceived by the Ephors , it deprived Sparta from the capacity to pursue politics of a panhellenic scope at that point in time.

1.4.1. The Spartan political system

The foundation of the Spartan political system is attributed to legislator Lycurgus, a figure grounded in both myth and reality.[51] According to tradition, Lycurgus reorganized the city after receiving a prophecy from the Delphic Oracle; the initial laws which he passed were termed the "Great Decree" and

---

51 According to Plutarch (Lycurgus), the wise legislator was the son of king Eunomus, who was killed while intervening in the clash of some citizens. After the death of his brother, Polydeuces, he became king; but he was forced to abandon Sparta to escape the conspiracies instigated by his sister-in-law. He travelled to Crete, Ionia, Egypt, India, Libya and possibly to Spain, and studied the local political systems. After the introduction of the new political system, he placed citizens under oath not to change anything until his return. However, he never returned: he went at the Delphic Oracle, where he died of hunger out of his own volition, believing that his death would ensure the power and stability of the Spartan political system (Smith 1870: 2/850-851). For issues related to the figure of Lycurgus and the relevant sources see MacDowell 1999: 12; Giouni 2006: 256-331.

formed the basis for the political system. The reforms he introduced are traced back to around the mid 8th c. BC[52] and revolved around three main points: (i) classification of the citizens not only according to tribal origin (the three Dorian tribes were the Hylleis, the Dymanes and the Pamphyloi), but also geographically, in large villages called "komai"; (ii) creation of the council of elders , comprised of 30 members (28 citizens and the two kings), power to draft and formulate bills drafts of which were to be submitted to the assembly; (iii) the assembly to convene at regular intervals to approve the Council's bills without having the right to debate (Sakellariou 1971α: 50-52).

Lycurgus

Chilo of Sparta

By the end of the 6th c. BC, when the Spartan political system assumed its final form during the classical period, additional reforms had been implemented, some of which were attributed to Chilo, one of the seven sages of ancient Greece. During his tenure as an Ephor (556 BC), he increased the Ephors' powers aligning them with those of the two kings, thereby reinforcing the oligarchic nature of the city-state (Sakellariou 1971b: 252).

In fact, Sparta was the dominant city-state within a broader political network, that of Lacedaemon. The population of Lacedaemon included the citizens (*homoioi*), the *perioeci* and the helots. The perioeci, who were of Dorian descent, inhabited all of Lacedaemon except for Sparta and Amyclae. Their municipalities were regarded as separate states with a certain degree of autonomy, but under the hegemony of the kings of Sparta. They were free citizens in the state of Lacedaemon, but without political rights in the state of Sparta. The perioeci paid regular dues to Sparta and were obliged to serve in the Spartan army, not as hoplites but as light-armed soldiers. They cultivated the least fertile lands of Lacedaemon, but they were free to exercise whatever profession they wished (Cartledge 2002: 153-159).

---

52 Regarding the issues with dating Lycurgus' laws and the relevant theories see Chrimes 1999: 305-347; Cartledge (2003b: 28-31), Salmon (1977: 97), and Cartledge (1977: 27) linked the "Great Decree" to the establishment of the hoplite phalanx and the increased hoplite power, placing it no earlier than the mid 7th c. BC.

The helots' origins were from those tribes that had been conquered by the Dorians (Messenians and Lacons). They belonged to the state and though they cultivated the land, they were required to surrender part of the crop to the Spartan owner of the allotment. They could not be sold outside of Messenia and Laconia and a limited number were conscripted to the army as light-armed soldiers or rowers. Children born of a Spartan and a helot parent were called "mothakes"; and although they were not considered citizens (homoioi), they received the Spartan education known as "agoge" (Cartledge 2002: 136-152; Hanson 2005: 92-95).

Spartan citizens, who represented the minority of the population, were called "homoioi" and had equal rights. For a Spartan to be considered an homoios, it was not sufficient to be born to Spartan parents with full political rights; he also had to be able-bodied and healthy from birth; he had to have endured and successfully completed the "agoge" ; he had to have been an elected a member of a team of fifteen men; he had to own a piece of land; he had to contribute to his team's activities as well those of his city(e.g., contribute to the monthly costs of the common meals[53]); in addition he could not have committed any offense which could bring "disgrace" (atimia) , resulting in the deprivation of his political rights (such offenses were desertion and retreating in the battlefield).

It is clear that inclusion into the corps of the homoioi demanded a long initiation process, of greater importance and of longer duration than the usual ceremonies signifying the shift from adulthood to youth. Furthermore, the Spartan citizens' status was not necessarily fixed for life; whoever was declared "disgraced" (atimos) or simply could not fulfill his obligation in terms of financial contribution to the common meals, was relegated to the class of subordinate citizens (hypomeiones), literally equals to perioeci (Sakellariou 1971b: 262).

The homoioi were preoccupied solely with military training and war preparation, even during peace time; they were prohibited from exercising any other profession; and their households were run by women who had a special place in Spartan society. The homoioi acquired the status of citizen at the age of 30, provided they had met the afore mentioned criteria and served as hoplites until the age of 60. After their discharge, they could participate in the council of elders. Essentially, their life was inextricably linked with the life and needs of the state.

---

53 All hoplites had to contribute on a monthly basis to the mess items such as flour, a pre-determined amount of wine and figs. The famous Spartan simplicity with reference to meals ("litotis") is evident from the contents of the mess: barley bread and the famous melas broth (soup made from pork meat; for more information, see David 1978).

The instruments of power in Sparta were the Council of Elders (Senate), the kings, the assembly and the Ephors. There were two kings, who in historical times, came from two different families claiming to be the descendants of Hercules, Argeades and the Eurypontides. They were heads of state for life, represented the municipality in front of the gods (e.g., submission of questions to the Delphic Oracle etc.) and carried the priesthood for Zeus Lacedaemonian and Zeus of Uranus. The kings were considered holy individuals and homage was paid to them as heroes after their death.

Due to their successes in war, the kings gained in status, which they often exploited in order to tilt the laws in their favor or in some cases to dominate the assembly; the case of Cleomenes is a prime example. Thus, in order to avoid unwanted developments, from the beginning of the 5th c. BC - possibly after the case of Demaratus and Cleomenes – the power of the kings was greatly curtailed to the benefit of the Ephors. They continued to be the leaders of the army, but exercised true leadership only on military expeditions. The Ephors made the decision to mobilize and mandated one of the kings as Commander-in-Chief; in fact, one of the Ephors would accompany the Commander-in-Chief on his expedition in a supervisory role. The restrictions placed on the kings' power on matters of foreign policy, state administration and dispensation of justice were of even greater importance. The balance achieved between these two poles of power is manifested in the following ritual: every month the kings swore under oath in front of the Ephors that they would implement the city's laws while the Ephors, who represented the city, swore under oath to each king that they would not terminate him as long as he adhered to his promise.

According to tradition, the institution of the Ephors (the chief magistrates) appeared around 754 BC. This institution was comprised five members, who functioning as a supervisory body, were tasked with protecting the political system. Its members were citizens elected by the Apella (the Assembly) for one year without the right of re-election. The Ephors' duties included safeguarding the law, receiving foreign ambassadors and determining the timing of the Apella's decision to declare war .

The Senate, the council of elders, preserved its character as an old aristocratic council. It was comprised of the two kings and 28 Spartans over the age of 60, who were elected by acclamation from the people's assembly. The Senate decided on which proposals would be voted on by the assembly and had judicial duties as well as.

Finally, all Spartans over the age of 30 participated in the people's assembly (Apella or Alea). According to the "Great Decree", the Apella convened every month on a specific date. Prior to the 6th c. BC, its presidency was exercised

by kings, but this later became the Ephors' duty. The assembly only approved or rejected by acclamation the Senate's proposals, without being entitled to discuss them (Chrimes 1999:397-428; Sakellariou 1971b: 254; Michell 1964: 137-164).

Despite the Spartan political system incorporating features of almost all the well-known ancient systems, it was not implemented in any other city-state. Although it is stereotypically regarded as un-democratic, particularly when examined in the context of the antithesis, both literal and symbolic, between Athens and Sparta. In fact, Sparta's political system incorporated many democratic elements, long before the Athenian city-state. It is noteworthy that the right to be elected and to participate in the assembly was bestowed upon all *homoioi* around the mid 7th c. BC; that is, before Solon's reforms in Athens. Additionally, in at least one other instance, the restrictions on citizens' eligibility to be elected were abolished first in Sparta; Spartan citizens always had the right to be elected Ephor, a right which was maintained even when this post became superior to that of the king. Certainly, it is true that Sparta did not proceed towards a direct democracy, but through the Ephors, it remained a representational democracy. Nevertheless, the strict hierarchy of the political system, its democratic ingredients and the discipline of its citizens ensured stability (Sakellariou 1971b:219-220).

On the basis of the number of land lots after the repossession of Stenyclaros in the mid 7th c. BC, Spartan citizens numbered approximately 9,000 while the *perioeci* were around 30,000. At that time, the state of Lacedaemon was experiencing signficant economic and cultural activity. The bronze works of art (mostly tripodes and lebes) and Laconic ceramics were in high demand in the Aegean and the eastern Mediterranean, while there is evidence that Lacedaemon imported ivory, amber and jewellery . This vibrant environment will be maintained until around the mid 6th c. BC, supported by the presence in Sparta of the poets Theognis and Stecichorus, as well as of foreign artists, such as sculptor Bathycles. However, shortly after, ceramics and copper works declined and exports ceased, while the measure of foreigner expulsion also begins. This is possibly linked to the fact that Spartan economy was never monetary. Sparta never minted money and it prohibited the possession of coins by its citizens, perhaps so as not to threaten the equal standing of the *homoioi* and by extension the stability of the political system. Lastly, starting in the 5th c. BC, the population decreased; a trend that accelerated in the coming centuries (Sakellariou 1971b: 222, 253, 264; Cartledge 2002: 273-272; Hanson 2005: 92-101).

1.4.2. Military training and Organization

Although in Athens political and military service constituted complementary aspects of α citizens' public life, such α distinction was not made in Sparta. The hoplite identity was not distinguishable from the identity of the citizen, as Spartans were soldiers practically their entire lives, ready to fight at any moment. As Demaratus told Xerxes, the governing law that applies to all Spartans revolved around one basic principle: Spartans are obliged to re-main on the battlefield until the end and they can either win or die (Herodotus, *Histories*, VII. 104.4-5).

In this city-state of hoplites, public as well as private life are intertwined with military life. The Spartans remain conscripted from the age of 7 to 60; their barracks were their home and the other hoplites were their families. The central goal of their education ("*agoge*") was to construct α powerful feeling of duty towards the city-state and simultaneously, to cultivate virtues of modesty and persuasion.

The Spartan army owed its reputation to the famous "*agoge*", meaning the way in which future hoplites were trained. At the age of seven, boys were taken away from their mothers and were handed to the state and trainers, who classified them into two groups simultaneously: the first consisted of children of the same age (*bouai*) and the second consisted of children of different ages (*ilae*). The *bouai* resembled α school class, whereas the *ilae* to military units, complete with an internal hierarchy (α young man from the previous class was the leader and the younger members had to obey the older ones). The *agoge* included military and sports training, the teaching of military techniques, survival skills and endurance training for tolerating deprivation and physical pain as well as the teach-ing of Spartan virtues (composure, "*laconismos*", discipline etc.). When the boys reached adolescence, they took part in an endurance competition of whipping and when the period of agoge was completed, they were called upon to prove their capacity to kill by joining the "*krypteia*": divided into teams, they would roam the countryside at night and kill any helots

Bronze statuette of a Spartan warrior (6th c. BC, Archaeological Museum of Olympia)

Statue of Spartan warrior identified with Leonidas (Archaeological Museum of Sparta)

they encountered (Xen. *Const. of Lac.*, ii-iii, x; Plut., *Lycurgus*, 16-25) (Chrimes 1999: 84-136).

When they completed their twentieth year, and provided they had successfully undergone the *agoge* stages, the youth had to be elected to a citizen group, named "*syssitia*" (common meals) or "*syskeniai*" (a messing together). This was the last trial before they were granted the identity of the hoplite. It essentially was a process of judgment and election. The aspiring hoplites offered themselves as candidates for those "*syskeniai*" where there were available spots. The members judged whether the candidates had the skills required by the *homoioi* model and a secret vote followed. Candidates received the identity of the citizen, only if they were accepted unanimously. From then on, they lived in their *syskenia* until they were 30 years old; after the age of 30, they had the right to spend the night at home. Apart from the obligation to exercise and to maintain a state of war-readiness, they participated in the assembly and could be elected as Ephors. After their discharge, at the age of 60, they participated in the life of the city-state, as counselors, members of the Senate (Gerousia) and trainers of the younger ones (Giarenis 2008α: 187-191; Birgalias 2001; Panagopoulos 1987; David 1978).

The strict military organization of the Spartan city-state obviously did not permit any Spartan to refuse to server in the army[54]. Besides, the social exclusion for hoplites who exhibited cowardice on the battlefield (*tresantes*) was absolute. The deserters were declared "disgraced" (that is, they lost their political rights and became *hypomeiones*) and any Spartan who encountered them in public was allowed to hit them (Giarenis 2008α: 187-191)[55].

The basic corps of the Spartan army was the hoplite phalanx, a model which was adopted by other city states in forming their own phalanx (Ray 2009: 10-11). It comprised several organizational levels and was ruled by strict hierarchy, allowing for greater ease of management compared to other

54 Nevertheless, according to the testimony of the Athenian orator Lycurgus, there was a law which foresaw the death penalty for those who were not willing to fight for their country (*Against Leocratus*, 129).

55 It seems that in some situations the castaways could be reinstated, if they demonstrated heroic behavior later. So, the Spartan Aristodemos, who had lost heart in the Thermopylae, wanted to make it up by participating heroically in the battle of Plataea (Herod., *Hist.*, VII.231, IX.71). Moreover, according to Thucydides, the Spartans who had surrendered in the battle of Sphacteria, were declared "disgraced", but after some time got their political rights back.

hoplite phalanxes. The smallest unit was called the *enomotia* (36 men); two *enomotiae* comprised one *pentecostys* (this term is a remnant of older times, when the unit totaled 50 men); two of these made up one company (*lochos*); four companies formed a *mora*; six *morae* made up a phalanx (3,500 hoplites). Each unit had its commander (respectively, *Enomotarchis, Pentecontarchos, Captain, Polemarchos*); the Commander-in-chief was the king, who carried full responsibility for the expedition and its operations. The Ephor who accompanied the king from the early 5th c. BC did not have the right to question him on the spot or to interfere with the king's orders, but the Ephor could prosecute the king and call on him to testify upon the army's return to Sparta, if there was just cause (Michell 1964: 233-258).

In addition to the phalanx, the light-armed infantry (*psiloi*), comprised of the classes of *perioeci* and helots, – also participated in military expeditions. The elite body of three hundred cavalrymen (*hippeis*), aged 20 to 30, who made up the king's bodyguard, is also worth highlighting. Despite their name, which must also be a remnant of earlier times, during battle they fought as hoplites; these were the same "300" who died alongside Leonidas atThermopylae. Sparta did not have a cavalry until the end of the 5th century B.C.; it more likely had to do with the power and prestige of the hoplite ethos rather than the lack of resources. However, during the Peloponnesian war, Sparta was forced to field a cavalry, primarily to deal with the destruction of farm production by Athenian raids (Gregoropoulos 2009: 34).

1.5. Athens: preparing for the "Golden Age"

The Athenians had a lot to be proud of – they were indigenous (while the Spartans were not) and Iones, mythical protectors of the Heracleids. In contrast to other city-states, Athens was not founded by a hero, but was created by its residents, who met the two key conditions to be considered indigenous: they were born in the region of Athens and they had never abandoned their land (Loreaux 2000: 13-18).[56] Even if they ultimately chose Athena's gift during the dispute of the gods for naming the city, it was not long before they appeased defeated Poseidon. At its peak, Athens was indeed the city of philosophers, of poets, of theater, and of art, while simultaneously the greatest naval power in Greece.

---

56 Out of the remaining Greeks, the only ones who were indigenous were the Arcadians. The inhabitants of Cynuria, who were also born into their land and had never abandoned it, had adopted the Dorian customs, so according to Herodotus (VIII.73.3), they could not be considered autochthonous (Loreaux 2000:14).

The city stretched across a plain 1,600 sq. km wide, situated between two hilltops. At the center of the plain, there was a group of smaller hills: the hill of Pnyx, the Areopagus, and the Acropolis, 60 m. tall, 300 m long, and 150 m wide. At the time of the battle of Marathon, the Acropolis had not yet acquired its glorious architecture which would be identified symbolically with democracy and the Athenian "Golden Age". However, it was a sacred rock, the center of worship of the patron goddess Athena. The other two distinctive areas of Athens were the Agora, the place of public life, the hub of commercial and political activity, and Kerameikos, the cemetery, the resting place of the dead heroes the role-models of war and political virtue.

To the southwest, 7-8 km away, lay the port of the city, Piraeus, and adjacent to it, the bay of Phaleron where the waters of the Cephisus River flows into the sea. The Cephisus River traverses the plain of Attica and branches out into three rivers. One of these tributaries, the main Cephisus , flowed to the west of the city between olive groves; the second tributary, Ilissus, flowed through the eastern suburbs; and the third tributary, Eridanus, flowed through the city (Evans 2010: 14-17; Loreaux 2000: 28; Lloyd 1973: 31-34).

According to Dicaearchus, Athens was a rocky, dusty city in a "poor location". It had about 10,000 residences, typically one-story houses, made of stucco or plaster, devoid of luxury. Most of the streets were narrow, more comparable to paths or passages. Yet, its water system was remarkable, complete with reservoirs, pipes and aqueducts which exploited natural springs. The famous fountain of Callirhoe was constructed at one of these springs in the south of the city (Lloyd 1973: 35).

The word 'Athens' referred not only to the city ("*asty*") but also to the entire city-state which included the countryside of Attica, with its scattered settlements and large villages. These villages were populated mostly by farmers who cultivated crops, olives and grapes. Due to the lack of arable land, stockbreeding was limited to the surrounding semi-mountainous regions, while sheep and goats were bred primarily for their wool and to a lesser extent for their meat (Evans 2010: 14-15).

According to lore, the beginning of the Athenian city came from "*synoikismos*"[57], meaning the unification of Attica's townships by Theseus. Theseus abolished the institution of monarchy[58] and the individual village councils, replacing

---

57 Both *synoikismos* and autochthony ensured Attica's inhabitants' common and cultural identity, see particularly Connor 1999: 34.

58 According to an alternative version, the institution of monarchy was abolished following the death of Codrus, around early 11th c. BC. According to this relevant myth, when the Dorians invaded Attica, king Codrus willfully sacrificed himself, because the Delphic Oracle foresaw that the Dorians would succeed in

them with a central council-chamber (*bouleuterion*) and a president's hall (*prytaneion*). After constructing a new constitution for the city, he installed himself as supreme magistrate and judge. He also renamed the "Athenian Games" to "Panathenian Games", in order to allow the inhabitants of the Attica region to participate. To help expand the city, he invited all important foreigners to become his "fellow citizens".

During the Archaic period and before the 6th c. BC, the Athenians were divided into four Ionian tribes (Aegikoreis, Argadeis, Geleontes, Hopletes), into clans "fratries"[59] and "gene"[60]. The nobles were the only active citizens. The wealthiest had the right to be elected while the less rich were part of the assembly. The division into four classes (*pentakosiomedimnoi, hippeis, zeugites,* and *thetes*) had already occurred by the time of Solon's reforms. Up until 683/682 BC, the magistrates held office for a decade. Subsequently, their tenure became annual and it was then that the institution of the three magistrates was created, the *Archon Eponymous* (=Magistrate Eponymous), the *Archon Polemarchos* (=Magistrate for War), and the *Archon Vasileus* (=Magistrate King).

The Archon Eponymous was head of the city-state and convened the Council and the Assembly. The *Archon Polemarchos* was head of the army and also adjudicated on military offenses. At a later date, he also became adjudicator of cases dealing with the metics (immigrants). Lastly, the *Archon Vasileus* served a primarily religious function though he also presided over cases which dealt with disrespect, murder, injury and arson. Around the mid 7th c. BC, a six-member committee of legislators was established. Though it was initially mandated with the job of recording the laws it was later also tasked with presiding over the trial of several cases.

It is possible that Areopagus was the council of aristocrats, its powers not defined as the laws had yet to be codified. The power of the Assembly was restricted, as it could be convened only by the decision of the magistrates and the Council once they pursued to secure their decisions (Rostovtzeff 1963: 83-88; Sakellariou 1971b: 230-231).

---

conquering Athens unless they killed its king (Smith 1897: 1/811). It is possible that this myth had been ignored when Theseus was being projected as the local hero of Athens.

59 Fratry (clan) is a group of people with close family ties, real or mythical. These controlled specific geographical areas because according to them, those areas were the places where their ancestors had been buried or where religious ceremonies established by one of their ancestors took place. They had a common sanctuary, their own priests and made sacrifices to the specific gods they considered their patrons. Within the social hierarchy, the fratry is in-between the level of the family (*oikos*) and the city (Frost 1994: 49).

60 By the term 'genus' we mean generation, which in this case is of aristocratic origin. Members of gene determined who would be accepted in the fratry (Frost 1994: 49).

The political turmoil witnessed in the last decades of the 7th c. BC was likely caused by the fact that Athens was experiencing a period of economic recession, as revealed by the archaeological findings. The most significant event of that period was Cylon's failed attempt, with the military support of his father-in-law, the tyrant of Megara Theagenes, to become tyrant. Cylon and his supporters occupied the Acropolis, which was almost immediately placed under siege by the Athenians; at the same time, the Assembly authorized the magistrates to handle the situation. After several days under siege, Cylon and his brothers managed to escape, but their followers and the Megarians went to the altar of Athena Polias (= "Athena of the city") as supplicants. Persuaded by the magistrates' promise that they would be put on trial, they abandoned the altar, but the besiegers captured and executed them (636 or 632 BC). This profane act, which was blamed on the magistrate Megacles, who belonged to the aristocratic genus of the Alcmeonids, was perceived as having tainted the entire city. According to lore, the Athenians invited Epimenides , a wise priest and prophet, to come from Crete to perform a ceremony so as to cleanse the city. Cylon was tried in absentia and exiled (Sakellariou 1971b: 232).

Draco's legislation (624 or 621 BC) must have been part of an effort to ease the tension stemming from this internal crisis which was troubling Athenian society, as demonstrated by the conviction of the Alcmeonids. The nature of the reforms supports the hypothesis that one of the demands was the enlargement of the body of active citizens. It is possible that Draco granted political rights to the hoplites. Moreover, he implemented the recording and codification of laws, created a special court for homicide cases, and passed a law against tyrants, who were punished with "disgrace" (deprivation of political rights and confiscation of property). Nonetheless, twenty-five years later, Athens faced yet another internal crisis, brought about by agricultural debts, which had resulted in the loss of property and personal freedom for many farmers (Forsdyke 2006: 334-340). As the demands for land redistribution became increasingly intense and the threat of a civil war was prevalent, the task of implementing reforms was assumed by one of the seven sages of ancient times, Solon.

1.5.1. Solon's reform

Solon was a prominent member of Athenian society and belonged to one of its most well-known families. Like the legendary legislator Lycurgus , he was well-travelled and "many were the men whose cities he saw and whose minds he learned". And like the famous poet Tyrtaeus, he had empowered Athenian

morale with his verses, mobilizing them to regain the island of Salamis, in an expedition, in which it is said, he served as General. In addition to dealing with the theme of military virtue, his poems expressed his concerns about the city's fate, his critical stance towards the magistrates as well as his faith in the values of *eunomia* (good government, good order)[61] and of moderation. Therefore, in 594 BC by unanimous decision of the Assembly, Solon was elected magistrate for one year, with temporary duties as mediator and legislator.

Solon

Solon's main concern was to create a political system which would ensure sound government and the dispensation of justice. A prime example of his beliefs was the measure that any citizen had the right to report an injustice, even if not personally involved (in other words, every citizen became guardian of justice and *eunomia*). The aim of his legislation was to provide a general code on all issues, based on common sense. Laws were intended to serve society, so this meant they could evolve alongside the needs of society.

Reform was implemented in three stages. The first one, which was implemented immediately, dealt with the cancellation of debts owed to the state, the abolition of borrowing against one's human capital (by pledging one's own being and personal freedom), the emancipation of those sold to Athenians as slaves to cover debts, and the pardoning of those who had committed certain injustices punishable by loss of political rights. These measures became known as "*seisachtheia*" (burden write-offs).

The second series of measures was focused on reforming the political system. The Assembly was given more power (including election of the magistrates) and its convocation at more regular intervals may have become compulsory. People's courts were established, as was a second council body with pre-parliamentary capacities, comprised of 400 members (100 from each tribe), who served annually and were elected directly by the citizens. The most important measure, however, was that for the first time, the *Thetes* –the small property owners who made a living as farmers - had political rights, even if restricted. Thus, all the adult male inhabitants of Attica, who belonged to tribes, fratries and gene, had become Athenian citizens. In accordance with

---

61 Regarding themes and techniques in Solon's poetry see particularly Stehle 2006; Blaise 2006; Noussia 2006.

the previous system, they were divided into four classes, depending on the annual production generated by their land ownership (the *"medimnus"* was the measuring unit): *pentakosiomedimnoi* (valued at 500 medimnoi of cereals annually), *triakosiomedimnoi* (valued at 300 medimnoi production annually) or *hippeis*, *diakosiomedimnoi* (valued at 200 medimnoi production annually) or *zeugites*, and *thetes* (valued 199 medimnoi annually or less). All citizens - even the thetes - participated in the Assembly and the people's court but only *pentakosiomedimnoi* and *hippeis* were eligible for the highest offices of the city-state (Council of 400, magistrates).

The third and final series of measures entailed the passage of laws dealing with financial and social issues, such as protecting injured war veterans, expense cut-backs, the prohibition of exports, and boosting imports (except for olive oil) so that the price of grain and other basic types of food could go down. Furthermore, all of Draco's penal code was abolished, except for laws dealing with homicide.

Although Solon exhibited modesty as a means of overcoming the internal crisis, resentment against the measures was not entirely absent. Some regarded the measures as extreme while others, particularly in the lower classes, criticized them as inadequate. A brief period of instability ensued but by 580/579 BC a general consensus emerged in the common battle against the danger of tyranny. So, that same year, the "government of ten" (*decandria*) was elected in place of the *Archon Eponymous* (5 nobles, 3 farmers and 2 laymen) (Evans 2010: 21-24; Parker 2007: 24-28; Mossé 2004; de Ste. Croix 2004: 74-104; Frost 1994: 50-51; Rostovtzeff 1963: 88-90).

Solon's political system was not democratic; on the contrary, while it enlarged the citizen body, it did not tamper with the essence of timocracy. However, his legislation created a framework which would facilitate the entrenchment of democracy after the Cleisthenean reforms. More specifically, it created a free class of peasants and small landowners, who a few years later would form the nucleus of Athenian democracy.

1.5.2. Peisistratus, tyrant of Athens

Almost 20 years after Solon's reforms, Athens seemed to be increasingly losing its foreign influence. Salamis was in the hands of the Megarians, Sigeion had been conquered by the Mytileneans and the openly hostile Aegina had increased its power. Domestically, the city was once again divided, as three parties had emerged, ostensibly representing local interests, but expressing

different social beliefs: the *Paralioi* (=those from the coast), under Alcmeonide Megacles, were in favor of a "moderate" political system; the *Pedieis* or *Pediaeoi* (=those from the plain) under Lycurgus were in favor of oligarchy, and the *Diakrioi* or *Hyperakrioi* (=the Mountaineers, coming from NE of Attica), led by Peisistratus, who projected himself as the defender of democracy.

Peisistratus managed to establish a tyranny, using democratic slogans to gain favour, particularly amongst the more dissatisfied classes. Though his victory against the Megarians and the repossession of Salamis surely enhanced his prestige, his rise to power proved to be a difficult matter in the end. His first attempt (561 BC) relied on a cunning plan: having staged his assassination, he managed to secure enough votes in the Assembly to create a group of club-wielding bodyguards for his protection. Thereafter, with the support of this personal guard, he seized the Acropolis and proclaimed himself tyrant. In response, Miltiades, a member of the Philaedes, whose mythical ancestors were Aeacus and Ajax, left Athens along with other citizens, settling in the Thracian Chersonisos (Gouschin 1999).

Peisistratus' first term as tyrant proved to be short as Megacles and Lycurgus joined forces to overthrow him. Peisistratus was tried and withdrew to Brauron, where he owned land. He returned to the fore twoyears later, at the behest of Megacles and certain nobles who were dissatisfied with Lycurgus. This time, the aspiring tyrant took advantage of Athenian superstition and craftily resorted to the following ploy: he had a noble's daughter dress in armor, put her on a chariot and soon afterwards, sent his men to Athens to spread the word that the goddess Athena was en route accompanying Peisistratus to the Acropolis. The Athenians believed him and welcomed Peisistratus as they bowed in front of the noble's daughter as if she was Athena; this incident is narrated by Herodotus who includes derogatory comments on the Athenians' gullibility (Her. *Hist.*, 1.60.3-5).

Once again, Peisistratus remained in power only for a short while (558/7-556/7 BC), as Megacles allied himself with Lycurgus against the tyrant. After his removal from power, he was tried in absentia and sentenced with "disgrace". He fled to Macedonia and with the permission of king Alcetas, founded a city in Raekelon, near the Thermaic Gulf. Shortly thereafter, he gained control of gold and silver mines in the Pangaeon mountains. He also established relations with the Thebans, the Eretrians and the Argives, while also recruiting mercenaries from Scythes and Paiones.

The events that transpired in Athens in the decade between Peisistratus' second and third tyranny is not precisely known. It is very possible that internal instability ensued, preventing the timocracy from stabilizing sufficiently

to deal with yet another coup d'état. This theory is corroborated by the fact that Peisistratus' influence was still significant while the governing powers of Athens were sluggish in preparing for a potential invasion of the tyrant and his supporters.

In 546/5 BC, Peisistratus disembarked in Marathon, to be joined by his supporters from all around Attica. His army was reinforced by 1,000 mercenaries sent by the Argives, as well as by a small force from Naxos led by Lygdames, who was counting on Peisistratus' future assistance to install himself as tyrant in Naxos. Exploiting the magistrates' delayed response, Peisistratus took the Athenian forces by surprise at the battle of Pallene. Having defeated the Athenian army, he entered the city. He proceeded to disarm the citizens (tantamount to discharging them from the army) and to exile those aristocratic families hostile towards him. The Alcmeonids had enough time to leave the city of their own volition.

Peisistratus' rule can be considered moderate. Although he installed friends and supporters in public posts and maintained his own private army funded by the public treasury, he did not implement any institutional changes. He also cultivated relations with the nobles and showed an interest in the lower classes, taking action to keep the poor peasants in the countryside. His ambitious public works program (Agora, Enneakrounos, Temple of Olympian Zeus, Eleusis santuary etc.) created new jobs, contributing to an econominc recovery. His contribution to religious life was also significant. He promoted the worship of Athena Polias and enhanced the festive atmosphere of the Panathenaea, with the aim of projecting and strengthening Athenian unity. At the same time, he helped the Eleusis Mysteries, which were practically under Athenian control since the 6th c. BC, gain Panhellenic recognition. Lastly, he succeeded in re-conquering Sigeion, once again establishing Athenian influence in the area (Evans 2010: 24-25; Rostovtzeff 1963: 91-93; Sakellariou 1971b: 253-254, 256-257).

Peisistratus died in 527 BC, bequeathing power to his three sons, Hippias, Hipparchus and Thessalos. In essence only Hippias exercised power since Thessalos was too young, while Hipparchus was too pre-occupied with his poetry. In an attempt to lessen Athenian opposition towards tyranny, Hippias curried favor with the aristocrats who had opposed his father, while giving the political system a veneer of "democracy". He was elected magistrate in 526/525 BC, followed by Alcmeonid Cleisthenes (525/524 BC), and Philaid Miltiades (524/523 BC), the nephew of the Miltiades who had emigrated to Chersonisos in 561 BC, and had served as General at the battle of Marathon. This period of stability however proved short-lived. Miltiades held the Pei-

sistratides responsible for his father's murder and in 516 BC, he set out for the Thracian peninsula with a trireme provided by the tyrants themselves; the Alcmeonids had already abandoned the city a few years earlier.

In 514 BC, the first ominous cracks in the tyrannical regime began to emerge. Hipparchus was murdered by Harmodius and Aristogeiton. This event coupled with the fact that his brother's murderers were worshipped as heroes, engendered Hippias to tighten his grip on power, by increasing the number of mercenaries, intensifying suppressive measures, and imposing the death penalty and exile. In addition to the reigning political dissatisfaction, economic problems began to emerge. The seizure of Sigeion by the Persians and the subsequent expansion of their dominance in Macedonia resulted in the loss of Athenian income from the Pangaeon mines. In order to pay his mercenaries, Hippias resorted to multiple tax increases, fanning popular dissatisfaction. Between 514 and 512 BC, two failed attempts to overthrow Hippias were made: there are no details regarding the first attempt except that it was organized by Cedon; the second, was led by the Alcmeonids and other exiled nobles. They entered Attica and set up camp in Leipsydrion, on the northeastern foothills of Mount Parnes (today known as Korakopholeza). Although they received some help from Athens, they were summarily defeated by Hippias' mercenaries, suffering significant losses. Cognizant of the fact that the anti-tyranny movement was gaining momentum, Hippias began constructing a wall in Munichia, intending to entrench himself there. However, Spartan intervention rendered his plans futile. In 511/510 BC, he abandoned Athens under a truce, fleeing to Sigeion where his half-brother Hegestratus governed under the suzerainty of Darius. Though the period of tyrannical rule came to a close in Athens for almost a century, political stability was not to be restored easily (Giarenis 2008a: 173-181; Lewis 1988; Sakellariou 1971b: 265-266).

1.5.3. Cleisthenis' democratic reforms

After Hippias had left Athens, Isagoras, the leader of the aristocrats was elected magistrate (508/7 BC). He indicated he would be willing to turn the Athenian political system into an oligarchy. In reaction to this possibility, Alcmeonid Cleisthenes, as a mere private citizen, proposed a series of radical reforms aimed at restructuring the body politic to the Assembly. His proposal was approved by the Assembly and he imposed himself as the new democratic leader. However, his reforms were to be implemented in a tense climate.

The constant interference of the Spartan King Cleomenes, at the request of Isagoras and the aristocrats, inspired the ire of the Athenian populace; this was possibly the first democratic uprising in history (Ober 2004). However, the temporary cancellation of the oligarchs' plans failed to appease the Athenians who feared that the Spartans would persist. Thus, with insecurity over Sparta's intetions gnawing at their sense of composure, the Athenians dispatched ambassadors to Sardis to explore the possibility of forging an alliance with Darius. The satrap Artaphernes did not refuse the offer, but rather demanded that Athens become subjugated to Persian rule. Though the ambassadors accepted the Persian offer, upon their return to Athens they were confronted with the comprehensive disapproval of the populace. In addition, they faced harsh punishment as they had exceeded the limits of their mandate.

As was highlighted in section 1.4., Cleomenes had indeed returnted o Attica with his Peloponnesian allies, with every intention of invading the city. While his allies ended up withdrawing due to infighting, the Boeotians and the Chalkideans managed to ransack Oinoe and other neighbouring areas along the northeastern coast of Attica. The Athenian army marched against the Boetians and the Chalkideans, defeating them and leading their captives to prison in chains, only to later free them after a ransom was paid. The victors took Oropos from the Boetians, but did not annex it to the Athenian city-state. The Athenians also confiscated land from the nobles of Chalkis, settling 4,000 cleruchs (allottees) there instead (Oswald 1988: 303-308). When Hippias returned to Sigeion and began urging the satrap Artaphernes to mobilize against Athens, hoping that by subjecting it to the suzerainty of Darius, he would regain control of the city, the Athenians again dispatched ambassadors to Sardis in an attempt to thwart Hippias' plans. This time Artaphernes put forward as a non-negotiable condition that Hippias be restored to power. His response was considered wholly unacceptable and automatically turned the Persians into enemies of the Athenians.

In the meantime, efforts to restore political stability continued in Athens with Cleisthenis' first wave of reforms passing in 508/507 BC and with the completion of the legislative project in 505/504 BC. As Cleisthenes and the Alcmeonids had been excluded from power at that time, it is possible that the reforms continued under the initiative of Xanthippus, Themistocles and Aristides. The first measures were finally put into effect in 501/500 BC.

The fundamental purpose of the reforms was to ensure that the citizens' real verdict was heard and to secure their substantive and equal participation in the political domain. It is interesting to note that this new political system did not exist in any other Greek city-state, but was rather invented by Cleisthenes.

Until then, the identity of the citizen was linked to his genus and his lineage, since to become a citizen one had to belong to a fratry. Cleisthenes distanced the concept of the city-state from the fratry and the tribes, replacing the fratry with the *demos* (township) and the four old tribes with ten groups of *deme* (which were also called "tribes"). These new "tribes" (*phylai*) were a form of electoral colleges. As such, Cleisthenes tried to ensure that they would have equal number of members, that they would not express one-sided tendencies or represent the special interests as dictated by the location of voter residence, and that they would not be vulnerable to the powerful local pressures. In order to achieve this, he split Athens into three zones: the city region or *asty* (Athens, Piraeus and the suburbs), the coastal region or *paralia*, and the inland region or *mesogaia*. In addition, he dictated that the deme would not be subject to the new tribes directly, but to an intermediary unit, known as the "trittys" (=third)[62]; ten trittyes would be derived from the "asty", ten from the "paralia" and ten from the "mesogaia". One trittys could include anywhere from one to eight or nine demes, depending on the size of their land area and their population. Every "tribe" would be comprised of one tritty of asty deme, one tritty of coastal deme and one tritty of mesogaia deme. As a result, the new "tribes" did have any particular affiliation with a specific area, but were spread out across Attica.

Inscribed stele, possible related to the reforms of Cleisthenes (end of 6th c. BC)

The four old tribes were not abolished, but they were disengaged from the city-state, playing a role only in religious or other social functions. In order to name the new tribes, Cleisthenes submitted to the Delphic Oracle the names of one-hundred Attican heroes; Pythia selected ten of these as patrons of the tribes, which bore their name.[63] The new tribes were named as follows: Aeantis, Aegeis, Antiochis, Erectheïs, Hippothontis, Cecropis, Leontis, Oeneis, Pandionis. Each tribe encompassed ten demes, so Attica consisted of one hundred demes (which later increased to 174).

---

62 The role of the "trittyes" was not exactly known. The fact that they had property and local worship denotes that they possibly operated in line with the deme, but on a peripheral level (Oswald 1988: 315).

63 Theseus was not elected as one of the eponymous heroes of any "tribe" – although three "tribes" were named after his close relatives (Aegeas was his father, Pandion his grandfather, and Hippothoön his half-brother). This likely happened because the hero had already acquired Panathenaic significance.

The implementation of these new measures resulted in the deme becoming a form of public corporation, which held general assemblies, had a mayor (who was elected directly by the assembly), a treasury and archives. The citizens' details were recorded at their demos' "registrar's office" and they were thereafter required to use both their name and their deme name as sign of their identity (e.g., "Socrates Sofroniskou Alopekithen", which means, Socrates, son of Sofroniskos, from the demos of Alopekis). The immediate relatives of every citizen automatically become members of the same demos, even if they decided to move elsewhere. This ensured a relatively even distribution of the population into demes, trittyes, and "tribes". It is also important to note that Cleisthenes bestowed political rights to resident aliens (metics), who had been excluded from political life up until that point. This also resulted in the enlargement of the body of citizens; these new citizens were known as *neopolitai*.

The "tribes" also had assemblies, elected authorities, wealth, and archives. Each "tribe" contributed fifty members to the Council (1/10 of Council) and the majority of the magistrates. In this manner, Solon's Council of 400 became the Council of 500, acquiring greater jurisdiction and limiting the power of the magistrates in the process, while contributing substantively to the governing of the city. While, the Areopagus maintained its previous role of adjudicating homicide cases, it also acquired the exclusive authority to try crimes against the state and was granted the right to call upon the magistrates to account for their actions.

Each tribe presided over the Council for 1/10th of the year (35-36 days), in order as determined by lot. The tribe's council members were known as *prytaneis* while the tribe itself was referred to as *prytanevousa*. The *prytaneis* also formed a sub-committee which handled any outstanding issues and also dealt with urgent situations ahead of the plenary of the council body. Every night a council member was named president of the *prytaneis* (*epistates*), essentially serving as head of state for 24 hours. All members of the Council were appointed to this post, but not more than once. In this way, the *Archon Eponymous* was no longer the pinnacle of power. Consequently, interest in this specific post waned and the risk that a magistrate would become tyrant was minimized.

In order to further protect the institution of democracy, the law of ostracism was implemented around this time. Lastly, from 501/500 BC the members of the Council gave an oath, swearing to use any means available to ensure the execution of anyone who attempted to overthrow the democratic political system (Evans 2010; 26-34' Lewis 2004: 292-308' de Ste. Croix 2004:

138-173; Oswald 1988: 309-325;
Munro 1939).

As per Aristotle's observation, the
reforms of Cleisthenes achieved in
making the Athenian constitution
more democratic than those of Solon,
facilitating the participation of more
citizens in public affairs. (Arist., *Ath.
Const.*, 21.2; *Pol.*, 1318b 19-24)[64].
The introduction of a new political
and administrative organization at a
local level through the establishment
of demes and the re-organization of
the "tribes" via the trittyes played a
definitive role in phasing out the old
local and religious groupings from
the political domain. Cleisthenes'

Athenian hoplite, in the end of the 6th c. BC (Acropolis Museum)

ultimate aim was to end the "dynastic" disputes between the aristocratic
classes, which had proven damaging to the city, as exemplified by the case of
Peisistratus. In order to achieve this end, he empowered common citizens with
the greatest participation in public affairs that they had ever experienced.
The addition of the patronym (father's name) and the name of the demos to
citizen's names for identification purposes helped abolish distinctions based
on genus. All citizens[65], irrespective of lineage or wealth, could now participate
in the Council and the Assembly, having secured equality of rights before the
law (*isonomia*) and equality of speech (*isegoria*).

Perhaps the most important element of the Cleisthenian reforms was that
political "intermingling" (see Arist., *Polit.*, 1319b 19: "every device must be
employed to make all the people as much as possible intermingled with one
another, and to break up the previously existing groups"). For the first time,
citizens from different parts of Attica were brought together under the auspices of these new "tribes" and were obliged to co-exist and co-operate on
political and religious issues, developing strong bonds in the process. These
bonds, forged at various gatherings, the Council and the Assembly (*ecclesia*),

---

64 It is worth noting that Stanton believed that the reforms of Cleisthenes were aimed at reinforcing the
genus of the Alcmeonids. For the contribution of Cleisthenes to the deepening of democracy, see also
Antonakopoulos 1979: 99).

65 At the end of the 6th c. BC, there were approximately 30,000 Athenian citizens. After taking into account the women, children and allottees, it is possible that the population of Attica reached 120,000; the
population of metics and slaves is not known.

provided another dimension and ingredient in the cohesion of the hoplites who fought in the Athenian phalanx. This was to prove of vital importance in the impending war adventures of Athens.

1.5.4. Military organization of Athens

In *Politics*, Aristotle notes that the constitutional make up of a political system must take into account the military requirements of the city (1267a 20-2: "It is essential therefore for the constitution to be framed with a view to military strength"). Indeed, Cleisthenes' reforms significantly influenced the military organization of Athens, both on a practical level (formation of units from tribes, election of generals and *polemarchos*) as well as from an ideological standpoint. The hoplites of the Athenian phalanx had already formed substantial bonds between themselves through their participation in the political sphere. At the same time, in addition to fighting for their motherland, they were defending the ideals of political freedom, equality before the law, and of democratic participation (de Ste. Croix 2004: 142-144)[66]. It is likely that the first time Athenian citizens had ever been called to defend their political rights was in the war against the Chalkidians and the Boeotians at the end of the 6th c. BC. About a decade later, they would gather in the plain of Marathon to battle once again for the same ideals.

The Athenian army was made up of ten units (*taxeis*), one from each tribe. Each unit was comprised of ten companies of one hundred soldiers. Only those citizens who could afford their own armor and weaponry participated as there was no state funding. The *thetes* served as *psiloi*,[67] armed primarily with javelins while there was also a cavalry. The tribes selected a commander of the infantry (*taxiarchos*) and a commander of the cavalry (*hipparchus*). The hoplites were deployed in the phalanx according to their tribal affiliation. Similarly, slain hoplites were recorded by tribes, with the funeral oration taking place in front of ten empty coffins.

The ten generals, one from each tribe, and the *polemarchos* were elected by the Assembly. Though their term was annual, there was no restriction on being re-elected, gradually leading to their emergence as key political posts. The institution of the ten generals was of particular importance. Firstly, the distribu-

---

66 For the military significance of Cleisthenes' reforms see van Effenterre 1976; Siewert 1982; van Schullen 2001: 168.

67 If the need arose, the state provided the weapons for *psiloi*. At a later point, once Athens required a larger military force, salary was paid (Hadjimihalis 1972: 3-8).

tion of military power amongst ten individuals reduced the risk that any one general would attempt to overthrow the state. Secondly, the principle of equality before the law was applied in the military domain as well, since the generals made decisions collectively and took turns in the leadership of the army. Lastly, the power of the *polemarchos*, the magistrate who wielded military leadership serving as Commander-in-Chief up until the battle of Marathon, was restricted. This system of military command, though faithful to the democratic leanings of the political system, did have the disadvantage

Warrior with full hoplite armament (5th c. BC)

of frequent changes at the top leadership levels (Parliament of Greeks 2010: 40-44; Kormallis 2010: 33-38; Steinhauer 2000: 66; Georgis 1995:44; Gerogiannis 1956: 3-5; Gedeon: 4).

In contrast to Sparta, where military training began at childhood, in Athens it represented the last stage of training for the youth before they were inducted into adult society (Giarenis 2008a: 182-187)[68]. While the Spartans became citizens upon completion of their military training and on the basis of their success in the related trials, in Athens, registration at the "registrar's record"[69], or the list of the members of a *demos*, occurred at the same time as enlistment into the army at the age of 18. The required prerequisite was for the already registered members of the *demos*, to cast votes and validate under oath that the candidate was of age and that he had been born free to Athenian parents. The list was verified by the Council and members of the

---

68 The training of children and adolescents in Athens did not strictly focus on military education. The functioning and perception of the state, in contrast to Sparta, contributed to the military ideal gradually becoming replaced by the athletic one (Soulis 1972: 11). Adolescence, the period preceding manhood, signaled the transition to adult life and was linked to the period of military training. Thus, pubescent boys who could bear arms and defend their hometown became citizens at the age of recruitment. For more detailon the period of adolescence and military training of the Athenians, see Pelekides 1962; Vidal-Naquet 1983; Adam-Magnesale 1998: 128-155. For the chronology of the institution of adolescence see Giannikopoulos 1990.

69 The "registrar's record" was kept at the Temple of Rhea (*Metroön*) in the Agora, which was also a kind of Archive for the laws and the resolutions of the city-state, see http://www.eie.gr/archaeologia/gr/02_DELTIA/Metroon.aspx.

demos were fined if violations of the requirements were discovered (Giarenis 2008α: 182-187).

The trainers of the newly-recruited (*paidotrivai*) and those responsible for their nourishment (*sophronistai*) were elected by the Assembly. Military training lasted two years. The first year, the adolescents were instructed in the use of weapons and they guarded Piraeus. They then manned the border fortresses (Anaphlystos, Thoricos, Sounion, Ramnus, Eleusis, Aphidnai, Phyle, Panacton) while studying military tactics and methods of fortification and also bearing responsibility for patrolling Attica. During their training, they were prohibited from participating in the public affairs of the city and from attending trials either as defendants or plaintiffs. At the end of this two-year period, at the age of 20, they were discharged with the skills necessary to serve their city as both citizens and hoplites (Giarenis 2008α: 182-187; Georgis 1995: 42; Gerogiannis 1956: 3-7). This double duty of defending both the city and the political system is captured in the famous oath taken by Athenian adolescents, which was immortalized by Lycurgus (*Ag. Leocr.*, 77):

Οὐ καταισχυνῶ ὅπλα τὰ ἱερά, οὐδ' ἐγκαταλείψω τὸν παραστάτην, ὅτῳ ἂν στοιχήσω. Ἀμυνῶ δὲ καὶ ὑπὲρ ἱερῶν καὶ ὁσίων, καὶ μόνος καὶ μετὰ πολλῶν. Τὴν πατρίδα δὲ οὐκ ἐλάττω παραδώσω, πλείω δὲ καὶ ἀρείω ὅσης ἂν παραδέξωμαι. Καὶ εὐηκοήσω τῶν ἀεὶ κραινόντων ἐμφρόνως, καὶ τοὺς θεσμοὺς τοῖς ἱδρυμένοις πείσομαι καὶ οὕστινας ἂν ἄλλους τὸ πλῆθος ἱδρύσηται ὁμοφρόνως. Καὶ ἄν τις ἀναιρῇ τοὺς θεσμοὺς ἢ μὴ πείθηται, οὐκ ἐπιτρέψω. Ἀμυνῶ δὲ καὶ μόνος καὶ μετὰ πάντων. Καὶ ἱερὰ τὰ πάτρια τιμήσω. Ἵστορες θεοὶ τούτων, Ἄγλαυρος, Ἐνυάλιος Ἄρης, Ζεύς, Θαλλώ, Αὐξώ, Ἡγεμόνη[70]

Upon completion of their military training, Athenian citizens were recorded in the lists of reservists and were responsible for maintaining their weapons and armor in good condition at home, to ensure swift mobilization if required.

Hoplite helmet and spear-head

[70] "I will not shame my sacred weapons, nor will I abandon my comrade with whom I will stand in battle. I will defend, by myself and with the help of all, the sacredness and holiness of my country and I will not leave her smaller than I receive her. And I will discipline myself to those who decide prudently every time and I will obey the current laws, as well as those that the demos unilaterally decides to put into effect. And should anyone be willing to abolish the laws or does not comply with them, I will not allow it, but I will fight him off by myself and with the help of all. And I will honor the homeland. Witnesses to this shall be the gods Agraulus, Ares Enyalius, Zeus, Thallo, Auxo, Hegemone". The Athenian adolescents gave this oath at the temple of Aglauros, at the Acropolis, either on the day of their recruitment or with the completion of their first year of training.

They were required to serve in the army until the age of 40, participating in both the defense of the city and in military expeditions. Between the ages of 40 and 60, they were no longer required to participate in campaigns, but they had to assist in the defense of the city in the event of an attack (Hadjimihalis 1972: 3-8; Gerogiannis 1956: 3-7).

Up until the first half of the 4th c. BC, the drafting of hoplites was made on the basis of lists compiled by the generals for a specific operation (Andrewes 1981: 1-13; Hansen 1986: 83-89). Later however the military draft was conducted by age groups (Giarenis 2008α: 182-187). The list of hoplite names had to be posted beneath the statue of the hero of each tribe, whereas the decree of mobilization announced the day of departure ("Tomorrow will be the marching out [Αὔριον δ' ἐστ' ἤξοδος]").

The trittys proved to be useful as a unit of mobilization, both for the infantry and the navy, as was demonstrated by the series of trittys landmarks which were located in the vicinity of the naval dockyard of Zea. The trittyes of each tribe formed along the streets leading to Athens. Therefore, the hoplites arriving from the coastal tritty, e.g. the Aegeis tribe (coastal demes of Rafina), en route to the city, united with the hoplites from the trittys of *mesogaia* (the inland demes, from Spata to Penteli), reaching Athens already in formation. In Athens awaited the hoplites from the trittys of *asty* (of the city). A similar method was used by naval crew as they boarded the triremes (Steinhauer 2000: 66).

Adolescents who refused to enlist or citizens who did not show up when drafted faced severe penalties. Their transgression was grouped into the category of public offenses[71], as it violated the city-state's interests. Any citizen had the right to charge them publicly ("*graphe*"). Typically, such military offenses carried the penalty of "disgrace" (partial or full revocation of political rights and up until the 5th c. BC the confiscation of property). The "disgraced" did not have the right to appear in the Agora, to enter sanctuaries, or address the Assembly (Kourakis 1985: 37; Giouni 1998: 73-80).

In addition to the hoplite phalanx, which constituted the main military force of the city, the Athenian army included cavalrymen, light-armed infantry ("psilous"), the naval crew, and from the beginning of the 4th c. BC, peltasts. Although at the beginning of the 5th c. BC there was a corps of 300 cavalrymen, there is no historical record of them participating in the Persian wars.

---

71 Examples of public offenses included failure to report for duty, refusal to join the army, desertion, and the embezzlement of public funds (McDowell 1978: 57). For every violation of military nature, there was a particular charge ("*graphe*"); the charge related to the failure to report for military duty was called "*astrateias graphe*" (Giarenis 2008a: 182-187).

However, after the mid 5th c. BC, and possibly as a consequence of their defeat at the hands of Thessalian cavalrymen in the battle of Tanagra (457 BC), the Athenians reorganized their cavalry.

In order to encourage the nobles to use their horses in the war, a special allowance was established (*katastasis*), whereas during the 4th c. BC, a law was passed with reference to the feeding of the horses (*sitisis*). Each year, one hundred cavalrymen were chosen from each "tribe", who had successfully passed the related ordeals. The person in charge of this cavalry (*phylarchos* = commander of the tribe) was the elected, and he grouped his men in 10 units of 10 men under the command of the "*decadarchos*" (=commander of ten men) Unlike what happened with the hoplites, there was no structured list for the cavalrymen; theoretically, any citizen who could afford a horse and passed the training could serve as cavalryman. The names of the cavalrymen per "tribe" were later recorded on boards and handed to the *taxiarchos*, to erase these names from the hoplite lists. There were two elected men in charge of the cavalrymen (*hipparchoi*), possible due to the tendency for the corps to be separated in two sections so as to protect the flanks of the phalanx. Although cavalry forces took part in particular battles, there is no testimony for mass mobilization of 1,000 cavalrymen (Gregoropoulos 2009: 31-33).

Certainly, the undisputed Athenian advantage was the city's naval power, which was formed under the initiative of Themistocles. The expense of the fleet's maintainance burdened the *pentakosiomedimnoi*, who were divided into groups (*naukrariai*) according to "tribe". The crew came from the *thetes* class, depending on the profession to be exercised by each. Thus, the seamen served in the triremes as sailors, while the rowers were either farmers or stockbreeders. Because the *thetes* played an important role in the acquisition of naval power, just like the hoplites in the past, they too acquired the right of election in higher offices, a fact which deepened even further the horizon of Athenian democracy.

Chapter 2

"King of the four quarters of the world": the empire of the Achaemenids

When Cyrus II the Great, seized Babylon (539 BC), he adopted the Babylonian royal title and from that moment onward he was called "Cyrus, king of the world, great king, mighty king, king of Babylon, king of Sumer and Akkad, king of the four quarters of the world" (Brosius 2006: 12). The title was probably fitting given that during the 30 years of Cyrus' rule, he had managed to transform the insignificant Persian kingdom into a vast empire, which would survive for more than two centuries. In fact, the Persians were the first to create a "global empire", extending from Egypt to India and from southern Russia to the Indian Ocean. More importantly, in spite of their successive failures to expand westwards (490-479 BC), the Persians maintained their control over all their conquered territories, until Darius' defeat by Alexander the Great (330 BC). To a great extent, this can be attributed to the policies adopted by the Persian kings, allowing the conquered regions to maintain a great part of their administrative infrastructure, language, customs and religion. Furthermore, the Persian kings themselves paid their respects to the local gods, initiated in their worship (Brosius 2006: 1-2).

For centuries (and to a certain extent up until this day), the Persians were considered "barbarians", especially when compared to the Greeks, according to Herodotus' account of the Persian wars. This comparison became more complicated and became the symbol of the conflict between enslavement andfreedom, despotism and democracy and lastly between Asia and Europe. The approach of Greek and foreign scholars to ancient history in the 18th and 19th centuries contributed to this perception.. In fact, the Persians were

never "barbarians", if this terminology insinuates the lack of any sense of civilization. The Achaemenid monarchs demonstrated great interest in the development of their vast dominion through the construction of key infrastructure projects (roads, bridges, canals), while they are credited with the establishment of the first ever postal service (Herod., *Hist.*, VIII.98). Their palaces were exceptional displays of architecture, while life in the royal court was characterized by a strict and at the same time equally refined protocol. Astrologers, engineers, architects, and poets-rhapsodists were welcome at the palace; the growth of the genre of romantic-epic poetry particularly, was facilitated by the latter (Brosius 2010: 2; Lloyd 1973: 116-118). Therefore, the essential point of differentiation with the Persians was not their cultural level, but primarily the political model upon which their government formation was based: absolute monarchy, where the king was not considered to be a "god" (as in Egypt), but nevertheless, governed by "divine right". In the Greek world, ther models of political government had been adopted (aristocracy, timocracy, democracy) and the kings' power was restricted (in cities where the institution was still present). In such an environment, acceptance of a despotic form of government , meant above all the non-negotiable subservience to the arbitrary will of a person, which derived its truth and validity not from reason or the collective consensus, but from the simple fact that this person was king. Under these terms, choosing resistance was self-evident.

Seal of Darius I

2.1 The creation of the Great Persian Empire: from Cyrus II to Darius I.

The Persians along with the Medes, Bactrians and Parthians constituted the group of Iranian tribes of Indo-European origin. Around 1,000 BC they settled in the plateaus of Iran and in the early 7th c. BC, they migrated to the southwest – in present day Fars (northwestern Iran) which the ancient Greeks referred to as Persis. The Medes settled in northwestern Iran around the city of Ecbatana, which became the capital of their state and extended to the boundaries of Azerbaijan (Young 1988α: 6-24). Around the same time, in the inland area of Asia Minor, the Lydians created an extended kingdom with

Sardis as its capital. In the northeast there was also the powerful kingdom of Phrygia, while the Assyrians empire stretched across the Middle East. The Carians and the Mysians were spread across small communities in southwest Asia Minor and near the Propontis respectively, while the Greeks inhabited the Asia Minor coast, Propontis and the Euxenus Pontus.

From the 8th century BC onwards the relations among the Greeks, the Lydians and the Phrygians were peaceful and involved trade and cultural exchanges. The Greeks imported amber from the Lydians, while the Phrygians, who since the mid 8th century BC had adopted the Greek alphabet, provided them with textiles, iron, and bronze. Furthermore, the Phrygian king Midas had excellent relations with the Delphic Oracle and married the daughter of the king of Aeolian Cumae, Agamemnon. The raids of the Cimmerians from the Caucasus region (late 8th Century BC) resulted in the destruction of the Phrygian kingdom (675 BC). Soon after, the king of the Lydians, Gyges, extended the borders of his kingdom, assimilating Phrygia and gradually turning against the Greek cities. Magnesia-upon-Maeander was conquered, but Miletus and Smyrna remained independent.

One Cimmerian raid proved destructive for the Lydians since Sardis, their capital, was plundered and besieged whilst Gyges was murdered (652 BC). The Cimmerians extended their reach as far as Ephesus and Miletus and settling in West Cilicia where they were finally exterminated by the Lydians, who once again launched a series of attacks on Greek cities, seizing Smyrna (600 BC).

The kingdom of Lydia reached its peak during the time of Croesus, who ascended to the throne in 560 BC. Shortly thereafter, the Aeolian and Ionian cities along the coast of Asia Minor, with the exception of Miletus, were captured by the Lydian king. However, shortly thereafter, Croesus had to face he Persian threat advancing from the East, which ultimately proved fatal for his nation (Sakellariou 1971b: 243).

The Persian empire was established in 559 BC when Cyrus II, son of the Persian king Cambyses I, ascended to the throne. Until this time, the Persians were under the rule of the Medes, who in the first half of the 6th c. BC, had fought off Scythian raids and had defeated the Assyrians, capturing their capital Nineveh (Huart 1972: 30-33). In 550 BC, however, Cyrus attacked Media and occupied Ecbatana. Initially, Persian independence from the Medes was perceived to be the motive for this operation. Yet, according to the Babylonian chronicles, the Mede king Astyages attacked Persis, but failed in his endeavor as part of his army abandoned him and joined Cyrus' forces

(Brosius 2006: 8-9)[72]. Commemorating his military triumph, Cyrus founded Pasargadae, where he built his palace and mausoleum. Immediately after, he conquered the region in the north of Media, reaching Lake Van before finally turning against Lydia.

Apparently, Croesus was expecting this Persian attack because he had sent ambassadors to the Delphic Oracle and the sanctuary of Apollo Ismenius near Thebes, asking for a divination. The response he received was that he had to ally with the most powerful Greek city-state and that, if he crossed the river Halys, he would destroy a powerful kingdom (Herod., *Hist.*, I.52-56). Once Croesus received the information that Sparta was the most powerful city, he struck an alliance with them and prepared his attack against Cyrus. He attacked the city of Pteria – without waiting for the Spartan army to arrive – where he clashed with the multitudinous Persian forces in an undecided battle. Hoping to receive assistance from Egypt and Babylon, he retreated to Sardis; but the Persians advanced aggressively and in the battle which ensued outside the Lydian capital, inflicted comprehensive defeat on their opponents[73], imprisoning the king himself[74] (547/546 BC).

Cyrus turned the conquered Lydia into a satrapy appointing the Persian Tavares as governor and assigning the Lydian Pactyes the role of collecting all of the treasure which once belonged to Croesus and transporting it to Persia. However, as soon as the king had departed, Pactyes began recruiting mercenaries and organized a Lydian revolution while urging the Greeks of Asia Minor to unite with his forces. Cyrus sent Mazares with a small force and Pactyes abandoned the operation before it even had the chance to develop into a battle. Mazares then turned against the Greek cities, which had joined Pactyes, capturing Priene and Magnesia-upon-Maeander. His successor Harpagus, who took over command of the province, finalized the conquest of Ionia (Cawkwell 2005: 30-45).[75]

---

72 It is a widespread yet questionable view that Cyrus was Astyages' grandson from his mother's side. It is likely that after the defeat of the Medes, he married Astyages' daughter – perhaps as a way to indicate symbolically the union between the Medes and the Persians under his rule (Brosius 2006: 9).

73 Herodotus notes(I.80) that Cyrus crippled the famous Lydian cavalry by implementing the following trick: he placed camels to lead the troops and the horses became terrified by their smell (Huart 1972: 39).

74 According to tradition which was already widespread in ancient times, the minute the Persians put Croesus to the stake, he shouted Solon's name. Cyrus asked to find out who this Solon was and when he heard the story about the two men meeting (and the famous saying of this wise man "Don't praise someone's happiness before his death"), decided to spare the Lydian king's life (Herod., *Hist.*, I 32, 86). According to Raubitschek (1963: 137-140), the meeting between Croesus and Solon was later contrived so as to explain this story

75 A little before Croesus was about to clash with Cyrus, he had summoned the Greek cities to revolt against the Lydians to no avail. After the destruction of the Lydian kingdom, the Asia Minor Greeks sent

After a series of expeditions against the Sacae and Bactrians, Cyrus conquered Babylon (539 BC). As he officially entered its capital, he proclaimed himself the new king who had received power from the Babylonian god Marduk. In the ensuing years, he expanded the borders of the empire, seizing Parthia, Bactria and Sogdiana, while campaigning against the Masagetes, east of the river Iaxartes, where he was killed in 530 BC (Brosius 2006: 9-13; Young 2008a: 24-47; Lloyd 1973: 100-108; Huart 1972: 34-35).

The successor of Cyrus, Cambyses II, continued his father's politics of conquest. During his reign, Cyprus fell to Persian rule while Egypt was added to the empire's satrapies (525 BC) with Memphis as its capital and Aryandes as its governor. Cyrene and Libya rushed to declare their allegiance with Cambyses - who carried on campaigning to the South, reaching the first Nile waterfall and the island of Elephantine, eventually reaching Nubia. Although Herodotus (*Hist.*, III.25) considers that the operation against Nubia was unsuccessful, the fact that Darius I included the Nubians among the nations of his empire implies that the Persians had gained control of at least some part of the country (Brosius 2006: 13; Young 1988a: 47-52; Lloyd 1973: 108-115).

The conditions surrounding Cambyses' death (522 BC) remain a mystery. It is said that as a child he suffered from epilepsy, which was exacerbated during the Nubian expedition, and upon his return to Memphis he had lost his sanity (Herod., *Hist.*, III 27-38). An uprising in Asia and a Mede's self-proclamation as Persian king, claiming to be Cambyses' brother Smerdis[76], forced the king to return to Persia, where in trying to suppress the revolt, he either committed suicide in despair or he accidentally wounded himself and died soon after (Huart 1972: 49-50).

Equally mysterious was the case of the Medeposing as Smerdis. According to one version of the story, Cambyses himself had ordered his brother's murder, fearing that he would conspire against him to take over the throne. The Mede impostor bore striking resemblance to the real Smerdis. So, he was able to deceive his subjects, the nobles and even the prince's wife, remaining in power for six months. The Persian nobles finally became suspicious of him and his act of fraud leading to his murder(Huart 1972: 50-51).

---

ambassadors to the Persian King asking that they remain his subjects as they were previously under Croesus' reign. When their request was rejected, they turned for Spartan assistance, who in turn send to Cyrus the message that he would have to confront them (Sakellariou 1971b: 254-255). The Persian king responded arrogantly that he did not know who these Spartans were (Herod., *Hist.*, I.153.1). These were the first official communication exchanges between the Greek world and the Persian empire.

76 Smerdis' name in Persian was Bardiya. In other Greek sources he is referred to as Tanyoxarkes (Ctesias, *Persica*, 13), Tanaoxares (Xenophon, *Cyropaedia*, VIII.7.11) and Mardos (Aeschylus, *Persians*, 774).

It is very probable that this story was contrived by the next king, Darius I. Although a noble, he was not a member of the royal family. His father Hystaspes was the Parthian satrap during the rule of Cyrus II and Cambyses II while he himself had followed Cambyses to Egypt. After Cambyses death, the throne was likely handed to his brother Smerdis since the king did not have a male child. However, neither did Smerdis, so it is likely that Darius organized the assassination of Smerdis in collaboration with other nobles. When he later entrenched his power and was crowned king, he manufactured the story of fratricide and the "pseudo-Smerdis" to cover up his involvement in the matter(Brosius 2006: 15-16). There are several clues which render this hypothesis possible or even plausible. Firstly, the sole source of all these specific events can be found on the famous inscription of Bisitun which was, of course, created under the command and dictate of Darius himself [77]. Setting aside the impossible fact that Smerdis had managed to deceive everyone for six months, a second indication revealed that after his ascension to the throne, Darius "constructed" a theory, which claimed that hewas the descendent of a certain Achaemenes (from which the governing dynasty derived its name), father of Teispes (and grandfather of Cyrus I). However, there is no mention of the Achaemene name in any previous source. It seems that Darius tried to legitimize his claim to the Persian throne by creating a family link to the royal dynasty; it is also interesting that he took it upon himself to reinforce this link by marrying both Cambyses' and Smerdis' daughters (Brosius 2006: 17-18). A final but equally strong indication was that, the first year of his rule was marked by nine revolutions, mainly in central satrapies (Media, Elam, Babylon, Bactria). It is plausible that one of the reasons for the unrest was the doubt and skepticism concerning whether his succession to the throne was legitimate.

Whichever the case, Darius I was the second important leader of the Persian empire after Cyrus I the Great. In the 36 years of his rule (522-486 BC) he confirmed his domination of all the lands comprising the dominion, he reorganised the kingdom's administration and the army, created an imperial system which survived until 330 BC and most importantly, he began the Persian expansion to the West. The king's first task was to restore order to his dominion; this he managed by waging 19 battles in 13 months. Once he cemented his position, he proceeded with a series of symbolic acts: he reconstructed the royal palace in Susa, the old former capital of the Elamites (Elam was the first satrapy which had revolted against him); he continued the construction work in the Pasargadae palace of Cyrus II, hence highlighting the continuation of

---

77 This version of fratricide and pseudo-Smerdis is narrated by Herodotus (*Hist.*, III. 30, 61-79). Apparently, it is this version which has survived the passing of time (whether invented by Darius or not).

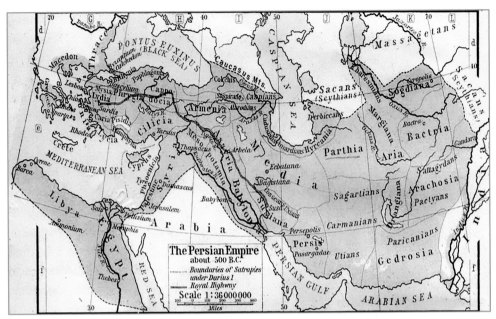

The Great Persian Empire

the Persian dynasty and the legitimacy of his rule. Lastly he founded his own royal city, Persepolis.

Darius I's strategy of conquest was smaller in scale compared to those of his predecessors, but no less ambitious. Around 518 BC, he campaigned in India, aiming to advance the empire's borders further eastwards than Cyrus II. Subsequently, he attempted something which no other eastern empire had previously undertaken: expansion to the West, to the "people beyond the sea" (Brosius 2006: 18-23; Young 1988b: 53-63; Huart 1972: 51-56). So, in 513 BC, he set off for Europe.

2.2. The expedition "beyond the sea"

The reasons that prompted Darius to campaign against Europe have spawned a variety of hypotheses. The rationale provided by Herodotus is based on the - familiar to the ancient historian - frame of revenge: Darius wanted to avenge the Scythians, because in the past, they had attacked the Median kingdom (Herod., *Hist.*, IV.1., 4). Other interpretations note that the real motive had to do with the gold mines of Dacia or that the Persian king wanted to satisfy the request of the tyrants in Ionia for the exploration of new markets as a way to

alleviate the economic depression plaguing the Ionic cities (Fol & Hammond 1988: 240; Pelekidis 1971: 282-283). While all of these factors may have played a role, it is more likely that Darius' real objective was to expand his empire into Europe, starting with the conquest of Thrace. It seems the empire had reached its natural boundaries. The Caspian Sea, the Caucasus region and the Black Sea were the empire's northern boundaries, in the west it reached the shores of the Aegean and eastern Mediterranean, while the Persian Gulf opened the way to India. Arabia seemed impenetrable due to the desert while the prospect of expanding further south than Egypt was not an attractive one, taking into account the fact that during the absence of Cambyses in the land of the Nile, there had been uprisings and disturbances in the satrapies (Huart 1972: 55). The only way out, thus, was to expand to the West (Cawkwell 2005: 49-50).

The transport of the Persian army to Europewas impressive. Darius ordered the construction of a float-ing bridge of 200 ships across the Bosporus, close to Calchedonia; an act which has been interpreted – for the most part – as a display of power and grandeur (Cawkwell 2005: 49). The exact number of Darius' army is not known. Herodotus (IV. 87) estimated 700,000 men and 600 ships, but later historians regarded these figures as extreme[78]. The ships which provided support to the land operations came from Cyprus, Egypt, Phoenice and the Ionian cities.

The bronze helmet and the gold mouth-cover of the "Gold Warrior". One of the most impressive archaeological findings at the excavations con-ducted by Anastasia and Pavlos Chrysostomou in Archontikon, Pella (August 2010)

Darius reached the Danube and annihilated any Ge-tae forces who resisted. Subsequently, he ordered the construction of a second floating bridge of Ionian ships in the river delta allowing him to cross it and continue his expedition in Scythia, ordering the tyrants of the Io-nian cities[79] to guard the construction until his return (or for 60 days: Herod., *Hist.*, IV.98). According to Herodotus (IV.137-138), the Scythians encouraged the Greeks to destroy the bridges, so that Darius would be trapped inland.

---

78 Pelekidis (1971:283) estimated that the forces of Darius were 80,000 men, namely the troops who remai-ned in Thrace under Megabyzus, after his return to Asia. Fol and Hammond (1988: 238), on the other hand, accepted the size of the fleet being 600 ships claiming that this must have been the naval force following the king in each of his overseas campaigns.

79 The tyrants of the Ionian cities were in charge of the ships taking part in the expedition. Herodotus (IV.138), mentions Daphnis, Hippoclus, Herophantus, Metrodorus, Aristagoras and Ariston from the Greek cities of the Hellespont; Strattis, Aeacis, Laodamas, Histiaeus and Aristagoras from the Ionian cities and the Athenian Miltiades –who later triumphed in Marathon – from the Thracean Chersonisos.

While Miltiades supported this proposition, Histiaeus turned it down because destroying the Persians would mean the collapse of the status quo of tyranny in Ionia[80].

There are limited accounts regarding the raid against the Scythians[81]. By implementing scorched earth tactics and withdrawal, Scythians avoided the conflict and lured the Persians further inland. Thus, Darius returned to the Danube and shortly thereafter, abandoned European terrain, leaving behind Megabyzus to act on his behalf with 80,000 men to continue the operations (Cawkwell 2005: 46-60; Fol & Hammond 1988; Huart 1972: 54-56; Lloyd 1973: 131-137; Pelekidis 1971: 282-284; Gerogiannis 1956: 11-14).

Votive plaque with representation of a male figure in Median garb. From the Oxus Treasure. 5th-4th c. BC. London, British Museum.

Megabyzus recaptured Byzantium, Calchedona and Perinthus, which had revolted during Darius' campaignagainst the Scythians, and subsequently he continued cementing Persian dominance in Thrace and Macedonia. These areas comprised a new satrapy where Sacae "beyond the sea" lived (possibly Getae), along with Thracians and "Iones wearing petasus" (meaning the Macedonians). It is claimed that the capital of the satrapy was Philippoupolis, due to its naturally fortified position. An equally important position was held by Doriscos, near Feres, where a powerful guard was stationed (Fol&Hammond 1988: 247).

The annexation of Macedonia to the Persian empire is linked to Herodotus' account, although questioned by most historians (Daskalakis 1960: 246-247, 255-256, 261-267). After the provision of "earth and water" to the Persian delegates dispatched by Megabyzus, the king of Macedonia Amyntas I held a splendid feast. The drunken Persians behaved inappropriately to the women

---

80 Cawkwell (2005:47-48) questioned the validity of this hypothesis, arguing that in this case, Darius would have undoubtedly discovered Miltiades' position; thus, he would have made sure to punish him upon returning from the expedition in the Danube. However, as each of the operations were finalized, Miltiades returned to Chersonisos where he remained tyrant until 496 BC, when he was forced to leave due to Scythian raids. According to Cawkwell, Herodotus' account comes from the testimony of Miltiades during his trial in Athens in 493 BC. The source may be Miltiades himself, but it may not necessarily be true.

81 Following his common practice, Darius sent messengers to the Scythian king asking for "earth and water". The messengers would return with a bird, a mouse, a frog and five arrows – this was the Scythian response. Darius felt it was a statement of subordination, but Gobryas interpreted these strange gifts as: if you cannot become birds to cross the air, mice to bury yourselves underground or frogs to hide in the swamp mud, you cannot escape our arrows (Herod., *Hist.*, IV, 131-132; Huart 1972: 56)

of the Macedonian royal court, whose presence was mandated by the foreign guests. Then, the son of Amyntas, Alexander I, who would have been between 15 and 18 years of age, urged his elderly father to retire. Subsequently, he dressed Macedonian warriors in women's attire and , he ordered theslaughter of the Persian emissariesjust at the right moment (Herod., *Hist.*, V. 17-21). The news spread throughout the Greek world, especially to Athens where Alexander I was particularly popular and considered a "Philhellene"[82]. A few years later, (possibly in 496 BC), Alexander I participated in the Olympic games and publicly declared his descent from the Heracleids – Temenides of Argos. His participation and action in the Persian wars has also led to various debates; yet, it is interesting to note the effect that all these relevant stories had in shaping the thinking of future generations: Alexander the Great, who proudly stated his descent from Hercules (from his father's side) and from Achilles (from his mother's side) obviously saw the anti-Persian campaign as the continuation of his predecessors' work and therefore, the "nemesis" for the

---

82 Within this framework, the marriage of Boubares, son of Megabyzus to the daughter of Amyntas is regarded as the triumph of Macedonian diplomacy which succeeded in the cover-up of the Persian slaughter (Daskalakis 1960: 264-266). Nevertheless, it must be noted that intermarriages between Persian nobles and women of aristocratic or even royal descent from the provinces was common practice, which obviously aimed at further establishing Persian rule.

In ancient times, the word "philhellene" was used to characterize any prominent Greek who was pervaded by panhellenic feelings, preached panhellenic ideas or offered services to the entire Greek nation. In other words, a "philhellene" was the Greek who did not limit his thought and action to a narrow local horizon of the city-state where he was born or lived; but, he who opened up horizons of panhellenic thought, spoke and acted not as a Greek citizen of a specific Greek city-state; in being Greek, he belonged to all of Greece. The fact that ancient writers, either philosophers or historians or orators use as almost as a rule the word "philhellene" in this sense leaves no room for doubt concerning this matter. See Thucydides i 57, 2: "Alexander the Philhellene who flourished during the Persian wars"; Dio Chrysostom., p. 25: "Alexander, called philhellene"; Harpocr., word 'Alexander': "He [= Alexander, Amyntas' son] is the one called philhellene"; Plato, *Rep.*, E 470e: "And won't they be philhellenes, lovers of Greeks, and will they not regard all Greece as their own and not renounce their part in the holy places common to all Greeks?"; Xenophon, *Ages.*, II.31: "Accordingly, [Agesilaus] having decided which of them showed the stronger signs of being a friend to the Greeks, he took the field with him. He inflicted a crushing defeat on the enemy of the Greeks, and helped to establish his rival"; cf. VII.3-4: "if the citizens should continue to live in peaceful submission to the laws, the fatherland would always prosper and that she would be strong when the Greeks were prudent. Again, if it is honourable in one who is a Greek to be a friend to the Greeks, what other general has the world seen unwilling to take a city when he thought that it would be sacked, or who looked on victory in a war against Greeks as a disaster?"; Isocrates, *Paneg.*, 96: "And yet how could men be shown to be braver or more devoted to Greece [philhellenes] than our ancestors, who, to avoid bringing slavery upon the rest of the Hellenes, endured to see their city made desolate [...]?"; Isocrates, *Evagoras*, 50: "At present, however, they have undergone so great a change that they strive with one another to see who shall be regarded as most friendly to the Greeks". And in another instance, Isocrates (*Phil.* 122), referring to Philip, who he considered a Greek from the Heracleids and fitting to take over the panhellenic struggle against the barbarians of Asia, wrote: "He is a man with a great vision and a philhellene". On some rare occasions, especially after the 5th c., a foreign leader who had offered great services to the Greeks was also called a "Philhellene"; this is the case with Pharaoh Amasis, mentioned by Herodotus (II.178), who had given his permission for the foundation of the Greek city Naucratis and had been generous to the Greeks in many ways (Daskalakis 1960: 343-344).

Detail from the Archers Frieze in Darius' palace at Susa (Paris, Louvre museum)

conquest of Macedonia by Darius. Even if we assume that the intention of Darius was to defeat the Scythians, it would be inappropriate to advocate that this first European campaign was unsuccessful. Quite the opposite: the empire had spread to the West, encompassing land which extended from the Danube to the Peneus River – land rich in minerals (especially gold and pure silver, both greatly sought after in Asia and Egypt) as well as other goods. Furthermore, he established a critical foothold in Europe, which allowed for further expansion while providing control of important territories – both from a financial and strategic point of view – for the city-states of southern Greece (Byzantium, Stageira, Potidaea etc.). As per G. L. Cawkwell's saying (2005: 52), the menacing shadow of Darius was now stretching over the Greek world.

2.3 Organisation and administration of the empire

During Darius' reign, the empire stretched from India to the Mediterranean and from the Caspian Sea to the Indian Ocean. Throughout this vast region, the king was the absolute monarch, acting as representative of the god Ahura Mazda[83] and ruling with the god's guidance. His right to reign was supported by his lineage stemming from the dynastic ruling house of the Achaemenids. As a rule, succession to the throne was smooth because the king nominated his successor. The criteria for selecting a successor included a prince's birth "in purple" (i.e. his father must have ascended the throne prior to the succcesor's birth) and his mother being a descendant of a Persian noble family. Nevertheless, the successor's abilities, especially his skill in archery, horse-riding and hunting[84] were also taken into account.

---

83 The worship of Ahura Mazda, god of good, justice and truth, became the official worship for Persian kings during the time of Darius I. However, the Persians were not willing to impose it upon their citizens (Brosius 2006: 32-33). For the religious practices of the Achaemenid empire refer to Huart 1972: 80-85 and Brosius 2006: 63-72.

84 In keeping with the analogies, hunting meant to the Persians what sporting events meant to the Greeks

After the king's death, his body was transferred for burial to Persis or later to Persepolis while funeral pyres were lit throughout the empire, signalling the period of mourning. During the reign of Darius I, a a glorious and symbolic ceremony declaring the new king was introduced. The successor, along with his escort, then traveled from Persepolis to Pasargadae where he appeared before the delegates from the satrapies dressed in the attire of Cyrus II, eating terebinth (a type of pistachio nut) and drinking sour milk as a symbol of the nomadic Persian past. Then, he would wear the royal Persian attire and receive the symbols of his power: the royal headdress, the scepter, the lotus flower and a special pair of shoes which were designed to make him look taller (Brosius 2006: 32-34).

In addition to the palaces in Parsagades and Persepolis, the king also had palaces in the capital cities of the conquered areas (Ecbatana, Susa, Babylon), which he would frequently visit so as to make his presence felt. On his trips, he was escorted by numerous members of the royal court and high-ranking officers, his mother, his wives[85], mistresses, children, Persian nobles, numerous servants, and of course, the elite military force of "Immortals". The famous "Royal Road" which connected the cities of the Persian Empire was used by the king on his journey. (Brosius 2006: 37).

The king was surrounded by the members of the seven Persian ruling houses who even had the right to appear before him without being pre-announced. Their role was an advisory one, but it is not known whether they constituted a unified body. The king would endeavor to secure their allegiance with gifts. Another privileged group were the so-called "King's Friends and Benefactors", members of which were not necessarily of Persian descent. With this title, the king paid his respect to all those who offered their assistance in all sorts of matters, primarily in military operations (Brosius 2006: 39-40).

Control and command of this vast empire was based on the system of provinces or satrapies, which had been introduced by Cyrus II. The satrapies were obliged to pay tribute to the king and also to provide men, weapons, horses and ships (where coastal areas were concerned) for the Persian army. Depending on its size, each conquered region constituted one satrapy. There were, however, instances of unification among many neighboring tribes in the same

---

since it gave them the opportunity to exercise and train in the use of various weapons (spear, dagger, bow). Hunting took place either in the palace's huge garden plots ("paradise") or in the wild (Brosius 2006: 44).

85 The women that belonged to the royal court (wives, daughters, sisters, etc.) bore the title of Princess. The king's mother and the successor's mother had the highest status in the royal court. In spite of the relevant information provided by Herodotus, the women of the royal court enjoyed great privileges, exerted far-reaching influence on the king and owned private property (pieces of land or even entire villages). See Brosius 2006: 41-45.

region. The king appointed the governors to head each conquered land; the governor was called "satrap" which means "protector of the realm". His duties included tax collection, peacekeeping, dispensation of justice and overseeing the economic growth of the satrapy. (Brosius 2006: 47; Huart 1972: 73-74).

If Cyrus II was considered the founder of the Achaemenid empire due to his conquests, Darius could claim the title of "co-founder", given that he created and systematized the imperial system of command, administration and most importantly, reformulated the imperial ideology. Until his time, the tribute imposed on the satrapies was

Gold Persian daric

not precisely defined and the satraps could also be nobles of the conquered land. However, from 522 BC onwards, the office of the "satrap" in the empire's 20 satrapies was assumed by members of the royal family or of the Persian nobility. Moreover, the king himself would appoint two additional officials reporting directly to him – the secretary and the general. Thus, the satrapies were in fact commanded by a group of three men who watched one another, while royal inspectors were also frequently dispatched to monitoring the situation(Goodspeed 1899: 251-252).

Each satrapy had to pay a tax which was determined by itsproductive and economic capabilities. The tax could be paid either in money or in kind.. Thus, Cyrene provided corn, Media sheep and horses, India hunting dogs and Babylon eunuchs (Huart 1972: 75). In order to facilitate the smooth functioning of the tax system and of trade within the empire, Darius introduced a monetary system modeled on the Babylonian one, which included 3 coins: the golden daric coin which had inscribed the figure of the king kneeling and holding a bow and arrow on the on one side, the silver stater, and the silver drachma (Goodspeed 1899: 252-253; Huart 1972: 76.)

Apart from tribute taxes, other taxes were levied not only on the conquered but also on Persians(tax for land ownership, customs duties, selling tax etc.). Imperial officials oversaw all the financial exchanges and enforced the royal decrees, while they also recorded every detail of revenues and expenses[86]. In

---

86 Darius' keen interest in financial matters is demonstrated by the fact that the Persians, according to Herodotus, called him "merchant" (*kapelos*) whereas Cambyses was refered to as a "despot", and of course, Cyros was regarded as "father", see *Hist.*, III.89.3: "the Persians called Darius the merchant, Cambyses the master, and Cyrus the father; for Darius made petty profit out of everything, Cambyses was harsh and arrogant, Cyrus was merciful and always worked for their well-being".

return for the cash flowing into its treasury, the central administration offered its subjects an organized system of infrastructure and transport (key road arteries, ports, canals, city water supplies), aid in the fields of agriculture and craft production (allotment of public land, raw materials, grain etc.) and the enforcement of the necessary peace and harmony (Greek Parliament 2010: 30-31).

Perhaps the most impressive of the imperial undertakings was the construction of the empire's infrastructure system. A network of road arteries criss-crossed the imperial land, facilitating communication and trading activity. The most significant one was the "Royal Road" which started in Persepolis, passed through Susa reaching Babylon; from there, the road led to Northern Iran where it branched out into two routes: the northern branch ended up in Cappadocia; while the southern branch, via Cilicia, led to Lydia and its capital Sardis. Eastwards "the Royal Road" led from Persepolis to Ecbatana of Media, where it continued its course around the Caspian Sea and further to the East to Bactria. The other branch of the "Royal Road" led to the south, via Arachosia and reached its final point in the southeastern satrapies. Finally, one other branch connected Persepolis with Egypt, via Jerusalem and Damascus; from Damascus the route again branched out northwards towards Asia Minor and eastwards to Media. All the main road arteries were lined with fortresses, inns, merchandise stations, royal storage areas etc. Thanks to this road network, the Persians were able to develop the first organized postal service of antiquity, which exclusively served the king's communication needs. Postmen would travel on fast horses and were entitled to receive an amount of flour and wine on a daily basis directly from the royal warehouses en route (Brosius 2006: 53-57; Huart 1972: 74; Goodspeed 1899: 253).

Although the Persian empire was primarily a land power, the conquest of Phoenice, Egypt, Cyprus, the Greek cities of Ionia and the Euxene Pontus also supplied it with a naval force. Hence, similarly to the main road networks, sea routes also served trade activity, starting from the eastern coast of the Mediterranean, extending to the Euxene Pontus and the Bosporus and reaching all the way to the Red Sea and the Gulf of Oman. Darius was the first king to be actively involved in the empire's naval development, ordering the completion of the canal – whose construction had begun during Pharao Nehu's time and which connected the Red Rea with the river Nile. As was customary, his attempt was engraved on the Inscription of Suez (Herod., *Hist.*, II.158; Brosius 2006: 57-58).

Nevertheless, military power, infrastructure works and economic development did not necessarily guarantee the stability of this vast empire. Darius'

substantial contribution was the formation of the empire's ideology and of a new rhetoric which aimed to transform his dominion into a cohesive state. The reference point for this ideology was the Great King who was no longer projected as purely a national Persian leader, but rather as the monarch of all the peoples of the empire. Within this framework, the rhetoric of piece, rule of law and just governing combined with the projection of – mostly military – power and tolerance were utilized. It is not accidental that upon entering the defeated peoples' capital city, one of the first actions undertaken by the Persian kings was to pay homage to the local gods ensuring they were presenting themselves as agents of the gods' commandments; this is what both Cyrus II in Babylon and Cambyses II in Egypt did. Likewise, after the conquest of the Ionian cities, Darius paid his respect to the god Apollo and his priesthood (Greek Parliament 2010: 18-26).

In terms of both functionality and ideology, the empire's main attribute was its inclusive and multicultural character. The Persians did not impose either their religion or their language on those defeated; in contrast, they allowed them to preserve their national and cultural identity. Even when the Persian language acquired its written form (also attributed to Darius), the local languages of the satrapies continued to be used in official documents (Brosius 2006: 39, 50).

This tolerance was most certainly a choice of political expedience as it guaranteed continuity at the administrative level, while it also did not provide an additional reason for the defeated to feel dissatisfaction. Despite its usefulness in achieving internal stability, this multiculturalism proved rather disruptive on the battlefield. The Persian troops deployed at Marathon were just an aggregation of diverse ethnic groups lacking any cohesive bond. Their only common element was the fact that they obeyed the Persian king's will. This, as it later became apparent, was not enough.

2.4 Military organization of the Persians

Medes, Assyrians, Bactrians, Hindis, Parthians, Chorasmians, Sogdians, Gandares, Libyans, Paphlagonians, Phrygians, Mysians: Herodotus needed approximately twenty paragraphs simply to enumerate the nations comprising the Persian army during Xerxes' campaign *(Hist.,* VII.60-81). Up to the battle of Marathon, this army had never been defeated while its reputation began to grow during Cyrus II's reign as he had based the entire empire on military might.

However, there were differences between the armies of Cyrus and Darius. Despite not having a detailed account of the army's composition and organizational structure, it can be assumed that, at least initially, it must have included a homogeneous body of Persian warriors; a fact which, to some extent, explains its effectiveness. The gradual expansion of the empire's borders, however, necessitated a proportional increase in military power and the Persian population was insufficient to cover the army's needs. Therefore, the Persian population continued to form the core of the Persian army while the satrapies provided the necessary number of warriors, weaponry and supplies to enable and support the great military expeditions.

Enlisting was mandatory for all citizens, aged 17-52. In order to meet recruitment requirements, the empire had been divided into districts, headed by the generals (*karanoi*) (Gerogiannis 1956: 8-11; Hadjimichalis 1972: 9). The Persians, who were to man the elite units, were trained in archery and horse-riding from the age of 5 until they turned 20. Then, at the age of 20, they joined the army, receiving an additional four years of training. From the time of their discharge at the age of 25 until the age of 50, they comprised the military's reserve force (Ray 2009: 31).

The most important corps of the Persian military was the cavalry. The Persians, similar to other Iranian tribes, were well-known horse breeders and possessing a fine horse conferred social standing and prestige. The Persian cavalry distinguished between the cavalry corps provided by each satrapy, the independent cavalry and the cavalry of the royal guard. The cavalry regiment (500-600 cavalrymen), which included squadrons of 100 cavalrymen, was the tactical unit ; two regiments comprised one body of a thousand (*khiliostys*), whereas two such bodies constituted a brigade.

The cavalry corps was equipped with bows, accompanied the infantry, and led the charge on the enemy. The independent cavalry, on the other hand, was armed with swords, spears or javelins and the riders bore light armor. Its mission was to search and pursue as well occupy the rear of the enemy. Finally, the cavalry of the royal guard – to which only Persians, Medes or Elamites were recruited - was also equipped with spears or javelins, swords and cuirasses. The cavalrymen wore trousers and tunics with sleeved overcoats which covered their bodies like a mantle. They also wore a soft felt hat which had extensions that allowed them to protect their mouths from dust and sandstorms (Gerogiannis 1956: 8-11; Hadjimichalis 1972: 9-13; Brosius 2006: 58)[87].

---

87 In addition tohorses, the Persian army also had camels which were ridden by the Bactrian cavalrymen, and chariots which were provided and led by the Scythians (Brosius 2006: 58-59).

A Persian footman, holding a light shield (work by Stelios Nidgiopoulos)

A Persian archer (work by Stelios Nidgiopoulos)

The Persian infantry, which outnumbered the cavalry, was divided into active, reserve and guard. The active army consisted of men from the satrapies as well as foreign mercenaries serving those satrapies. The reserve army had a similar composition and would assemble whenever large military campaigns were being organized or otherwise in the event of emergency affecting the empire. Lastly, the guard army was the permanent guard which manned the fortresses along the "Royal Road" or in a number of remote satrapies (e.g., in Doriskos or the island of Elephantine where Jewish mercenaries comprised the guard). The infantry tactical unit was a body of 10,000 soldiers (*myriostys*), while its subdivisions were the body of a thousand soldiers (*khiliostys*), the brigade (100 soldiers), and the company (25 soldiers); every myriostys included 10 *khiliostys*, 100 brigades and 400 companies. In peace time, the *myriostys*, were grouped into triads, with each group of three comprising an army corps. In wartime, the reserve army was also summoned, boosting the number of each army corps to 300,000 men; 200,000 of which were warriors, with the remainder performing various support services (Geroniannis 1956: 8-11; Hadjimichalis 1972: 9-13).

The infantry soldiers were armed primarily with long-range weapons (arrows, slingshots, javelins) and the majority did not bear defensive armor. The mercenaries proably bore swords, axes or spears as well as a light shield. From the early 5th c. BC, a light rectangular wicker shield (*spara*) began to be used. The shield-bearers (*sparabara*) would line up in the first two ranks

A Persian footman from the elite corps of the Royal Guard (work by Stelios Nidgiopoulos)

A Persian cavalryman, with a light cuirass and two javelins (work by Stelios Nidgiopoulos)

forming a wall of shields to protect both themselves and the archers behind them from enemy arrows, while the archers of the next ranks fired at the enemy. The Persian spear was smaller than the Greek counterpart and did not have a butt-spike (*sauroter*). The soldiers used it to defend the shield-bearers in the first ranks since, in contrast to the hoplites, they did not advance towards the enemy, but instead tried to pin the enemy, enabling the archers to rain arrows down on them with devastating affect(Ray 2009: 30-31).

The main weapon used by the Persian army was the bow which was regarded as particularly prestigious by the world of the East; it is important to note the portrayal of the king as archer on the daric coins. The Persian bow was of large dimensions and was strong, allowing it to cover large distances. Its maximum range was estimated at around 300m while its effective range was up to 200m (Gerogiannis 1956: 8-11).

The elite infantry corps, the "Immortals", comprised 10,000 Persian, Medes or Elamites soldiers. The name "Immortals" was given to elite unit because as soon as a member was killed or injured, he would be replaced so as to maintain the number of soldiers constant. They bore a long spear, with a silver pomegranate at the butt, bows and arrows and a light wicker or leather shield. The king's personal guard was comprised of 1,000 soldiers, of Persian noble lineage, chosen from the Immortals. To make them distinguishable

from the rest, their spears bore a golden apple at the butt ("apple-bearers"). The king's personal guard also included 1,000 cavalrymen, who were also drawn from the Persian aristocracy (Goodspeed 1899:253-254; Huart 1972: 77; Brosius 2006: 58).

The Persians did not have a navy of their own. However, after conquering Phoenice, Egypt, Cyprus and the Greek cities of the Aegean and Asia Minor, they acquired the fleets of the defeated lands. The core power of the fleet was 600 vessels from Phoenice, Cyprus and Egypt while during military campaigns reinforcements were provided by the Ionian cities of the Aegean (Greek Parliament 2010: 28-30). Although the fleet was utilized in the campaigns against Europe, in reality the Persians never developed a naval strategy nor did they promote the element of naval power. The Persian perspective emanated from its dominance as a land force. Thus they saw vessels, not as a means of maritime domination, but rather as a mobile wing of their land forces. In general, the fleet's role was to support land operations either by replenishing supplies or by transporting reinforcements to the rear of enemy lines (Cakwell 2005: 254-257).

The king was in command of all military forces, and as such he had to be well-skilled in warfare tactics; besides, a good king was considered one who was a good warrior, capable of defeating his enemies and achieving victory for the empire (Brosius 2006: 60). During battle, he was positioned at the center of the army, in a chariot, wearing his red tunic and his crown. The Immortals and 10,000 cavalrymen were lined up on either side of him. However, his presence was not required in every single military operation. Cyrus II and Cambyses II led their troops to battle during the time of their greatest conquests as did Darius in the expedition of 513 BC; yet, the leadership of small-scale operations was assigned to either one of their generals or the satraps. Moreover, Xerxes not only led the expedition to Greece, but also watched the naval battle of Salamis, from mount Aegaleon, where a special throne was erected. After failing to conquer Greece, Persian kings would appear in battle less frequently, perhaps due to the absence of any imminent threat until the second half of the 4th c. BC. when Alexander the Great's expedition to Asia forced them to assume their role as military leaders yet again (Brosius 2006: 61-62).

The warfare tactics of the Persian army were defined by their main weapon, the bow, and by the use of the cavalry. The typical formation of combat troops was the infantry *myriostys* in deployment, with spaces about 25m and arrangements of 30-100 ranks. The elite bodies, the Persians and the Sacae, were placed at the center, while the soldiers from the satrapies were deployed at the flanks, by ethnic group. The cavalry body took positions in the two flanks

of the infantry; the independent cavalry was at the rear; while the royal guard cavalry was positioned at the center of the formation. Finally, armed chariots were placed approximately 50m ahead of the infantry, constituting the outpost line (Ray 2009: 32; Gedeon 2002: 3-4; Gerogiannis 1956: 8-11).

Since its main weapon was the bow, the Persian army's dogma was inherently a defensive one. The large troop body would wait for the enemy to approach before unleashing a countless barrage of arrows – in today's equivalent, this was effectively annihilation of the enemy by fire. As a result, battle formations had to be extremely dense and deployed in multiple ranks, to facilitate the simultaneous firing of a large number of arrows. The customary formation, therefore, was the arrangement of the *myriostys* in a quadrangle full of soldiers, with a front line and depth of 100 men (see figure). The last row aimed beyond the ranks in front and with the objective being for its arrows to be effective at a distance of at least 100m from the first row.

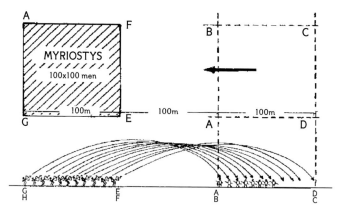

Assuming that a good archer could launch 4-5 arrows per minute, the entire *myriostys* would fire 50,000 arrows at the same time. Consequently, a heavily armed opponent -who would need approximately two minutes to cross the fire zone at an attacking pace – would be subject to an enormous amount of arrows (approximately 80,000-100,000). Theoretically, any opponents who attempted to cross the line of fire would have to be placed out of battle (Gerogiannis 1958: 8-11; Hadjimichalis 1972: 9-13).

These tactics may have been effective for the wars in Asia, where the same type of warfare primarily prevailed; however, it proved inadequate in dealing with the hoplites. The heavy defensive armor worn by the Greeks allowed them to pass through the line of fire uninjured and to fight in close quarters. The Persians were both unprepared and ill-equipped for such type of warfare (Gerogiannis 1956: 8-11). The plethora of troops deployed by the Great King did not play a role in this case.

"...save the Ionians from slavery":
The Ionian Revolution

While for the Greeks the Ionian revolution was the prelude to the Persian wars[88], for the Persians it was nothing more than another revolt by subjugated nations, which the empire had to confront. Its suppression was integrated within the operations focusing on European expansion. In this sense, it did not expedite the European forays of the Persians, especially the attack against Greece, but may have rather slowed down Darius' plans. Having established an important bridgehead in the regions of Thrace and Macedonia, the Persian king would surely not allow much time to pass before further expanding his empire towards the west; nothing prohibited him from attempting his next campaign in the first decade of the 5th c. BC. Had that been the case, the outcome would have been far from certain, given the internal problems endemic in Greek city-states and the fact that they were not prepared – at least psychologically – for this confrontation (Cawkwell 2005: 80). Thus, the Ionian revolution bought the Greeks some time: in the critical decade of 500-490 BC, Athens had the opportunity to consolidate its democratic reforms, which to a large extent, contributed to the formation of strong internal bonds amongst its citizens, enhancing the ideal of democracy, which they would soon be called upon to defend. Moreover, three key figures, who would also prove to be of vital importance for the immediate confrontations, emerged during these turbulent political times: Miltiades, Themistocles and

88 Herodotus considered it "the root of all evil" for both the Greeks and the Persians (*Hist.*, V. 97). According to his approach, the Persians burned the gods' temples in Ionia and later the Acropolis during their campaign against the Athenians as a means of avenging the revolutionaries for destroying the temple of Cybele in Sardis (*Hist.*, V. 102); while the Athenians, in turn, created the Delian league to avenge the Persians. Alexander the Great would put an end to this chain of retribution from both opposing groups, by destroying the Persian empire (Murray 1988: 466).

Aristides. Finally, the Athenians and the Eretrians, who were sent to reinforce the Ionian revolutionaries, managed to gain direct insight into the Persian standard practice of warfare. Thus, even if the Ionian revolution signaled the end of the Greek cities' prosperity in Asia Minor, it constituted an event of vital importance to the Greeks "beyond the sea".

Herodotus

The only written source for the events that unfolded from 499-494 BC is Herodotus (*Hist.*, V-VI). However, even those historians who do not reject all of Herodotus' work, acknowledge that his narration of the Ionian revolution is the most problematic area of his work (Murray 1988: 466)[89]. In addition to citing the Ionian revolutionary activity as the cause of the Persian wars, he deemed the Milesian tyrants Histiaeus and Aristagoras responsible instigating this activity, depicting them as acting with ulterior motives. However, the story of Histiaeus did not appear to have a relationship with the outbreak of the revolution even if one were to accept in good faith that he did send a secret message[90] to Aristagoras (Murray 1988: 472). Furthermore, because of the inconsistencies in Herodotus' narration in relation to these two tyrants, various interpretations have been formulated by scholars concerning their actions and their motives.

In Herodotus work, Histiaeus appeared for the first time in the scene of the Danube bridge, where he rejected the plan to destroy it, arguing that should the Persians be defeated, the tyrants of the Ionian cities would lose their supporters. Darius wanted to reward him for his loyalty[91]. Histiaeus requested and received Myrcinus, a city of political significance both due to its location[92]

89 Generally speaking, Herodotus regarded the Ionian cities usually with reservations and sometimes with implicit |, possibly due to his Dorian heritage. For a critical approach of his position, see Murray 1988: 470-473; Cawkwell 2005: 61-68.

90 The story with the slave bearing the revolt's message tattooed on his head meant that Aristagoras had to shave his head in order to read it (Herod., *Hist.*, V. 35). This has been the topic of lengthy debate as to its veracity (for a brief yet critical examination see Cawkwell 2005: 69-70). However, as correctly noted by Manville (1977: 84), the story's apparent impossibility does not suggest we should conclude that Histiaeus and Aristagoras did not communicate in other more conventional ways.

91 In the previous chapter, the issues arising from this incident are mentioned, pointing out that Darius did not punish Miltiades who had agreed to the destruction of the bridge. Nonetheless, according to Evans (1963: 14), proof that Miltiades had fallen into disfavor was that the Persians did not assist him in dealing with the Scythian raids in the Chersonisos during the years 511-510 BC, which resulted in his abandoning the city.

92 The Persians placed particular emphasis on securing control of the coastal route of the Hellespont-Macedonia region because it guaranteed communications with the Strymon valley, the great northern commercial route

and its proximity to precious mineral deposits . However, when the Great King decided to return to Susa, he ordered Histiaeus to accompany him, as he was indispensable to the royal court[93]. So, Histiaeus set off for the empire's capital, appointing his son-in-law and nephew Aristagoras as commissioner of Miletus. It is likely that the two men remained in contact but whether Histiaeus encouraged Aristagoras to revolt or tried to prevent him from doing so is a matter of interpretation[94]. Regardless, after the outbreak of revolt, he left Susa with Darius' permission and the promise that he would appease the Ionians. He went to Sardis where he faced the hostile and distrustful Artaphernes (perhaps due to his involvement in a conspiracy against the satrap); he escaped and attempted to return to Miletus. However, he was not well-received by the Milesians, so he headed for Chios where he convinced the inhabitants to help him, claiming he was the mastermind behind the revolution. His second attempt to return to Miletus failed, so when Chios stopped offering assistance, he went to Lesbos, where for a short while he became involved in pirate activity in the area near Byzantium. After the fall of Miletus, he captured Chios, but then after a failed attempt to reinstate his power in Myrcinus he turned his attention to the capture of Thasos. Upon receiving word that the Persian fleet was leaving Miletus for Aegean waters, he returned to Chios. Forced to carry out raids inland in Asia Minor due to the lack of supplies and the inhabitants' refusal to assist him, he was arrested by Artaphernes and Harpagus. Despite making it known that he was one of Darius' advisors, Artaphernes executed him and sent his head to the Great King (Herod., *Hist.*, IV-VI; Manville 1977).

Despite differing opinions as to the degree of Histiaeus' involvement in the revolution, most scholars agree that his main motive was thirst for power (Blamire 1959; Evans 1963; Manville 1977; Califf 2002: 21-23)[95]. Herodotus'

towards Europe as well as the point of intersection of the main routes whose starting point was the Thracian goldmines. That is why Darius expelled Paeones from the area. Myrcinus was a neighbouring country to that of the Paeones, so its strategic importance was obvious (Blamire 1959: 143-144).

93 According to Herodotus, Darius' decision is due to the envy of Megabates, who pointed out that control of Myrcinus would make Histiaeus powerful; Megabates was constantly undermining Histiaeus to the king. However, it is rather improbable to assume that Darius was unaware of the region's strategic importance; besides there is no indication that Histiaeus' invitation in Susa meant that he would definitely lose Myrcinus. The decision of Aristagoras to flee there after the revolution's failure indicates that the city was still under the control of Miletus. Moreover, it would be irrational to assume that Darius needed some sort of an excuse to remove his subordinate tyrant from the command of the city. So, it is most likely that he did need him in Susa (Blamire 1959: 145; Evans 1963: 116-117).

94 According to Manville (1977: 84-85), Histiaeus' message to Aristagoras was not just pre-emptive but rather threatening; yet, Aristagoras lied about its content so that he could have the support of his father-in-law's friends for his plans. Cawkwell (2005: 69-70) claimed that Histiaeus may have informed his son-in-law about Persian intentions to resettle the Ionians in Tyros, Sidon and in the Persian Gulf.

95 Cawkwell (2009: 69-71) was more precautious with Histiaeus' negative assessment, claiming that

observation that he fell victim to Persian officials' animosity did not appear to be unfounded (Manville 1977: 87-89; Keanevey 1988: 78-81). Additionally, after his departure from Susa, all his actions appear to be geared towards acquiring negotiating leverage. Thus, his effort to become entrenched in Chios was possibly linked to his endeavor to regain Darius' favor, since he could claim that he had suppressed the rioters and restored the island under the Great King's scepter. Also, the pirate activity targeting ships transporting wheat to Miletus has been interpreted as a means to blackmail the Milesians into accepting him back as their tyrant (Manville 1988: 89-91). Although all of the above are but mere speculations, they do provide a reasonable inter-pretation of Histiaeus activities. Opportunist or not, it appears that he had not lost his imperial favor: when his head arrived in Susa, Darius demanded that it be washed and buried with all the honors befitting a king's friend and benefactor (Herod., *Hist.*, VI. 30.2)

The case of Aristagoras is much more interesting. Herodotus also viewed him as an "opportunist" who tried to avoid Persian punishment after his im-prudent, as it was proven, proposal to attack Naxos. Many later historians partly adopted this perspective, although in a more moderate form, inter-preting Aristagoras' departure from Miletus (496 BC) as abandoning the battle for purely selfish reasons. A diametrically opposed view, argued by de Sanctis (1931) and Cawkwell (2005: 76), was that Aristagoras was the "first hero of Greek freedom", a truly inspired leader of the Ionian revolution. Manville (1977) attempted a third approach, somewhere in the middle of these two opposing views; on the one hand he recognized Aristagoras' role as substantial in the revolution, but on the other argued that his basic mo-tive was the competition between him and Histiaeus to rule of Miletus. In this context, Aristagoras' decision to abolish tyranny in the city and to declare *isonomia* (equality before the law) was a kind of coup d'état against Histiaeus. At the same time, it was a demagogic choice, since, despite his declarations of democracy, Aristagoras operated "with the authoritarianism of a tyrant" (Manville 1988: 86).

Herodotus characterized him as self-interested and motivated by pro-Persian sentiments so as to allow Miltiades' personality to gain prominence. Despite this, he agreed that his role in the Ionian revolution was unimportant, projecting Aristagoras as the leading figure. Cf. Murray's view (1988: 486-487) that Histiaeus – as described by Herodotus – seemed to fit the character of the "Trickster", which was familiar in Greek tradition, Ulysses being its prototype; this means that Herodotus' narration, whether consciously or not, was in line with some common narrative patterns – at least where the assessment of the acts and motives of Histiaeus are concerned. It should be noted at this point that, from ancient times, Herodotus was regarded as "the most Homeric of all authors" (see Longinus, *On the Sublime*, XIII.3), which should to be taken into account when reading *Histories* (Murray 1988: 463, 467).

The bifurcation in historians views on Aristagoras serves as a reminder of the fortune of the great revolutionaries in world history who are either characterized as "heroes" or "traitors", depending on the author's perspective and the circumstances. Undoubtedly, Aristagoras' presence was of crucial importance to the revolution. This does not mean that mistakes or miscalculations made, should be exclusively attributable to him. Also it was not coincidental that after his departure there were no attempt at collective attacks by the revolutionaries. From the data available, there was no indication that Aristagoras was being disingenuous in declaring *isonomia* in Miletus. As for his "authoritarianism" (the exact nature of which is not well-defined), one should take into consideration that both the city and the whole of Ionia were in a state of war, thus, forcefulness and determination were necessary; in the same light, Dionysius of Phocaea could be characterized as authoritarian, taking it upon himself to train the Ionian ship crews shortly before the naval battle of Lade, causing much displeasure and negative reaction (Cawkwell 2005: 64). Aristagoras' actions could be interpreted as a manifestation of his personal pursuits and ambitions (given that these are merely guesses regarding his secret motives), but also as a manifestation of real patriotic and democratic convictions. The second version is preferable, not because of its emotional force, but because it does not further compound the interpretive preconditions beyond what is necessary, constructing scenarios based on consecutive hypothetical propositions.

3.1 A national, democratic revolution

Why did the Ionians revolt? As we saw in the previous chapter, Persian policy with regard to the subjugated nations was not to assimilate them. Its main consequences were visible mainly in the commercial sphere, and this was primarily after Darius' rise to power as he determined the maximum tribute tax and organized the tax collection system. The Ionians could have continued living as they had before Persian rule: worshipping their gods, speaking their language, trading and philosophizing. As long as they remained loyal to the Great King, they had nothing to fear. Nevertheless, in 499 BC they decided to revolt and indeed, at a time when Darius was extremely powerful: he was not facing internal problems and his successful operations had paved way towards European expansion. For some reason, Persian policy did not seem to be effective in Ionia.

The Persian king's standard practice and rhetoric was based on two points: to project himself upon the subjugated nations as the liberator from previous authoritarian situations; and to exploit religious sentiment to his benefit, thus, acquiring the omnipotent priesthood's support in the East and showing respect to the local gods. However, in Ionia the circumstances were not conducive to either of these. Croesus had of course annexed the cities, but he was more negligent in tax collection nor did he demand the participation of local populations in his army. Thus, the rhetoric of "liberator" could only but fail.

The Persians' policy of appointing tyrants from the local aristocracy also proved ineffective. Even if we consider that tyranny could be perceived as transitional stage from aristocratic governing to a more "democratic" one, this would have only been valid in the early years of Persian conquest. But in 5th c. BC, tyranny was regarded as an unacceptable form of government since its historic role had ended. The Ionians, however, did not have the freedom to implement democratic reforms, such as the ones adopted (although to a different extent) by the Greek city-states beyond the sea. The Persians had imposed upon them lifelong tyrants since the meaning of government reform was completely foreign and unfamiliar to them.

But what happened to the gods of Ionia? As was customary, Darius tried to secure Apollo's "recognition" a god he regarded as the most important of the Greek gods, given the PanHellenic influence of Delphi and Delos. Thus, he, in one of his official letters, he threatened to punish the satrap Gadata, for being imprudent in collecting taxes from Apollo's priesthood and in ordering them to cultivate the land belonging to the god. This was yet another ineffective act which, at best, may have positively predisposed the priesthood of Apollo in Ionia or of the Delphic Oracle, but it did not have the slightest influence on the Ionians' or the rest of the Greeks' attitude. Besides, what Darius chose to ignore or failed to understand was that, the polytheism of Greek worship no longer reflected a strict vertical hierarchy, but functioned with the logic of internal balance. Though each city had its own god-protector, he or she had not been given the privilege of absolute power over the other gods. Apollo was not Marduk; and foremost, he did not show any desire to "recognize" Darius (Murray 1988: 475-476).

The failure of Persian policy reveals in part the causes of dissatisfaction which led to the revolution. The empire's expansion had been detrimental to trade due to both warfare operations and the fact that the Persians had direct control of vitally important areas for Greek interests. Moreover, Darius' practice of providing land to aristocrats in exile or former kings who fled to Susa, possibly placed additional financial burden on the Ionian cities, since

The Ionian revolution and its spreading

the king's gifts to the Greeks of his court would come from their areas[96]. Lastly, the obligation of the Ionians to send men for the Persian army would have not only had financial repercussions but also would have made the sense of subjugation more pronounced (Murray 1988: 476-480). However, despite the economic difficulties, there is no apparent indication that the cities were experiencing economic decline (Blamire 1959: 146; Cawkwell 2005: 71-72). Besides, Herodotus himself pointed out that on the eve of the revolution, Miletus had reached the peak of its prosperity (*Hist.*, V. 28: "at about the same time Miletus, at the height of her fortunes, was the glory of Ionia") and it was at this point that the unrest began. While one cannot preclude that economic reasons played a factor in the revolution, they do not appear to one of its primary causes. This is confirmed by the fact that there was no mention of economic

---

96 An example of this is the case of Metiochus, son of Miltiades, who was arrested by the Persians while his father was departing from Chersonisos (493 BC). Darius gave him a house, property and a Persian woman to marry (Herod., *Hist.*, IV.41; Murray 1988: 480).

problems neither in discussions in the Ionian assemblies nor in Aristagoras' speeches to the Spartans or the Athenians.

So, why did the revolution take place? This is exactly what Darius asked his advisor, Histiaeus who briefly responded: [Insert Ancient Greek Text] (It would seem, then, that as soon as I was out of sight, the Ionians did exactly what their hearts had long been set on). Is it possible that the then deposed Milesian tyrant was aware that his words, even if they did not contain a hidden meaning, could be interpreted in such a way as to recognize the link between political emancipation and national liberty? Histiaeus himself governed Miletus in a dual capacity: not only was he a tyrant, but he was also one appointed by the Persians. Therefore, the revolutionary reaction towards him and towards the other tyrants of the Ionian cities emanated from this dual capacity. The overthrowing of tyranny and the establishment of democratic governments was tantamount to shaking off Persian rule; a democratic form of government necessitated the liberation of the Ionians.

Aristagoras' abolishment of tyranny in Miletus and declaration of *isonomia* reveals that the desire for democratic forms of government already existed – whether Aristagoras took advantage of the situation for personal reasons or because he was sympathetic towards it, is a different story. Another fact which reinforces the revolution's political dimension is that, after the defeat in the naval battle of Lade, Darius did not interfere with the democratic governments already in place; apparently, so as to assuage one of the reasons of the Ionian peoples' dissatisfaction. This was obviously a decision of political expediency: the democratic government, in this case, was intended to lay the foundation for safeguarding subjugation (Blamire 1959: 476; Murray 1988: 474-475).

The Ionian revolution was essentially the first whereby the political and national demands were inextricably linked[97]. Its most significant outcome, from an ideological standpoint, was the creation of political polar opposites between despotic Persia and Greek democracy. During the Persian wars, this manifested itself as the conflict between eastern despotism and Greek freedom (Murray 1988: 475). Finally, this ideological framework allowed the Greeks to redefine themselves as a nation as they clashed with the Persians on the battlefield. The road had once again been paved by the Ionians.

---

97 Evans (1963: 118-119) characterized the Ionian revolution as purely national. Also, Cawkwell (2005: 72-73) considered that the only cause of the revolution was the liberation of the cities; however, although he persuasively argued for the dismissal of the economic reasons, he rather casually skips the issue altogether of democratic reform.

3.2 Naxos and Aristagoras

It is paradoxically coincidental that the ultimate catalyst for the national-democratic Ionian revolution was the democratic revolt in Naxos. At the end of the 6th c. BC, the municipality abolished the aristocratic form of government and established a democratic city-state. The exiled aristocrats fled to Miletus to seek help in reclaiming power. As Histiaeus was in Susa, they were welcomed by his commissioner Aristagoras who claimed he did not have the authority to assist them. Instead he addressed the matter to the Lydian satrap Artaphernes. The fact that Aristagoras acted without informing Histiaeus has been interpreted as indicative of his intentions to overturn the tyrant or even as a way of taking control of Naxos himself, by using Artaphernes (Manville 1977: 83). However, in reality there was no reason why he should have sought the opinion of Histiaeus on such a matter. It is likely that Aristagoras assumed his father-in-law wouldn't oppose supporting the aristocrats and he would have been right since this was the standard practice of the tyrannies in Ionia.[98] Moreover, turning to Artaphernes was a prerequisite since any initiative required informing the Persian rule, especially when military force was involved.

The manner in which Aristagoras presented the case to Artaphernes reveals not only his political acuteness, but also his knowledge of Persian geopolitics. After mentioning Naxos' riches and its proximity to Ionia, he emphasized that seizing it would facilitate the expansion of the Persian rule to the Cyclades and Euboea; and promised that Miletus and the Naxian aristocrats would pay for the operation's expense. Artaphernes was convinced and upon gaining the approval of Darius, organized a fleet of 200 triremes from the Greek cities of his satrapy, headed by Megabates along with competent military forces consisting of both Persians and other soldiers.

In 499 BC, the fleet set sail from Miletus - seemingly headed for the Hellespont - and awaited favorable weather conditions in Chios before attempting a surprise landing in Naxos. At this point, Herodotus (*Hist.*, V.33.2-4) noted the strife between Megavates and Aristagoras, which according to Herodotus was the cause of the failure of the Persian attack. Ascertaining that one of the ships had been left unguarded, Megavates ordered his guards to arrest its commander, Scylax, thrust him partly through an oar-hole of the ship and

---

98 Herodotus did not mention anything in relation to this, but it seems unlikely that Histiaeus did not know what was happening since Artaphernes – before attempting any move on Naxos – informed Darius. Apparently, Darius must have sought his advisor's opinion; and the fact that he agreed to the attack on Naxos, implies that Histiaeus must have regarded the operation as beneficial.

Ruins of the ancient Agora in Miletus

bind him there, so that his head was outside the ship and his body inside. Upon hearing this, Aristagoras pleaded with Megabates to stop abusing Scylax. When this plea went unanswered, he took matters into his own hands to free Scylax. He then proceeded to reprimand Megavates in front of the crew, arguing that he should obey his orders as instructed by Artaphernes. Infuriated by this humiliation, Megavates warned the Naxians at night of the impending attack.

Several issues have been raised with respect to Herodotus' account. First of all, it seems improbable that Aristagoras would have provoked Megavates in such a way. One should not forget that Aristagoras was not the tyrant of Miletus, but rather an installed administrator until the return of Histiaeus while Megavates was the cousin of both Darius and Artaphernes (Cawkwell 2005: 67-68)[99]. Even if one were to assume that there was a dispute or rivalry between Aristagoras and Megavates, it seems very unlikely that Megavates would tip off the Naxians, thus sabotaging the operation and depriving Darius of a significant conquest (Cawkwell 2005: 68; Murray 1988: 473)[100].

---

99 Evans (1963: 119-121) accepts the narration of Herodotus regarding the incident (even though not to the point concerning Megavates' attempt to inform the Naxians) claiming that, with this action, Aristagoras became a "hero" in the eyes of the crew, a fact which secured popular support for the revolution.

100 The least convincing view of Keanevey (1988) might as well be noted, supporting that Megavates did

The course of events confirmed that the Naxians were indeed aware of the Persian movements. However, they could have equally well been warned by Aristagoras himself[101], or an Ionian crew member, or the inhabitants of Chios or even by a fisherman. The main point is that when the Persian attack materialized, Naxos was prepared for a long siege, in contrast to the besiegers, who were forced to depart empty-handed four months later, having run out of both money and supplies.

The failure of the attack put Aristagoras in an extremely difficult position. Firstly, he had to answer to Artaphernes as the mastermind of the entire undertaking and perhaps, even to Histiaeus, who would have definitely demanded an explanation (Manville 1977: 84). Moreover, he had promised to cover operation's expenses along with the Naxians. However, it as it turned out, it is more likely that the cost was to be borne entirely by Miletus. The revolution seemed to be the most convenient solution and the opportunity was literally in front of his own eyes, since the fleet of 200 triremes had not yet been disbanded, but was docked in Myus. So, Aristagoras summoned a meeting in Miletus to announce his intentions. The only person to react was the famous historian Hecateus, who pointed out that Darius was very powerful. Despite his concerns, he formulated what proved to be an extremely rational proposition in retrospect: to use the treasure from the temple of Apollo Didymaeus to pay for a fleet, foreseeing that the defense of the Ionian freedom required naval power. Unfortunately, this suggestion was ignored. Subsequently, Iatragoras was dispatched to the Ionian ships to secure crew participation. The Ionians seized the fleet, overturned the tyrants and established democratic governments in their cities. Aristagoras himself had abolished tyranny in Miletus declaring *isonomia* (Murray 1988: 473-474; Cawkwell 2005: 75-76).

The seizure of the fleet and the persecution of the tyrants hinted at the possibility of coordinated action and preparation. It is possible that after the meeting in Miletus, the "Ionian Confederacy" (the *Koinon* of the Ionians)[102] was assembled for the first time at Panionium (the temple of Poseidon Elikonios)

---

inform the Naxians since he disliked Aristagoras and as he intended to accuse him for the failure of the operation.

101 The involvement of Aristagoras cannot be excluded, but this would mean that he would have already organized the specifics of the revolt and that the attack on Naxos was part of his plan; this view was supported among others by Grudy (1901: 84-89). Nevertheless, in this case, it would have made more sense if he had avoided going against Megavates so as not to arouse his suspicions.

102 The *Koinon* of the Ionians had been set up in the mid 7th c. BC by twelve Ionian cities (Miletus, Myus, Priene, Ephesus, Colophon, Levedus, Teos, Clazomenae, Phocaea, Chios, Erythrae, Samos, see Herod., *Hist.*, I. 142). During the Ionian revolution, cities not belonging to the initial group of these twelve Ionian cities also participated.

in Mycale in order to inform the Ionian cities. If this did in fact occur, then Iatragoras departed for Myus from Mycale and not from Miletus – obviously having the approval of the *Koinon* for his subsequent activity (Cawkwell 2005: 75). It is not known how often the *Koinon* assembled nor if it did function as a kind of "central committee" for the revolution. The *Koinon* certainly approved the fleet's mission in order to reinforce the Cypriots, so it is possible that it had also approved, or at least discussed, the plans for the joint Ionian campaigns in the Hellespont and Caria. Despite this fact, the *Koinon* did not appear to have military command of the operations. The military forces of each city had its own Generals, without there being a supreme commander. If joint operations were to take place, the Generals would meet - just like a warfare council - and collectively would decide on the course of action. Only in the naval battle of Lade was there a unified command although it was a voluntary decision dictated by circumstances rather than standard practice (Murray 1988: 482).

In the winter of 499/498 BC, Aristagoras departed for continental Greece in search of allies as the ambassador of the *Koinon*. The first city-state he turned to was Sparta. Its former intervention in favor of the Ionians must have cultivated hopes for an affirmative response and any Spartan military assistance would definitely reinforce the revolt. Upon meeting with king Cleomenes, Aristagoras started by referring to the subjugation of the Iones - with whom they shared the same bloodline ("the sons of the Ionians are slaves and not free men" [N.B. insert ancient Greek text]) - requesting from the Spartans, as leaders of the Greek world, to save them from enslavement ("save your Ionian kinsmen from slavery" [N.B. insert ancient Greek text]). He subsequently described the enemy, by saying that they were not as brave and that they fought with bows and short spears wearing trousers – obviously a sign of self-indulgence[103]. After a lengthy report about the peoples and riches of Asia, he ended with the enticing - in his view– prospect that through the campaign the Spartans would become masters of Asia, stressing the fact that this "trophy" would mean postponing the wars and the rivalry with the Messenians, the Arcadians, and the Argives over small strips of land (Herod., *Hist.*, V.49). However, Cleomenes was not moved by any of these arguments as he was unwilling to become involved in an expedition so far away. We do not know if the underlying reason for his refusal was related to the problems the Spartans were facing with Argos, or the conviction that the revolution was

---

103 The affiliation of the Asians with luxury and self-indulgence must have, since then, become stereotypical (Goldhill 1988: 190-191). Initially, the Greeks attributed this to the Lydians, whom they easily replaced with the Persians. This issue in connection with the tyranny is taken up by Georges 1994: 38-43, 200-201.

almost doomed[104], or the shift of the Ionian cities towards democracy, or even apprehension at how the legendary Asian riches[105] would influence the hardened Dorians. Nevertheless, the Milesian departed having achieved very little.

Aristagoras' next stop was Athens. In his address to the Assembly, he repeated most of the arguments he had made to Cleomenes. However, he made sure to add that Miletus was an Athenian colony, so it would only be just that Athens ensure Miletus' salvation (Herod., *Hist.*, V.97.2: "he said that the Milesians were settlers from Athens, whom it was only right to save seeing that they themselves were a very powerful people" [N.B. insert ancient Greek text]). The attitude in Athens was quite favorable because the claims made by Artaphernes to reinstate Hippias as tyrant had caused strong anti-Persian feelings. Thus, upon his return to rebellious Ionia, Aristagoras had secured Athenian and Eretrian assistance. However, this appeared almost symbolic in nature: 20 and 5 triremes respectively (Murray 1988: 482; Cawkwell 2005: 76-77; de Souza et al. 2004: 17-21; Califf 2002: 21-23; Lloyd 1973: 141-151).

3.3 The war operations

It should be noted that the military activity of the Ionians was primarily reactionary to Persian initiatives. It was possible that Aristagoras may have had a high level plan[106] in mind. Thus, the attack and capture of cities which were the headquarters of the satrapies (Sardis, Dascylium, Colossae, Celaenae) would make it difficult for the satraps to organize a Persian counter-attack (Cawkwell 2005: 77). Seemingly Aristagoras hoped for the spread of the revolution to

---

104 It is possible that this climate of defeatism surrounding the Ionian revolution could have been partly due to the divination, received by the Argives at the Delphic Oracle when they set out to inquire about the fate of their city; the second part of the divination foretold the fall and destruction of Miletus (Herod., *Hist.*, VI.19). The Oracle's role and position during this phase of the Greek-Persian opposition merits further discussion. It must also be noted that Argos was one of the cities to medize. In fact, in one of his campaigns to Greece, Xerxes – in what may be considered as an exceptional diplomatic gesture – called upon the Argives to remain neutral, underlining that the Persians were descendants of the Argives since they came from Perses, son of Perseus and grandson of the king of Argos, Acrisius (Herod., *Hist.*, VII.150.2-3). For an in-depth examination, see Georges (1994: 66-71.

105 Apart from describing the riches of Asia, Herodotus mentioned that, after Cleomenes' refusal to assist Aristagoras, the Milesian attempted to bribe him. The king's young daughter, who was present at the time, told her father that if the foreigner did not leave immediately, he would completely corrupt the king (*Hist.*, V.51).

106 According to Herodotus (*Hist.*, V.49) Aristagoras suggested to Cleomenes that he embark on an expedition up from the Asia Minor coasts into the inland (*anabasis*); yet most scholars regarded this reference as an anachronism, corresponding to the principles of Panhellenism, which was formulated after the end of the Persian wars (Cawkwell 2005: 77).

the rest of the conquered nations, mainly the Carians and the Lydians (Tozzi 1978: 168), and quite possibly also hoped for the assistance of the Thracians, since he had informed the Paeonae, who Darius' had displaced in Asia, that they could return to their homeland (Grundy 1901: 93-94). However, such a plan was rather vague and did not provide for any alternative scenarios.

Equally problematic was the collaboration of the revolutionary military forces. While the Ionians managed to organize their fleet for joint operations, they failed to do so with their land forces. Thus, in the siege of Sardis, the forces which had participated, were mostly from Miletus along with the Athenians and the Eretrians. A possible explanation is that the ideal of *isonomia* greatly mobilized the fleet crew in taking joint action, while the aristocrat cavalrymen and hoplites of the Ionian cities (except for Miletus) were willing to defend their native lands only (Murray 1988: 482).

The attack on Sardis (498 BC) was the first joint land operation of the alliance. With Ephesus serving as their base, the Milesians and their allies along with the Athenians and the Eretrians – under the command of the brother of Aristagoras, Charopinus and a citizen called Hermophantus – took by surprise and seized the Lydian capital, forcing Artaphernes to withdraw; the satrap fled and entrenched himself in the Acropolis where the guard consisting of Lydians and Persians put up strong resistance.

The success was short-lived. During the siege, fire was set on some houses and soon the larger part of the city, together with the temple of Cybele, burned down. Upon learning of Persian reinforcements advancing, the revolutionaries withdrew to the south along Pactolus River where they reached mount Tmolus. Persecuted by the Sardian guard, they crossed Tmolos and deployed in the valley northwest of Ephesus. The time had come for the first battle.

The exact number of the revolutionary forces is not known but it is estimated that Miletus and Ephesus had sent 2,000 hoplites while the rest of the Ionian peoples 1,000 in total. Together with the 800 Athenians and the 200 Eretrians, the troops must have totaled about 6,000 hoplites and 1,000 psiloi. The Persian forces were estimated around 14,000 (6,000 shield-bearers from the Sardian guard, a number of Lydians, bearing similar armor to that of the hoplites but with a shorter spear, and Mysian peltasts) and 1,600 cavalrymen. They formed a front line of 1km, with the Mysians deployed and the cavalry ready to attack at the right time. The Ionian warriors probably deployed in a phalanx of equal length and 6 shields deep. The Ephesians were in the right flank, the Milesians in the center and the rest of the Ionians followed along with the Eretrians and the Athenians to the left, with the latter holding the riverbank of Cayster in order to protect themselves from the enemy's cavalry.

As soon as the battle began, the Persian shield-bearers proceeded up to the effective bow range while the cavalry, forming a four-sided array, moved next to the exposed right flank. At the same time, the Ionian phalanx, under heavy fire, speedily marched against the opponent; however, their attack was rebuffed by the enemy's wall of shields and the Lydian hoplites. Unfortunately, the Ionian hoplites had not been trained in the tactic of *othismos*, which could have allowed them to break up Persian lines or to go beyond the cavalry's cover-up and sur-round the enemy's left flank. The 1,000 Athenians and Er-etrians were not a factor much because the effectiveness of *othismos* depended on hoplite cohesion and holding their tight lines. So, they were literally pinned in their positions, trapped between archers and cavalrymen. The Ionian psiloi could not hold the enemy cavalry for long, since most of their ammunition had been exhausted in the opening skirmishes; hence they scattered in the first cavalry

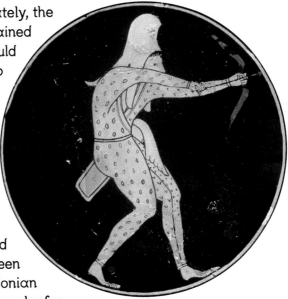

Persian archer (Attic red-figured kylix, 510 BC)

attack, leaving the left flank of the front exposed. The Ephesian lines were broken up and soon the phalanx collapsed. At that moment, the Eretrian leader, Eualcides was killed; he was a famous athlete and his victories in the Olympian Games had been praised by the poet Simonides of Ceos (Herod., *Hist.*, V.102.3). The forces who survived the battle and the subsequent relent-less pursuit of the cavalry, scattered in the cities; shortly after, the Athenians and Eretrians abandoned Ionia (Ray 2009: 33-35; Murray 1988: 483; Theo-doratos 2007: 13-15).

The outcome of the operation painted a clear (yet painful) picture of the land-based operations, where the revolted cities had little hope. Although the Persian army's dogma was defensive, their cavalry's supremacy made them truly invincible. The phalanx was of no use, since the hoplites were inexperi-enced in its warfare tactics. Without the ability to make effective use of their armor and shield's weight, the hoplites easily fell prey to the light-armoured shield-bearers and archers of the Persian army. Moreover, if there was any

hope for the accession of the Lydians to the revolution, the burning of Sardis would have definitely destroyed it.

However, the revolution was not yet lost. In 498 BC, the Ionian fleet had achieved victories in Byzantium and the Hellespont, where it later set sail to the south in order to incite the Carians. Around this time, Onesilus overthrew his brother Gorgus, the king of Salamis in Cyprus, then seized power and declared the revolution. Soon enough, all the island's cities joined him, apart from the Phoenician Amathous, Citium and Lapethus. Persian reaction was immediate because the occupation of Cyprus was of immense strategic importance for all naval operations in the eastern Mediterranean. Thus, a great number of the Persian army was transported by 300 Phoenician ships from Cilicia to Cyprus, in an attempt to recapture the island. In the face of danger, Onesilus addressed the Ionian cities for help and the *Koinon* responded by sending triremes to Salamis.

Possibly, at the start of the summer in 497 BC, the first dual land and naval battle was conducted, initiating a practice which would characterize the confrontations between the Greeks and the Persians in Greece. The Ionian ships were in charge of obstructing Phoenician action, while the Cypriots faced the Persian army on land. The conflict took place near Salamis, on the eastern tip of Mesaoria. The army consisted of forces sent by Salamis, Paphos, Soloi, Enkomi, Curium and Idalium totaling 10,000 hoplites and 2,500 psiloi. The revolutionaries had also 200 strong war-chariots which took the field in squadrons of 50. It is therefore possible that Salamis, Curium and Soloi each sent a squadron (total 150), while the chariots from Paphos, Enkomi and Idalium altogether made up one squadron. Each chariot carried a rider, armed with a sword and small shield, and an archer. The Salamis forces headed by Onesilus were lined up in the right flank adjacent to the Solians and followed by the rest of the hoplites; while on the left side, the warriors from Paphos were lined up in a depth of eight shields. The Psiloi and the chariots were divided up on both flanks (the squadrons from Salamis and Curium on the right and the other two on the left).

The Persian forces, headed by Artybius, were around 8,000 soldiers (6,000 shield-bearers from the satrap's guard in Cilicia, 200 cavalrymen and 1,800 peltasts). Alongside the Persians, were the troops of the Phoenician cities of Cyprus, estimated to be only half of the Greek forces namely 100 chariots and 4,800 heavy-armored warriors (hoplites and peltasts with heavier equipment including a small round shield, helmet, *linothorax* and two javelins) and 1,200 peltasts. The Persians were lined up in the left flank, so that they could face the best Greek forces; the front line was 600m in length with a depth of 10

shields. The peltasts and the cavalry were positioned on the left flank. The forces of the Phoenician cities were drawn up in the right flank, creating a front line of 600m in length with a depth of 8 shields; while on the right side, they were protected by chariots and the light-armored peltasts.

After the first skirmishes, the Persians and the Phoenicians proceeded by throwing arrows and javelins, while the Greeks also moved forward, both sides preparing for the lash. However, the Persian and Phoenician front lines managed to immobilize them. Apparently, the Cypriot hoplites were also not well trained in *othismos* and their phalanx did not have the required cohesion, not allowing them to break the enemy's lines. While it appeared as if the battle would be a repeat of the conflict in Ephesus, the Greek chariots on the right flank successfully faced the Persian cavalry exposing the left Persian flank. at the same time, Onesilus managed to kill the Persian leader Artybius. The revolutionaries could have hoped for victory, but at the critical moment, the troops and chariots from Curium and headed by Stesinor abandoned their lines, joined the Persian army[107] and surrounded Onesilus. Shortly after, Onesilus was killed and the Persian cavalry attacked the Greeks from the right and the rear. The Ionian lines broke up and the hoplites disorderly retreated; the last to fall in the battlefield was Aristocyprus, king of Soloi (Ray 2009: 36-40; Murray 1988: 483-484).

Persian cavalryman, holding an axe (work by Stelios Nigdiopoulos)

Meanwhile, the Ionian fleet which was right off the coast of Salamis had successfully defeated the Phoenicians, but this was not enough to salvage Cyprus. Upon successive attacks and sieges, the Persians succeeded in recapturing all the Greek cities and by 497/496 BC, the revolution in Cyprus had been suppressed.

---

107 Obviously, Onesilus had not managed to curb Gorgus' followers influence in Salamis, who conspired with Stesinor so as to bring the deposed king back in power. Gorgus was present in the battle, on the Persian side (Ray 2009: 39).

Archaeological excavations in Paphos have shed light on important findings which allow for deduction with reference to Persian besieging tactics: the city was protected by a semicircular trench, behind which a strong wall had been erected. Instead of trying to weaken the wall (which was the case such as in the siege of Soloi), the Persian raised a siege towers which they gradually pushed into and across the trench. From the siege towers, they shot arrows upon the besieged, who responded with javelins and stone balls. The detection of four passageways under the wall and the siege towers revealed that the besieged attempted to overturn the towers, where the Persian archers were positioned. In summary, the conclusion drawn for the besiegers is that of an experienced army, which used standard besieging tactics; in contrast, the besieged, although quite possibly led by an experienced leader, did not appear to be accustomed to warr – their defense was based on the use of all means available (Murray 1988: 488).

Immediately after the siege of Sardis, the Persian forces had regrouped in three armies led by the three brothers-in-law of Darius: the first, under the command of Daurises, was assigned the Hellespont; the second was headed by Hymaeës [need to check name] who deployed his forces in the Propontis; and the third, under Otanes and Artaphernes attempted to recapture the cities of Aeolia and Ionia, starting from Cumae and Clazomenae. Soon, Daurises achieved the conquest of the besieged cities of the Hellespont (Dardanus, Abydos, Perkote, Lampsacus, Paesos, Parion) and he was able to restore the empire's communication with the Northern Aegean and the coastal areas. However, he was forced to move with his forces further inland in order to confront the Carians[108], who had revolted in response to the Ionian's invitation.

The first confrontation between Daurises and the Carians occurred in Marsyas, a tributary of the river Maeander. The Carians had rejected Pixodarus' prposal – to line up along the country's northern boundary having Maeander River behind them, so as to facilitate their escape – because they felt it was inappropriate and unworthy of their experience and reputation as warriors. Hence, they opted to fight in an area south of Maeander and lined up eastward from the Marsyas. This position enabled them to face the enemy's cavalry by anchoring against the stream bank. Their forces consisted of 8,000 hoplites and 2,000 peltasts, some of who may have borne heavier armour. The Carian front extended for 1km and 8 shields in depth while the peltasts covered the right flank.

Daurises army included 6,000 shield-bearers, 4,000 Lydian hoplites, 4,000

---

108 The Carians fought much like the Greek hoplites, with whom they had also served as mercenaries in the army of the Pharaoh Psammetichus I.

Mysian peltasts and about 800 cavalrymen. The shield-bearers were posi-tioned in the center and the Lydians were divided up in both flanks (both at the depth of 10 men), while the Mysians and the cavalry along the right flank. As soon as the Persians moved in order to reach shooting range, the Carians moved speedily, so as not to be exposed to the enemy's arrows and aiming to engage in close quarters fighting. Their attack, however, was ineffective; pos-sibly, because their shields were unsuitable for *othismos*. The conflict turned into a kind of duel taking place in the first lines, with neither of the opponents managing to break each other's formation. Finally, the shower of arrows and the pressure of the spearmen found in the Persian first line suppressed the Carians. The battle in Marsyas is regarded as one of the most fierce and bloody battles of the Ionian revolution. The revolutionaries' casualties are estimated from 3,500 to 4,000 men while the Persians had about 2,000 dead (Ray 2009: 41).

In 496 BC, the Carians regrouped in Labraunda and while they disputed about whether they should surrender or abandon the country, they received reinforcements from Miletus and other Ionian cities. The allies forces amounted to 3,000 hoplites and 750 psiloi while the Carians had still 5,000 hoplites and more than 1,000 peltasts. The forces, which were deployed in phalanx forma-tion over 1km in length and with a depth of 8 shields, had the Carians in the right flank, the Milesians in the left and the rest of the Ionians in the middle. They were facing 12,000 Persian infantrymen and 750 cavalrymen. At the center of the Persian phalanx there were, as usual, 6,000 shield-bearers at a depth of 8 men while on the right 3,500 hoplites were positioned. The 3,500 Mysian peltasts withdrew at the start of the fight while the cavalry was either in the rear or in one of the two flanks. The Carians attacked under a shower of arrows, but their phalanx did not manage any better than it had done in Ephesus, Salamis, or the Marsyas River. They were soon immobilized while the barrage of arrows descended upon them. After a while, they witnessed their left flank collapsing, the Persian cavalry and Mysians destroying the psiloi, the Milesian lines were shaken, and soon the entire formation broke up. The battle ended with the pursuit of the defeated by Mysian peltasts and the slaughter of those who did not succeed in escaping (Ray 2009: 42).

By the end of the summer of 496 BC, just before the compulsory suspension of military operations, Daurises decided to finish off the Carians, organizing a series of attacks against the cities in central Caria. Aware that they were unable to face Daurises in battle, the Carians followed Heracleides' advice (who in 480 BC would have been glorified at Artemisium and praised for his naval stratagems) to set up an ambush. Hence, they spread a rumor that

their forces had regrouped in Pedasus, and Daurises, confident of all his recent success, proceeded towards the trap.

Persian footman, holding javelin and bow (work by Stelios Nigdiopoulos)

The Persians began their advance at night, through a hilly terrain, so as to have the advantage of a surprise attack. According to their standard practice, about 700 cavalrymen led the shield-bearers, the auxiliaries and the Lydeans came next, while the Mysians followed last. The total number of the infantrymen was 8,000. The Carians were left with very few forces: 2,500 hoplites and 500 peltasts, and at best, about 2,500 reserve troops. However, because they were aware of the Persian army's standard order in similar cases, they were positioned in the slopes in such a way that the hoplites could confront the shield-bearers and Lydians at the center; the peltasts were divided up on both ends to obstruct the rearguard and the enemy's escape. Covered by darkness, they caught the Persians by surprise and attacked them with a raging vigor that it did not take long to eliminate them. Daurises and four of his Generals lost their lives in that battle. The Carians had, for the first time, prevailed; shortly after, they would give up their weapons after persistent negotiations (Herodotus, *Hist.*, V.118-121; Ray 2009: 40-44; Murray 1988: 484-485; Pelekidis 1971: 285-286).

Nevertheless, neither the victory in Pedasus nor the naval achievements could save the revolution. Since 497 BC, when the Persian counterattack had been launched forcefully, Aristagoras called a meeting in Miletus suggesting that his supporters follow him to Sardenia or Myrcinus. Then, Hecateaus noted that if they were to abandon the city, it would be best to fortify Leros and use it as a base to recapture Miletus. His proposal was not accepted though, since it did not secure the salvation of the Milesians. Thus, Aristagoras' view prevailed, who in the end, departed for Myrcinus with a number of Milesian inhabitants. Herodotus hastily brands his act as cowardly (*Hist.*, V.124.1), depicting him as abandoning his men and his city at a moment most critical in order to save his life. Naturally, there is another possibility: upon witnessing the doom of Miletus, Aristagoras tried to at least saveit's the city's inhabitants (Cawkwell 2005:

77; Grundy 1901: 115-116). It should be noted that he decided not to settle in Sardenia, but in Myrcinus which was once again within the boundaries of the Persian empire. Could it be the case that he was hoping to exploit the wealth of Myrcinus in order to organize an army or was it, that in his mind, the idea of another revolution had been generated, at a more suitable time, within a region of vital importance to Persian interests, yet rather far away from the empire's center? We will never know. Shortly after his arrival in Thrace, he and his men were killed in a raid (Murray 1988: 485-486).

3.4 The naval battle of Lade (spring 494 BC)

After the defeat in Pedasus, further large scale military operations do not take place. Notwhithstanding, the majority of the cities in both the coastal zone and further inland had succumbed. Miletus, where the revolution had started, remained standing. Although Persian land forces had proved extremely effective, the fall of Miletus required the use of the navy. During its siege by the Lydians in the early part of the 6th century BC, the city had endured eleven years due to its strong fortification and most importantly, because it could be supplied via sea. As long as the Milesians and Ionians prevailed at sea, the siege on land would prove unsuccessful. Hence, in 496-495 BC, the Persians focused on organizing their fleet; and in 494 BC, they were finally ready to attack Miletus both by land and by sea (Cawkwell 2005: 77-78).

The Ionians gathered in Panionium and decided that the Milesians should have control over the terrestrial defense of the city while they would confront the Persians at sea. The allied fleet (353 triremes) assembled in Lade and included 100 triremes from Chios, 80 from Miletus, 70 from Lesvos, 60 from Samos, 17 from Teos, 12 from Priene, 8 from Erythrae, 3 from Myus and 3 from Phocaea. The ship leaders of each city decided to appoint one commander, so that basic organizational and coordination issues could be addressed. Dionysius from Phocaea was chosen because, like all Phocaeans, he possessed naval experience in confronting the Phoenician ships.

As soon as he assumed leadership, Dionysius began crew training[109] in the naval tactics used by the Phoenicians called *"diekplous"* (ramming). The

---

[109] Herodotus (*Hist.,* IV.12) mentioned that the Ionian crew members proceeded to mutiny after being dissatisfied by the relentless training. According to Murray (1988: 488) this incident was contrived, so that the treacherous negotiations between the Samians and the Persians could be justified. In fact, the Persians had approached troops or crew of isolated cities with the assistance of deposed tyrants, who were with the Persian army, and attempted to secure their cooperation through offers or with threats. Seemingly, the same transpired with the Samians.

Phoenician standard manoeuver was to sail in column through the opposing line of ships, turn sharply through rigorous rowing, positioning themselves side by side with enemy vessels, catching them by surprise. Immediately, the Phoenician sailors would board and capture the enemy's vessel. The critical success factor of the *diekplous* was the rowing speed, which enabled the rowers to turn the trireme quickly and pull up right next to the enemy vessel (Cawkwell 2005: 63-64, 221-225)[110]. Although Phoenician triremes were heavier than the Greek ones, the Phoenicians had mastered the manoeuver, and Dionysius attempted to instruct the Ionians on its execution. Moreover, with the aim of using sailors as hoplites, he assigned 40 heavy-armed men to each trireme. Cimon would also emulate this strategy in the naval battle of Eurymedon, about 30 years later.

As it turned out, Dionysius' training was to bear fruit. Herodotus (*Hist.*, VI. 15.2) noted that the Chians captured many enemy ships[111], but lost most of their own. A short while later, however, the Samian triremes set sail; only 11 Samian triremes remained as their commanders opted to continue the fight despite orders[112]. The triremes of Lesvos as well as of other cities followed. Only the Chians did not give up the fight and managed to escape with a few ships.

The outcome of the naval battle decided the fate of Miletus and that of the revolution. Having prevailed at sea, the Persians cordoned off the siege surrounding Miletus and captured it in the summer of 494 BC. The city was destroyed and most of its inhabitants were enslaved[113], with Chios enduring a similar fate. The revolution had been suppressed.

After his victory, Darius did not want to impose suppressive measures on the Ionian cities. With a few exceptions, he left the democratic political systems untouched; neither did he disassemble the *Koinon* of the Ionians. Furthermore, he specified that any differences between them - from that moment onwards - would be resolved with the satrap's mediation. After carrying out an immedi-

---

110 The *diekplous* was also implemented in the naval battles of the Persian wars; the only difference being that, instead of capturing enemy ships, the objective was to ram and destroy them. Due to the weight of the Phoenician triremes, the *diekplous* required an open sea so as to facilitate setting course and sudden changes. For this reason, after the naval battle of Artemisium, Themistocles chose to confront the Persian fleet in the straits of Salamis; here, light Athenian triremes could overpower the Phoenician warships (Cawkwell 2005: 64).

111 The Persian fleet included 600 triremes from Phoenice, Cyprus, Cilicia and Egypt (Ioannides 2010).

112 Afterwards, possibly after the Persian wars, the ship commanders were honored and praised by the city; their names were inscribed on a column, which was erected in the Agora of Samos (Murray 1988: 488). Nonetheless, Pelekidis (1971: 287) mentions 11 triremes which belonged to Lesbos, not Samos.

113 The news of the fall of Miletus shocked Athens. When the tragic poet Phrynichus taught his tragedy titled *The fall of Miletus* – today lost– the Athenians fined him 1,000 drachmas for reminding them of a calamity deemed their own ("familiar misfortunes").

Athenian warship (late 6th c. BC)

ate investigation, Artaphernes imposed a new yet fairer taxation. According to Herodotus (*Hist.*, V.105.2), the Great King's rage was turned against the Athenians and he became determined to extract revenge. He even ordered a slave to remind him three times daily not to forget the Athenians ("[N.B. Insert Ancient Greek Text].").After the Ionian revolution, Darius must have been supremely confident that further expansion into Europe would be unobstructed. The heavy-armed Greek infantrymen had proven powerless against his superior cavalry and his agile shield-bearers and archers. However, soon enough, he would come to the realization that the hoplites of the Greek cities would be using much more advanced tactics than those employed by the Ionians (Murray 1988: 488-490; Ioannidou 2010; Ray 2009: 44; de Souza et al. 2004: 21-27; Pelekidis 1971: 288).

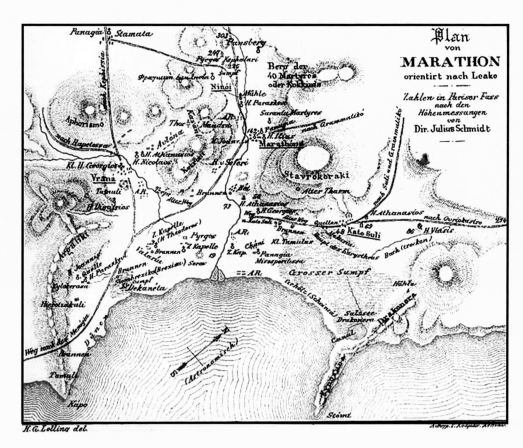

The plain of Marathon according to W.M.Leake's description. Map drawn by J. Schmidt

Chapter 4

The apex of Persian expansionary policy:
The 490 BC campaign and the battle of Marathon

The Ionian revolt had delayed Darius' expansionary plans by almost a decade, but it gave him the opportunity to reinforce and corroborate the imperial ideology. His policy towards his subjects was along the double axis of severity and munificence. Thus, after the exemplary punishment of the Milesians and Chians, the Persian fleet sailed into the Hellespont and Bosphorus area in 493 BC burning and destroying the cities that had sided with the insurgents. The Hellenes of Byzantium and Chalcedon abandoned their cities and settled in Mesembria on the Black Sea while Miltiades left the Peninsula and headed for Athens. Shortly afterwards the refugees (but not Miltiades) were invited to return to their cities. The Great King adopted a conciliatory policy, as an example of his "fatherly" pardon (Hammond 1988: 493).

When peace was restored, Darius was able to continue untrammelled his initial objective started in 513 BC – that of expanding towards Europe and creating his own imperium sine fine. He already had a foothold in Thrace but it had to be strengthened. Moreover, Aristagoras' previous recommendation to subjugate Naxos and other Cycladic islands was strategically correct and the fact that it had not implemented by 499 BC did not mean it should be abandoned all together. Thus, a new campaign led by his son-in-law Mardonius was launched in 492 BC, with a sizeable land and naval force.

Mardonius set off from Cilicia and sailed along the coast deposing the tyrants of the Ionian cities and setting up democratic governments. He then headed to the Hellespont and advanced towards Thrace and Macedonia without meeting any resistance since Thassos, the strongest naval force in the North Aegean had already surrendered. However, the expedition was

marked by two unexpected events. The first was the destruction of a large part of the Persian fleet in a storm off the coast of Mount Athos; according to Herodotus (*Hist.*, VI.44.3) he lost 300 triremes and 20,000 men. The second was the sudden Bryge attack on the Persian camp which inflicted significant losses and resulted in Mardonius being wounded. Subsequently, the troops and the fleet returned to Asia as the campaign was coming to an end (Hammond 1988: 494-496).

If Herodotus' view is accepted (*Hist.*, IV.43.4), it can be reasonably concluded that Mardonius failed since the objective of the campaign was to punish Athens and Eretria. However, this does seem to be the case. Firstly, if the objective was indeed to launch an attack against the two Greek cities that had supported the Ionians, Mardonius would have emulated Datis and Arthaphernes action plan two years later, capturing the Cycladic islands first and then continuing towards Euboea from there. Instead, the Persian fleet sailed along the Ionian and Aeolian coast heading towards the Hellespont. Obviously, Darius would not attempt to use force against southern Greece without first ensuring that the Northern Aegean, Thrace and Macedonia were firmly under his control.

It may be assumed that Mardonius' mission was to establish Persian rule in Thrace and then advance southwards to attack Eretria and Athens; in other words follow the same tactic as Xerxes in 480 BC. In this case, the Persian forces would have had to spend the winter in Macedonia or Thrace since as we mentioned before their return to Asia after the destruction of the fleet coincided with the end of the campaign period. However, there is no indication of such a plan. Furthermore, Darius had not sent envoys demanding "earth and water" as he did in 491 BC, one year before the Datis and Arthaphernes campaign. Finally, had Mardonius failed he would have surely faced the Great King's wrath or at least his discontent and his punishment would have been held up as an example for Darius's court to see. Herodotus did not provide any information to that effect.

Another factor to be considered is that Darius usually acted very methodically with respect to his expansionary plans. It is indicative that during the Ionian revolt he could have mobilized a larger military force in order to carry out parallel operations against the rebels. Instead, the Persians launched successive attacks conquering one city before moving to the next one. It is possible that this tactic was aimed at curbing the moral of the rebels or even to project a certain image of the empire: there was no reason for the Great King to act quickly and spasmodically, since on the one hand he was not afraid and on the other he knew that sooner or later all cities would surrender one after the other. The same tactic was probably implemented against Greece. Darius was

Green line, shows the sea route followed by Mardonius, red line shows the overland campaign in 492 BC, and blue arrows show the course followed by Datis and Artaphernis in 490 BC	The Persian campaigns in 492 and 490 BC

surely aware that the sequential operations solved many practical problems but also served as a show of force[114] for his future subjects. Thus, he initially sent Mardonius to take care of the situation on the empire's European territory and possibly expand its western border to the "Iron Gates" (Demir Kapu) of Axios; from this viewpoint, the campaign was successful, even though the fleet was destroyed (Hammond 1988: 495-496, Lloyd 1973: 152-154, Pelekidis 1971: 293).

The disadvantage of this tactic was that it gave time to the Hellenes to get organized to confront the Persians. But Darius was not worried. His army had not faced defeat up until that point and surely many cities would follow the example of Thassos. Even if some united against him, he was certain it would not take him long to crush them.

---

114 Cawkwell (2005: 49-50) believed that the construction of a floating bridge in the Hellespont in 513 BC was a show of force, which he characterizes an "extreme folie de grandeur gesture".

However, the Greek cities were far from forming a common front against the Persian threat, which had not yet been detected by 513 BC, but had become all to apparent by 492 BC. During the year of the naval battle of Lade, the Spartans where again at war with Argos. It is possible that beyond the traditional antagonism between the two cities there was also the fear that the Argives would offer land to the Persians to establish a base in the Peloponnese. Cleomenes planned to invade Argolida by land, but the omens of sacrifices were discouraging. When a sacrifice to Poseidon confirmed that circumstances were favorable, he loaded his army onto ships provided by the ally cities of Aegina and Sikyona and landed in Nauplia without any resistance. The battle took place in Sipeia and though the Spartan hoplites crushed the Argives, their victory was overshadowed by sacrilege. Cleomenes ordered his troops to slaughter the survivors who had fled into a sacred grove and then set it on fire (Hammond 1988: 497).

In Athens, the situation was also tense. The "more democratic society" of Cleisthenes was not yet established and the tyranophiles had formed an alliance with the oligarchs and disenchanted followers of the reformer legislator. It is possible that the recall of Athenians sent to reinforce the Ionian revolt was attributable to the increased influence of this group that opposed the Ecclesia (the Assembly). Naturally, this was a strange alliance but the Alcmaeonidae had cooperated in the past with the followers of Pisistratus clan. The result of this alliance was the election of Hipparchos, chief of the tyranophiles to the highest office in 496/495 BC. Seemingly, a pro-Persian sentiment prevailed in the city for a period, as demonstrated by the condemnation of Phrynichus for teaching the tragedy the *Capture of Miletus* (Μιλήτου άλωσις).

However, the demos elected Themistocles in 493/2 BC. Realizing that Athens could survive a possible show-down with the Persians, only if it transformed itself into a naval power, he began the construction of fortifications in Piraeus and planned to simultaneously proceed with building a fleet . However, the return of Miltiades from the Peninsula interfered with these plans. The conservatives perceived him as a capable leader: even though he had been a tyrant in Thrace, Miltiades was an enemy of the Pisistratus clan and of the Persians and his advantage was that he had inside knowledge of the condition and tactics of the Persian army. Perhaps that was the main reason he was brought to trial at the beginning of 492 BC indicted for being he tyrant not only to the barbarians but to the Hellenes as well while in Thrace . Even though there were suspicions that Themistocles was behind this , it is most probable that the masterminds of this political prosecution were the tyranophiles and those on the side of the Medes. Miltiades however, was exonerated with the

help of Aristides the just and his political friends and was elected general in 490 BC (Hammond 1988: 497-154, Pelekidis 1971: 292-293).

Therefore, the Greek cities were immersed in their internal and external problems. Of course, there was the Peloponnesian League under the leadership of Sparta, where Boeotia, Phokida, Aegina and all Peloponnesian cities participated except Argos and possibly Achaia. If they joined their forces, these cities could form an army much greater than the armies of any other city or alliance in Greece. Moreover, after the destruction of the Ionian fleet, it had the most powerful Greek naval force, while its cavalry was second in strength only to the Thessalians.

Themistocles

It did not take long to prove that the existence of the Peloponnesian League did not necessarily mean the adoption of a common stance with respect to foreign policy issues. Thus, when the emissaries of Darius arrived in Greece in 491 BC, Aegina sided with the Medes while Sparta (and Athens) killed the ambassadors in a symbolic (despite it being considered sacrilegious) act of rebellion.

The pro Persian stance of Aegina served to further intensify its old rivalry with Athens. As we saw in the previous chapter, Athens sought the help of Sparta in order to kidnap the leaders of oligarchic Aeginians aiming to keep them hostage and thus ensuring the island's neutrality in the event of a Persian attack. Indeed, Cleomenes and Leotychides overcoming various obstacles delivered the oligarchic Aeginians to Athens. Even though Cleomenes probably took this initiative to demonstrate that the two cities were united before the Persian threat, the ambassadors of Aegina who arrived in Sparta shortly afterwards, publicly accused Leotychides for this incident. In order to avoid a rift with the oligarchs of the allied city, the court handed Leotychides over to the Aeginians who then demanded that Athens release the hostages. The Athenians refused arguing that both Spartan kings should be present thus repeating the trick that the Aeginians themselves had used on Cleomenes.

Though a line was temporarily drawn under the affair, a cold war sentiment prevailed between Aegina and Athens. Finally, in 490 BC, before the Persian campaign, the Aeginians kidnapped some prominent Athenians who had gone to Sounion to attend the festivities in honor of Poseidon and

declared that they would keep them hostage. The Athenians did not let the challenge go unanswered. As Athens possessed only 50 triremes, they rented 20 more from Corinth and defeated the Aeginian fleet. The war continued on the island where 1000 soldiers arrived from Argos but suffered significant losses at the hands of the Athenian army. On March of that year, the Aeginian fleet sailed unexpectedly into open sea, and upon finding the Athenian fleet in disarray proceeded to seize 4 triremes along with their crews (800 men). However, the military operations were interrupted due to the Persian campaign in the Aegean.[115]

It is possible that Darius did not know, even in general terms, the internal circumstances of the Hellenic world. Apart from his spies (the eyes and ears of the Great King), exiled Hellenes found refuge in Seleucia or the satrapies (Hippias and later Demaratos) while as we saw his advisor was Histaios of Miletus. There were also other Hellenes in his service, such as his doctor Demokedes, who came to southern Greece and Italy together with Persian officials to collect information on the ports and anchorages (Herodotus, *Hist.*, III.135-137). In any case, the fighting Hellenic cities, many of which were facing internal instability problems, did not appear to pose a significant impediment to his plans. Thus, in the spring of 490 BC he gave the order to launch the third great campaign in Europe, prepared for one more military and political success. However, he would soon be proven wrong (Hammond 1988: 498-502, Hanson 2005: 106-107).

4.1. From Cilicia to Attica

The campaign of 490 BC had many interdependent objectives. Establishing full control in the Aegean region would provide naval supremacy to the empire, something it did not have up to that point. At the same time, it would ensure the capture of Euboea and Attica, thus helping create a foothold for the expansion into the Peloponnese. Moreover, the punishment of Eretria and Athens would act as an example for any Hellenic cities which had not yet surrendered, confirming that the Persians were unbeatable and promoting the power of the Great King. The commanding generals were Datis, who was a Mede and had taken part in the operations against the Ionian revolt and Artaphernes, the nephew of Darius and the son of Artaphernes the satrap of Lydia. Alongside the generals, was the deposed tyrant Hippias who was

---

115 Some historians place the war between Athens and Aegina after the Medes campaign, believing that Herodotus was mistaken as to its timing. For refutation of their view, see Hammond 1988: 501.

meant to assist in capturing Athens. The army included warriors from Iraqi empire populations while most of the ships were Phoenician.

There have been many hypotheses and many pages dedicated to the size of the Persian force. Herodotus' reference (*Hist.*, VI.96) to 600 triremes is generally disputed under the argument that the ancient historian always provided this number for all Persian naval operations.[116] Plato on the other hand (*Menex.*, 240a6-7), mentioned 300 triremes - a number accepted by many ^ historians - and 500,000 land troops, while other ancient sources cited 200,000 or 300,000, perhaps also counting the crews of the triremes (Pelekidis 1971: 294, Greek Parliament 2010: 58). Modern historians reject these numbers as exaggerations but fail to agree as to the size of land forces. Indicatively mentioned: 40,000 infantry troops (Munro 1899: 189-190), 24,000 infantry troops and 400 triremes (Maurice 1932: 18), 48,000 infantry troops and 600 triremes (Gerogiannis 1956: 21-31), 30,000 infantry troops (Lloyd 1973: 179), 25-30,000 infantry troops, 1200 horses, 800 riders and 300-400 triremes (Hammond 1968: 32-33, Hammond 1988: 504, Green 2004: 90 and Hanson 2005: 107-119 agreed only as to the number of infantry troops), 25,000 army including 1000 cavalry and 600 triremes (de Souza et al. 2004: 38), 30,000 infantry troops, undefined number of riders (Cawkwell 2005: 88), 9-10,000 infantry, 500-600 cavalry and 300 triremes (Ray 2009: 60). These variations are largely due to the manner by which each historian attempted to reconstitute the narration of Herodotus regarding the Persian military operations, mainly with respect to the battle of Marathon. It should be noted that most researchers chose to accept the veracity of some of Herodotus' information while considering some other information as false; however if aggregated, the information considered to be false by most researchers would correspond to the entire work of the ancient historian.[117] The issue at hand is that there is no objective criterion for accepting or rejecting any of the information. It seems that each historian has formed an a priori theory on the battle of Marathon

---

116 Notably Cawkwell (2005: 88) stated that Herodotus's reference of 600 triremes participating in the 513 BC campaign, during which there was no need to transport the troops nor were any naval operations planed, was therefore unreliable for both campaigns. With respect to this, it should be noted that Cawkwell's approach does not take into account the logical possibility that Herodotus may indeed overstate the Persian naval force in 513 BC but the number may be accurate with respect to the 490 BC campaign.

117 See the relevant comment of Hammond 1968: 28. See The excellent study of Whatley (1964), on the difficulties arising when attempting to reconstruct ancient battles. Whatley notes inter alia, that often historians approach ancient battles having in mind subsequent forms of war and tactics, and they seem to accept a priori certain information or principles and usually cannot fathom that ancient generals made mistakes in strategy (1964: 128). Another source for problems and misunderstandings is that many historians ignore or overlook basic information such as for example, the number of soldiers a trireme could carry in addition to the crew, at what speed it could sail or how would the cavalry land (Hodge 1975: 157-158).

and picks the elements that corroborate it from Herodotus. Obviously, this procedure has a distorting effect while at the same time producing narrations that may seem plausible and consistent but do not necessary reflect reality. In other words, many historians tell us how things could have happened (οἷα ἂν γένοιτο) and not how they happened (τὰ γενόμενα) - but that is the work of a poet and not of a historian as noted at the time by Aristotle (Poetics, 1451a 36-39); and even if a historian attempts to narrate how things could have happened either out of choice or due to lack of information, he must present his work as a probable state of affairs and not as a final historical narration .[118]

It is important to examine all the facts available currently. Herodotus noted that 300 triremes were destroyed in Mardonios' campaign (*Hist.*, VI.44.3). If we assume that the empire's naval force was indeed 600 triremes, then half of the fleet was ready to do battle. Given that Darius would take into account the likelihood that Athens, Eretria, Megara and Corinth would unite their fleets (200 triremes total) to face the Persian fleet, he would have sent at least 300 triremes to Greece, which were already at his disposal. In fact, Herodotus tells us that he ordered the construction of (horse) transport ships (ἱππαγωγὰ πλοῖα, ἱππαγωγοὺς νέας) (*Hist.*, VI.48.2, 95.1), but it may be excessive to assume that it took two years to build them. The main characteristic of the 490 BC campaign was the combination of marine and land operations of a large scale while naval supremacy was the key prerequisite for their success (Hammond 1988: 503; Lloyd 1973: 162). Thus, it is possible that Darius waited two years in order to acquire such supremacy and cover the fleet losses with new triremes. Therefore, the participation of 600 triremes in the 490 BC campaign should not be rejected in principle.

Each trireme had a crew of 200 and the capacity to transport 40 soldiers. It is possible that one or two rows of oars could have been removed to make room for more soldiers; in this case, each trireme would be able to carry 60 or 120 soldiers, respectively (Hodge 1975: 164-166)[119]. Thus, the size of the

---

118 Specifically with respect to the battle of Marathon, a form of ideological prejudice is detected in many modern historical works. It has been known since the ancient times that this battle was considered a key event in the encounter of the Hellenes with the Persians, which the Athenians used as the axis for the city's ideological constitution. Therefore, because some historians suspect the facts have been magnified for ideological reasons (which cannot be ruled out), they seem to degrade its importance and diminish the feat of the Athenians professing that in reality they faced a small number of Persians. See indicatively, Ray 2009: 61, however it should be noted that the writer is prone to contradictions because he initially professes that 300 triremes were "sufficient for a punitive operation" (p. 60), and a few paragraphs below he refers to the "ambitious nature of this campaign" (p. 61).

119 Based on these assumptions, the 500,000 soldiers Plato refered to would not fit in 300 triremes unless each ship carried more than 1600 persons, which was impossible. Remarkably, the historians who accepted the number of ships provided by Plato rejected his information on the land forces without commenting on this disparity.

Persian army ranged theoretically between a minimum of 12,000 soldiers (300 triremes x 40 soldiers) and a maximum of 72,000 soldiers (600 triremes x 120 soldiers) – not counting the riders. As mentioned above, Herodotus makes reference to transport ships. The number of transport ships is unknown and it is not clear whether the vessels transported soldiers (transport capacity unknown) or various auxiliary troops, supplies, etc. However, it should be noted that after capturing the islands, the Persians took a large number of people with them to reinforce their force.

It is certain that Darius expected resistance at least from Sparta and Athens since the two cities had killed his ambassadors and probably from Megara, Corinth and Eretria as well. According to his information, these cities could collect an army in the range of 30,000: in the battle of Plataea Sparta sent 10,000 hoplites, Megara 3,000 and Corinth 5,000; the Athenians and Plataeans deployed 10,000-11,000, while Eretria had approximately 2,000 hoplites in 490 BC (Hammond 1968: 32, note 89). Therefore, the size of the Persian army was at least in the range of 30,000 (Hammond 1968: 32-33, Lloyd 1973: 179, Hammond 1988: 504, Cawkwell 2005: 88). However it is reasonable to assume that the force deployed by the Great King would be twice the size (including the cavalry),[120] for strategic reasons and as a show of force.

Duel between a Greek hoplite and a Persian warrior (5th cent. BC kylix)

The troops gathered in the Aleian plain in Cilicia, boarded the ships and initially sailed along the southern Asia Minor coast. After a short stop in Rhodes, where one of the Persian generals dedicated weapons to the temple of Athena Lindia (Hammond 1988: 503), the Persian army continued along the Miletian coast. But after reaching Samos, the ships changed course, heading towards Ikaria and after sailing among the islands, they reached Naxos. The inhabitants of Naxos were caught by surprise, perhaps because they expected the Persian fleet to head north again

---

120 Since the cavalry constituted the indisputable advantage of the Persians, it is calculated at 500 to 1000 cavalrymen. Whatley (1964: 135) believes that the number of cavalrymen must have been small taking into consideration the boarding and landing difficulties.

towards the Hellespont and Thrace. Hence, the island was captured without any resistance; the temples and the city were burned and residents who did not have the time to flee to the mountains were displaced. The fleet then subjugated other Cycladic islands and took hostages; in Delos Datis offered sacrifices to Apollo and Artemis without carrying out any military operation (Hammond 1988: 503-504).

The dispersal of the Persian fleet bewildered mainland Hellenic cities since they could not predict the next target of the invaders. In August however, Datis re-assembled the triremes and arrived in Karystos. The citizens of Karystos closed the gates to the city and refused to provide hostages. The Persians then ravaged the surrounding area and besieged the city, forcing the residents to surrender.

Since Karystos was equidistant from Eretria and Athens it was not clear which of the two cities would have to face the next Persian attack. The Eretrians requested help from the Athenians who sent the 4,000 allotees they had installed in Chalkis. Indeed, upon arriving in Eretria and discovering that the city was divided as to whether it should resist the Persians or surrender, the force of 4,000 returned to Chalkis, crossed the channel to Oropos and arrived in Attica by land.

Having destroyed Karystos, the first city that resisted, the Persians continued towards Eretria. To avoid any chance of an attack,[121] they landed in three different locations, one of which, Tamynes was approximately 24 kilometers from the city. However, the Eretrians had decided not to defend their coast and therefore had three options: to fight in an open plain, to stay within their walls or flee to the highlands. After the experience of the Ionian revolt, prompted the Erertrians to follow the most reasonable option which was to remain in the city.

The siege lasted six days and both sides suffered considerable losses. On the seventh day, two Eretrians named Ephorvos and Philargos, opened the gates. The Persians razed the city, burned the temples and deposed the residents. Datis then organized his base in the area, since the Lelantine plain was suitable for the cavalry and he prepared his next move (Hammond 1988: 505-506, de Souza et al. 2004: 38, Green 2004: 90-91, Gerogiannis 1956;

---

121 In order to land the triremes had to come very close to the shore in calm water without currents. The horses and riders disembarked in the water and came to shore swimming. Thus, they were an easy target for enemy troops (Hammond 1988: 505). That is the reason why landings in ancient times were carried out as far as possible from areas of concentration of enemy forces; this is also corroborated by the fact that after the battle of Marathon the Persians did not land in Phaliron because they saw the Athenian army in position there (Whatley 1964: 138).

14-15, Pelekidis 1971: 294).[122] Although he had other alternatives,[123]he decided together with Artaphernes to attack Athens while it remained without help and while the punishment of Eretria was still fresh in people's memories. Thus, after leaving part of his force in Eretria, he loaded the cavalry and approximately 25-30,000 soldiers onto ships, sailed down the Euboea straights and arrived at Marathon in September of 490 BC.[124]

4.2. In Marathon

The Marathon valley is situated on the eastern coast of Attica and is on the southern Euboea gulf. Its northern and western sides are surrounded by the peaks Agriliki and Kotroni of Mount Penteli and Stavrokoraki of Mount Parnitha while

122 Maurice (1932) presented a different version of the facts, believing that the Persian army was divided in two sections: the first under Artaphernes besieged Eretria while at the same time the second under Datis was deployed to Marathon to attack Athens. According to his interpretation, the Athenians did not only send the Chalkis allotees but their entire military force to help Eretria. On the way they learned that the Persians had landed in Marathon and they changed course to face them. This interpretation however does not account for the moves of the Plataeans. Maurice assumed that the Eretrians turned to them for help also or the Athenians asked them to join and then notified them not to head towards Eretria but towards Marathon instead (p.21). The view on the division of the Persian army is rejected by the majority of contemporary historians - some without any reference (e.g. Whatley 1964: 137). As mentioned before, parallel operations was not a tactic that the Persian army used often. In this case, especially, Datis would want to use the destruction of Eretria to show to the Athenians what was in store for them (see relevant comment of Munro 1899: 186).

123 Since Chalkis had been abandoned by the Athenian allotees, Datis could head into Boeotia, hoping to gain the support of Thebes that was an enemy of Athens, and subsequently to continue north in order to unite with the Persian forces in Macedonia; the Persian fleet sailing along the coast could deter any resistance on the way. Another alternative was to head for the Peloponnese and cut communication between Sparta and Athens with the help of Argos (Hammond 1988: 506).

124 Whether the battle took place in August or September of 490 BC has been another point of dispute. The German scholar Philipp August Böckh (1785-1867) was the first to date it on 12 September in his work *Zur Geschichte der Mondcyclen der Hellenen* (1855), associating the denial of Spartans to campaign during the Karneia festivities taking place every September. Recently however, American astronomer Don Olsen, argued that the Spartan calendar was different from the Attic calendar, Karneios, the month of the Karneia festivities in Sparta did not coincide with Metageitnion (August-September) as Pausanias thought but with Hekatombaion (July-August); based on this he calculates that the battle took place on 13-14 August, see *Sky & Telescope* 2004. Pelekidis suggests the same date but for different reasons (1971: 293-294, where all relevant views are presented) and Ray (2009: 60), without justification. However, most historians have agreed that the battle took place in September (see Hammond 1968: 40, point 119, 121). It should be noted that the ancient Greek calendar was lunar and not solar and the full moon was always on the 15 of the month. According to one version in Attica, the new year started after summer solstice (21 June); the first month was Hekatombaion (22 June-21 July), the second was Metageitnion (22 July-19 August) and the third was Boedromion (20 August-18 September). On this month were the celebrations in honor of Artemis Argotera, where the Athenians sacrificed to thank the goddess for helping them win in Marathon (Mommsen 1864: 49, 52, 61, 280-281, Drew 2003: 179-181). However, Pritchett (1991: 119-120) notes that victory anniversary celebrations did not have to coincide with the day of the battle and the exact chronology required further research. On the history of ancient Greek calendars, see Greswell 1862, Meritt 1961, Samuel 1972: 19-28, 57-78.

to the northeast the long tip of the hill Drakonera extends into the sea forming
a narrow cape called Kynosoura. There were four passes through this natural
wall from where the roads to Athens pass. The first passage was to the south
between Agriliki and the small marsh, just to the north of present-day Nea
Makri; from there passed the road to Mesogeia which ended in Athens through
the flat land between Mount Hymettus, Mount Penteli and Pallini. The second
passage to the west, crossed the small valley between Agriliki and Kotroni,
climbed to the peak Aforismos and passed through Dionysos and Maroussi
(ancient Ikaria and Athmonia respectively); this was the shortest road to Athens.
Most probably, the ancient town of Marathon was situated at the entrance to
the small wedge-shaped valley to the northwest, between the peaks Agriliki
and Kotroni, in the location of present-day Vranas. The third passage to the
north was between peaks Kotroni and Stavrokoraki curved around Kotroni
to the north with a road that ended up in Athens through Dekelia. Lastly, the
forth passage did not lead to Athens but to central Diakria. It was formed on
the northern side of the valley between Stavrokoraki and the large marsh, in
the location of present-day Kato Souli (Gerogiannis 1956: 19-21).

The Marathon valley has a long rectangular shape where the long side,
approximately 8km long, runs parallel to the coast and the short side, approximately 2.5km long, stretches to the northwest. During ancient times, this
valley was separated in two sections, of almost equal in size: the north-eastern
section was almost completely covered by the large marsh, impassable at the
time and the south-eastern, which was crossed by the Haradros ravine and the
passages to Athens (Gerogiannis 1956: 19-21, Pelekidis 1971: 296).

Marathon's location had many advantages. Due to its proximity with Eretria,
resupply and deployment of enforcements from the reserve forces stationed
there would not require much time, while the area was ideal for the cavalry
since it offered grazing pastures and water as well as good camp sites. Additionally, it was sufficiently far from Athens and therefore the risk that the
landing would be blocked was rather small, and had many passages towards
the city.[125] It was Hippias who insisted on Marathon, calculating that the old
followers of the Pisistratus clan would hasten to provide their support as they
did during Pisistratus' third attempt take regain power in 546 BC (Hammond
1988: 506-507, Ray 2009: 61, Whatley 1964: 138, Bury 1856: 96).[126]

125 Oropos and Lavrio were two more bays connected to Athens by road. The disadvantage of Lavrio was
that it was far away from Athens and Eretria. Oropos on the other had was across the channel from Eretria
but the road to Athens passed from Parnitha through the Dekelia pass which was difficult to guard and
capture (Panagiotidis 1927: 6-7).

126 Munro (1899: 186-187) considered that the proximity to Eretria and the suitability of Marathon for the
deployment of the cavalry are sufficient yet not necessary reasons for the selection of this area. According

Schinias beach and cape Kynosoura

The Persians disembarked the Eretrian hostages on the island of Aegielia and landed in Marathon. Their exact landing site and campsite are not known. The geomorphology of the area suggests the beach of Schinias as the most probable landing site while the camp must have been between the Haradros ravine and the large marsh, which was protected by Stavrokoraki

to his approach, the Persians in essence lured the Athenians to Marathon - a view supported by Bury earlier (1896: 97) – so that the pro-Persian group would rise to power with a coup and deliver the city to Datis and Hippias. In this way, Munro explains why the two sides delayed their engagement in battle and the famous shield signal. Munro's approach is an almost exemplary conspiracy theory; Whatley's opinion (1964: 128) that was based on a deduction theory and may not be too extreme.

It should be also noted that Maurice (1932: 16-17) cannot explain why Marathon was selected, assuming that the Persian forces did not have any cavalry. In his view, if the goal was to influence the pro-Persian group in Athens, the most suitable areas would be Aegina, Salamina or the western plains of Attica. Still, his assertion on the parallel operations in Attica and the siege of Eretria does not convincingly justify the selection of Marathon over some other area.

from the north and was close to the Makaria spring. The fleet anchored at the north-eastern tip of the bay, between the marshes and point Kynosoura (Gerogiannis 1956: 19, Green 2004: 91, Greek Parliament 2010: 58-59).

The Athenians learned almost immediately that the Persians had arrived in Marathon thanks to their successful surveillance system; it is certain that news of the fate of Eretria had raised alarm bells in the city. Their options were very specific: meet the Persians in Marathon, wait for them on the Pallini road or stay within the walls of the city and endure the Persian siege. Miltiades insisted on the Marathon option and indeed suggested that a number of slaves be freed to fight with the Athenian forces. There were many reasons for this. Given what had happened in Eretria, no one could rule out the possibility that the Athenians who had sided with the Medes would not attempt to deliver the city to the Persians in the same manner. Furthermore, the fortification of Athens was too weak to withstand the besiegement tactics of the Persians, something which Miltiades would be cognizant of. The exit to Marathon had the advantage that it would surprise the Persians and keep them away from the city (and also from their conspiring associates), would protect Attica from their attacks and finally the terrain allowed the deployment of a phalanx (Hammond 1988: 507, Soulis 1972: 9).

The general's suggestion was accepted. The Plataeans were immediately notified while the messenger Pheidippides (or Philippides) was sent to Sparta to ask for help. The Athenian hoplites (9-10.000)[127] took off for Marathon taking the road between Penteli (Agriliki) and Parnitha (Kotroni). According to Herodotus (*Hist.*, VI.108.1), they camped near the holy temple of Heracles; there are many conjectures as to the location and the most prevalent places the camp on the Agriliki heights ridge, close to present-day Vranas. From this position, they could protect the passage to Athens and check the movements of Persians while having access to two supply lines from Attica and as well as having the option of being supplied with water from Marathon and from the spring above Oenoi in the event of an emergency. Due to the landscape, the camp was protected from a possible cavalry attack, but Miltiades further enforced the defence ordering trees to be cut down and wooden barriers to be made[128], in order to fortify the left side (Hammond 1988: 507-508, Gerogiannis 1956: 21-31, Theodoratos 2007: 18-20).

---

127 The calculation is based on the obligation of every tribe to send 1000 hoplites; however, a number of hoplites must have stayed behind to guard the city. However, Ray claimed (2009: 62) that in 490 BC each tribe sent 500 hoplites, based on the inexplicable and obviously arbitrary assumption that the army corresponded to the Boule of 500.

128 This is how Cleomenes faced the Thessalian cavalry, which came to support Hippias in 510 BC (Ray 2009: 62).

Miltiades

Enforcements from Plataea (800-1000 hoplites) arrived that same night or at dawn the next day, under general Arimnestos. Two days after departing from Athens, Pheidippides arrived (Herodotus, *Hist.*, VI.106-7), with the Spartan reply: they would send help but could not be in Marathon before the 18th of the month as they could not advance before the full moon.[129] There was dichotomy in the war council of Athenian generals[130], as half wanted to avoid conflict with the Persians due to their obvious supremacy in numbers and the presence of their cavalry. This time Miltiades did not succeed in convincing those who disagreed on how important it was to do battle, arguing that the morale of citizens would be shaken in the opposite case, which could result in their siding with the Persians. Thus, he addressed the polemarch Callimachos, who would determine the result with his vote, stressing the significance his opinion would have on the freedom of Athens and its future position amongst Greek cities. Among the most notable points of his speech was that the legacy of the decision of Callimachos would be greater than the legacy of Harmodios and Aristogeiton, an element demonstrating the ideological culmination of the antithesis between Hellenes and Persians as a conflict between democracy and despotism (Herodotus, *Hist.*, VI.109). Callimachos was finally convinced and sided with Miltiades, but it was agreed they would fight when the appropriate opportunity presented itself. After this, the four generals who had supported him from the beginning gave over their command for the day[131] (Hammond 1988: 508, Despotopoulos 1971: 297-298).

Aristagoras may have described to Cleomenes the Persian army as an unworthy enemy (at least according to Herodotus), but that was not the case in reality.[132] The Persians had extensive war experience with many campaigns

---

129 It is possible that the real reason was the problems Sparta had with the Argives or with the Messinians (Plato, Laws, 698e, Kargakos 2004: 472).

130 Only the names of five of the ten generals are known (Miltiades, Aristides, Themistocles, Xanthipos and Stesilaos).

131 There was also the opinion that Miltiades had been elected commanding general by the war council or that Callimachos allowed him to determine the plan and time of the attack (Despotopoulos 1971: 298).

132 See Herodotus comment on the battle of Plataea that the Persians were not inferior to the Hellenes in strength and courage, but their main disadvantage was they did not have defensive armor or training for the hoplites (*Hist.*, IX.62.3: λήματι μέν νυν καὶ ῥώμη οὐκ ἥσσονες ἦσαν οἱ Πέρσαι, ἄνοπλοι δὲ ἐόντες καὶ πρὸς

in distant places and had solved key transportation, organization and supply problems. Their generals also had extensive military experience and were effective in combining the cavalry, the psiloi and the infantry (How 1923: 119-120, Maurice 1932: 13-14). Being no stranger to Persian army tactics, Miltiades did not make the mistake to underestimate his opponent. Although he understood that the delay could prove dangerous because those on the side of the Medes could take advantage of the absence of the Athenian army and potentially conspire to hand over the city to the Persians, he could not launch an attack before resolving a series of basic problems, which would in essence tip the balance in his favor. Specifically, the Persian cavalry should be incapacitated in some manner, limit the exposure of his hoplites to enemy archers to the extent possible and minimize the risk of the Athenians and Pla-taeans being surrounded by the larger in size Persian army. Until Miltiades has a plan in place, a fact that is justly considered a sign of high strategic intelligence, he avoided enemy invitations to fight and studied the area and the terrain. He may have also hoped that the Spartans would arrive before the indicated time or calculated that the delay would have a negative effect on the morale and strength of the Persian army.

The reasons for Miltiades' delay were understandable, however, this was not the case with Datis. Thus, many historians have assumed that his delay is due to a different strategic plan. Based on Bury's comment (1896: 96-96) that the Persians wanted to lure the Athenians away from the city, Munro (1899) expressed the theory that they literally wanted to keep them pinned in Marathon until those that sided with the Medes and the tyranophiles of Athens could take over power with a coup and inform them (through shield signals) that everything was in place for an attack against the city. Yet, the famous signal[133] was given while the Persians had already boarded their ships and here headed towards Phaliron. Nonetheless, by that time the city was already informed about the victory of the Athenians and hence the conspiracy plans were de facto invalid (Maurice 1932: 17-18). Furthermore, if such a conspiracy was indeed organized, it is unclear why the Persians brought the main body of their army to Marathon when they could pin the Athenians with fewer forces and at the same time use part of their army and reinforcements from Eretria to attack the city.

ἀνεπιστήμονες ἦσαν καὶ οὐκ ὅμοιοι τοῖσι ἐναντίοισι σοφίην).

133 The shield signal issue has triggered many discussions, see indicatively Reynolds 1929 (who however believed that the signal did not communicate the success of the plan but its failure); Hudson 1937, Hodge & Losada 1970. Herodotus mentioned the shield incident (*Hist.*, VI.6.115, 121), rejecting the allegation that the Alkmeonides where involved in the conspiracy case.

Maurice (1932) suggested a different interpretation and completely dismissed the chronological order of events, as delivered by Herodotus. In his view, Datis waited in Marathon for Artaphernes to complete the siege of Eretria and to join his forces (see 294, Greek Parliament 2010: 59). However, Maurice himself contended that the siege of Eretria did not require a strong army, only 3-4000 (p. 19-20), and therefore the expected reinforcements would not offer a great advantage to Datis. On the other hand, if Datis believed that his army of 16-20,000, which according to Maurice (1932: 20), had taken up positions in Marathon, was not sufficient to face the Athenians, dividing his forces would not be logical in the first place.

Possibly the explanation is extremely simple and self evident. As noted by Whatley (1964: 137-138), such delays occurred in half of the ancient battles, mainly due to the necessary preparations (landing of forces, setting up camp, scouting the terrain, etc.) and the hope that the enemy would make a fatal strategic mistake. In the case of Marathon, an additional reason for the delay was that the Athenians had camped in a fortified position that did not allow the Persians to use their cavalry (Ray 2009: 62). Finally, it should be noted that according to the war ethics of the time, both opponents had to agree to fight.

4.3. Without cavalry (Χωρὶς ἱππεῖς)

Miltiades addressed the issues posed by the Persian archers and numerical supremacy of the Persian force in a truly inspired manner. In order to avoid being outflanked, the Athenian line should be as long as the enemy line. However, this would not be possible if the phalanx had the same number of ranks in depth through its entire length. Thus, Miltiades despite weakening the center, with 4 ranks instead of eight. he gained an additional advantage. It was known that the Persians placed their elite troops at the center of their formation leaving the weaker troops for the wings, and Miltiades targeted exactly that weakness. His goal was to cut off the center of the Persian formation from the wings in order to attack it with his entire force. The thin Athenian center formation would retreat at first but when the two wings broke the enemy line, they would return to surround the Persian center.

The problem with the archers required calculation of two important factors: the distance between the two lines and time. The hoplites had to charge quickly in the fire zone and not be immobilized by enemy missiles. At the same however, the hoplites would have to surprise the Persians by literally falling on

them with sheer force of Othismos (ωθισμός), namely the impact caused by the hoplite phalanx charging and pushing the enemy lines. However, the weight of the armor, which reinforced the effect of Othismos pushing the Persian line back, restricted the speed of the hoplites particularly within the close ranks of the phalanx. As a result, Miltiades decided to push his base forward for the attack and each night extended gradually his camp with new barriers made of tree trunks. Having narrowed the distance between the two armies (on the eve of battle the distance was about 1.5km) he ordered his hoplites to accelerate once they were inside the range of enemy missiles.

However, identifying a strategy to neutralize the threat of the Persian cavalry remained an issue. The Persian riders wore chest armor and could fight from a distance with javelins and arrows or in close quarters with spears or swords. Of course they were trained to fight against armies with light armor and not a solid line of hoplites; the cavalry was useless against the dense formation of the phalanx. Despite this shortcoming against the phalanx, the Persian cavalry could inflict significant damage to the exposed side or rear of the formation and attack broken lines with a massive assault or by launching missiles from a distance (Hammond 1988: 510-511). Thus, Miltiades waited for the moment when the cavalry was away from the Persian army formation for some reason. Finally, just before dawn on the eve of the battle, the Ionians who had deserted the Persian camp sent notice that the cavalry had left the valley.[134] This was exactly the opportunity that the Athenian general was waiting for.

Two interpretations have been provided regarding the absence of the cavalry.[135] According to the first, Datis ordered the cavalry to board the ships planning to lead the fleet to Phaliron and attack Athens (Bury 1896: 96).[136] The second interpretation is based on the fact that the cavalry could not remain in the open valley overnight; it retreated behind the large marsh, close

---

134 The information is delivered by 4th century BC ancient historian Ephoros, the roman historian Cornelius Nepos and the byzantine lexicographer Souidas who notes that the phrase "without cavalry" (χωρὶς ἱππεῖς) has been used ever since proverbially to denote breaking of ranks. See Souidas: "χωρὶς ἱππεῖς. Δάτιδος ἐμβαλόντος εἰς τὴν Ἀττικὴν τοὺς Ἴωνάς φασιν, ἀναχωρήσαντος αὐτοῦ, ἀνελθόντας ἐπὶ τὰ δένδρα σημαίνειν τοῖς Ἀθηναίοις, ὡς εἶεν χωρὶς οἱ ἱππεῖς· καὶ Μιλτιάδην συνιέντα τὴν ἀποχώρησιν αὐτῶν συμβαλεῖν οὕτως καὶ νικῆσαι. ὅθεν καὶ τὴν παροιμίαν λεχθῆναι ἐπὶ τῶν τάξιν διαλυόντων"

135 Maurice (1932: 16-17) argued that there was no cavalry in 490 BC campaign and believed that the horses offloaded in Euboea were the horses of officers. To the contrary, Ray (2009: 63) argued that the cavalry was present in the battle, positioned far back behind the Persian army, but either did not dare get involved or it failed (see Whatley 1964: 136).

136 Discussing this possibility, Whatley (1964: 136) dismissed the involvement of Ionians arguing that in this case the movement of the cavalry would be rather noisy and heard by the Hellenes. Cawkwell also considered most probable that the cavalry was boarded on the ships (2005: 88-89).

The camps of the Greek and the Persian army

to the Makaria spring to find pasture and water and returned at dawn. On the night in question, there must have been some mistake as to the time of return because the waning moon set after dawn (Hammond 1968: 39-41, Hammond 1988: 511).

Irrespective of the reason, Miltiades whose turn it was to be commanding general, acted very fast and ordered his hoplites to form ranks in their predetermined positions. On the right wing were the Aeantis, Akamantis, Hippothontis and Oeneis tribes with their generals and the polemarch Callimachos whose position according to the custom was always on the right. In the center were the Leontis and Antiochis tribes led by Themistocles and Aristides, respectively. Finally, on the left wing were the tribes Pandionis, Aegeis, Cecropis, Erechteis and last were the Plataeans (Despotopoulos 1971: 300-301, Garoufalis 2003: 92). The length of the front line was initially 1375 meters (125m for each tribe and 125m for the Plataeans). Earlier, most historians assumed that the right side of the formation was on the north side of the Agriliki heights while the left side was on the southern tip of the Kotroni heights (Tsambazis 1956: 121, Gerogiannis 1956: 21-31, Hammond 1968: 38-39, Hammond 1988: 508-511).

However, such an arrangement would leave the Athenian rear and the Pallini road unprotected. Thus, more recently and after the findings of archaeological excavations, it is considered that the Athenians had most probably Agriliki to their rear and were arranged at an angle to the beach and not facing it (Greek Parliament 2010: 60-62).

Similarly, the Persians should not have had their rear to the sea since that would leave a small margin for manoeuvres or to retreat. Therefore, it is speculated that they were arranged with their right flank on Stavrokoraki and their left towards the beach, having the Harados ravine to their rear (Greek Parliament 2010: 60-62). At the center as always were the elite Persian and Saka warriors, the Medes on the right wing and the Ethiopians and Assyrians on the left.[137] The warriors in the first one or two ranks were armed with light shields (spara). The front line was approximately 1600m long. Calculating that each warrior required about 1.40m to be able to use the bow, there were approximately 1100 to 1140 warriors on each rank along the entire front. In depth, the Persian formation must have had 30 ranks covering about forty stadia (see Xenophon, *Kyrou paideia*, VI.3.19: ἐκεῖνοι τύνοιν, ἔφη, πάντες τεταγμένοι ἐπὶ τριάκοντα τὸ βάθος καὶ πεζοὶ καὶ ἱππεῖς πλὴν τῶν Αἰγυπτίων ἐπέχουσιν ἀμφὶ τὰ τετταράκοντα στάδια; consequently arranged opposite the Athenians and Plataeans was a Persian army of 30-34,000.

After the preparatory moves, Miltiades re-arranged his forces so the two fronts were of equal length. Thus, he removed 4 ranks from the center to elongate his line. Now the two wings were 8 ranks deep and the center was in weak formation, 4 ranks deep. After the customary sacrifices gave good omens, the bronze men (χάλκεοι ἄνδρες) of the phalanx got ready. It was time for the battle to begin.

4.4. Forward, sons of Greece (ὦ παῖδες Ἑλλήνων, ἴτε): the battle

The battle, distinguished in three phases, took place between the Haradros ravine bed and the small marsh, around the tomb that survives today, in a semi-crescent area 10km long and maximum width of 3km in the middle of the battleground. As we saw, Miltiades' plan was based on the hoplites running through the fire zone and attacking the enemy with force along the entire line. The Persian battle plan aimed to annihilate the hoplite attack with a hail of arrows and javelins and break their formation. Then, the Persian center would

---

137 According to Ray (2009: 63), the Medes were distributed in the two wings, while the Ionian hoplites were placed at the right end. The archers covered both wings but not the Ionian ranks.

break the ranks of the Greek formation and would subsequently turn against the two flanks, if these had withstood the pressure of the corresponding Persian flanks. However, the outcome of events was destined to be very different.

First phase: March / charge

When the order to attack was given, the hoplites marched across the greatest part of the distance separating them from the Persian forces (approximately 1.5km) and broke into a run in the last 200 meters with their 2.5 long lances extended (Herodotus, *Hist.*, VI.112.1: δρόμῳ ἵεντο ἐς τοὺς βαρβάρους[138]. Seeing them charge against them without cavalry and without archers, the Persians thought they had gone mad - says Herodotus (*Hist.*, VI.112.2-3), but even if that was not the case it is certain they were surprised and unprepared for such an attack.[139] The impact was fierce along the entire length of the front and especially at the two wings, 500m on the right and 600m on the left. As the formation at the wings of the Athenian phalanx was dense and had more depth, the entire mass of hoplites fell on their enemies like a metal wall with a force that was doubled due to the speed of the running attack. The application of Othismos, which both the Athenians and Plataeans were trained on executing, was very effective and its impact amplified by their defensive and offensive armor (shield, cuirass, helmet, greaves, spear, sword) and the coordinated actions of 8 ranks of hoplites. The Persian troops were not able to resist for long. Their first ranks were forced to backtrack pushing the ranks behind them and overthrowing them, the lines broke across all 30 ranks with the Persian troops fleeing in panic.

In the center however, the hoplites were not able to achieve the same result. Even though the Persian shields where much lighter that the Greek and the Persian center was not as dense as the Athenian was, the pressure of a 4-rank deep formation was not able to break the resistance of a 30-rank deep formation. Heavy defensive fighting ensued after the attack. In a truly titan effort, the hoplites of the Antiochis and Leontis tribes led by Aristides and Themistocles managed to keep the Persian center busy long enough until

---

138 This is considered a significant development in war tactics and probably the earliest example of a charging attack. It is characteristic that later a hoplite who wanted to say he fought in Marathon he would simply say "I ran" (Ray 2009: 63). After the battle of Marathon the charging attack was adopted as standard procedure in dealing with archers (Lloyd 1973: 193).

139 According to Ray (2009: 63-64), the Persians also advanced a few meters to approach the hoplites and have them within range. However, they could only throw but a few arrows because the hoplites crossed the fire zone at great speed not caring to hold their formation; obviously Ray overlooked the fact that if their formation was broken the hoplites would be vulnerable to enemy missiles on the one hand and on the other they would not be able to apply the push forward tactic.

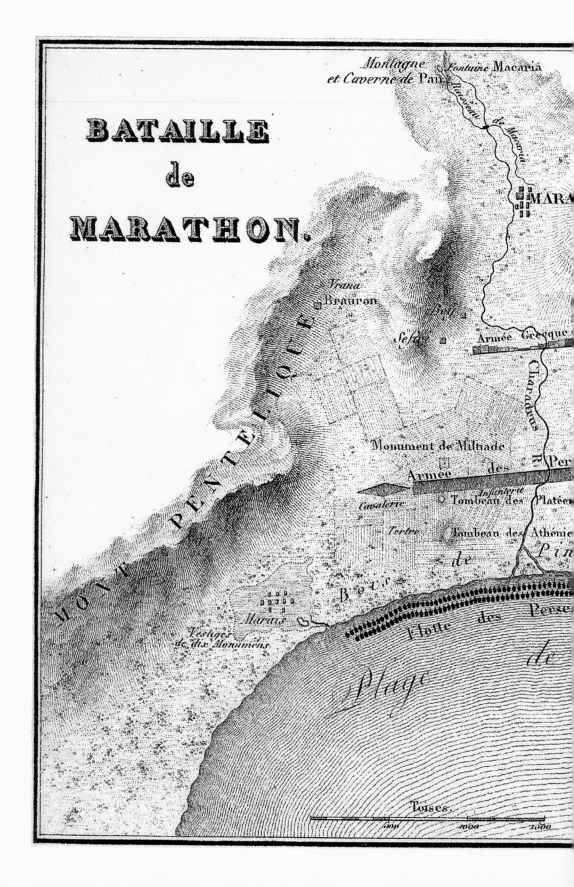

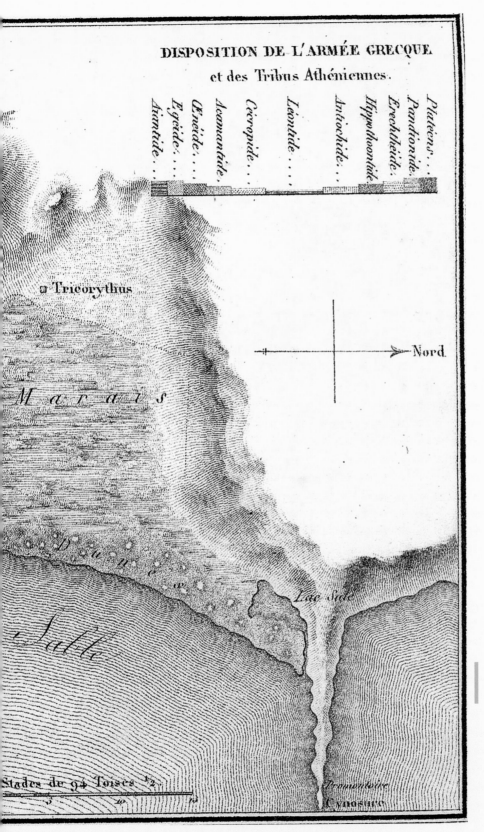

DISPOSITION DE L'ARMÉE GRECQUE
et des Tribus Athéniennes.

Platéens....
Pandionide..
Erechthéide..
Hippothoontide.
Antiochide....
Léontide.....
Cécropide....
Acamantide..
Œnéide.......
Égéide........
Aiantide......

◦ Tricorythus

─┼──────────►Nord.

M a r a i s

D u n e c

◦ cp

Lac Sac

Sat t e

Stades de 94 Toises ½

5   10   15

Promontoire
Cynosure

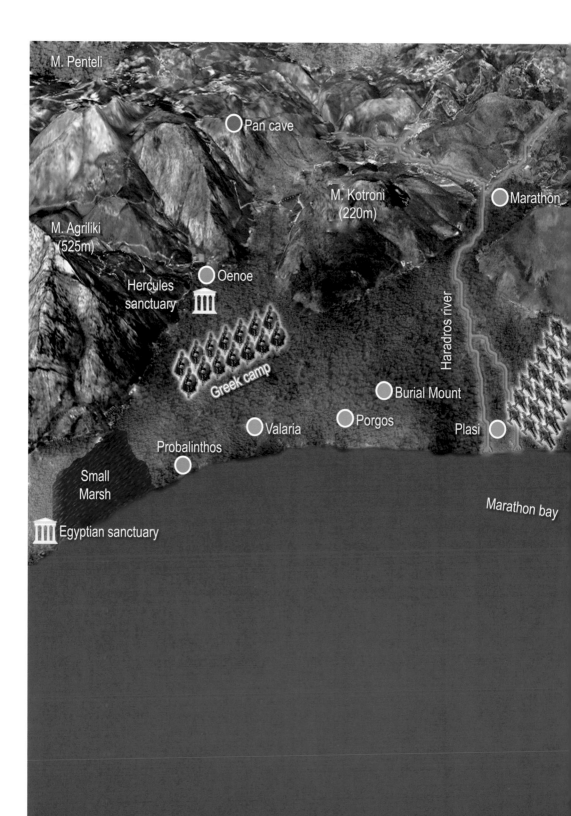

M. Stavrokoraki
(340m)

Persian headquarters

Trikorythus

Persian cavalry

Macaria spring

Euboean Gulf

N

Great
Marsh

M. Drakonera
(210m)

Persian fleet

c. Cynosoura (90m)

The camps
of Greek and
Persian army

M. Penteli

Pan cave

M. Kotroni
(220m)

Oenoe

M. Agriliki
(525m)

Hercules
sanctuary

Plataeans
Pandionis
Erectheis
Hippothontis
Antiochis
Leontis
Cecropis
Acamantis
Oeneis
Aegeis
Aeantis

Sacae   Immortals   Scythians

Valaria

Probalinthos

Small
Marsh

Egyptian sanctuary

Marathon

M. Stavrokoraki
(340m)

Persian
headquarters

Macaria spring

Plasi

Persian cavalry

Great
Marsh

N

hon bay

Persian fleet

*The boarding
of the Persian
cavalry
started before
the battle*

Marathon

M. Stavrokoraki
(340m)

N

Macaria spring

Great
Marsh

Persian cavalry

athon bay

Persian fleet

*First phase
of the battle:
The Athenian
centre falls
back towards
Agiliki. The
Persian wings
retreat*

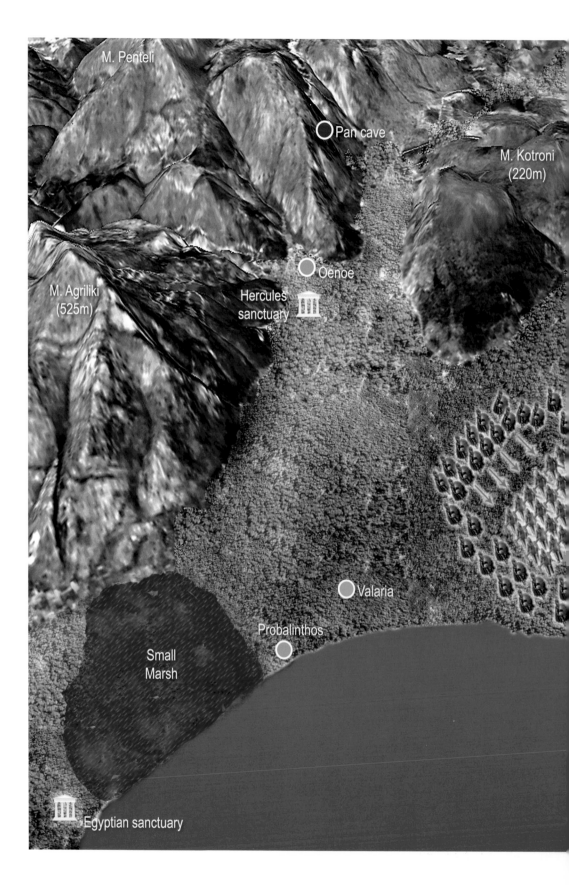

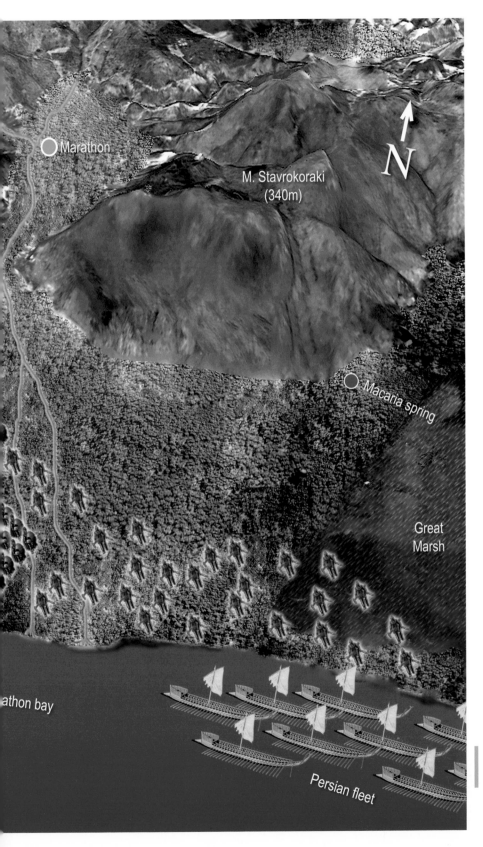

Marathon

M. Stavrokoraki
(340m)

N

Macaria spring

Great
Marsh

athon bay

Persian fleet

*Second phase
of the battle:
bilateral
outflanking
manoeuvre*

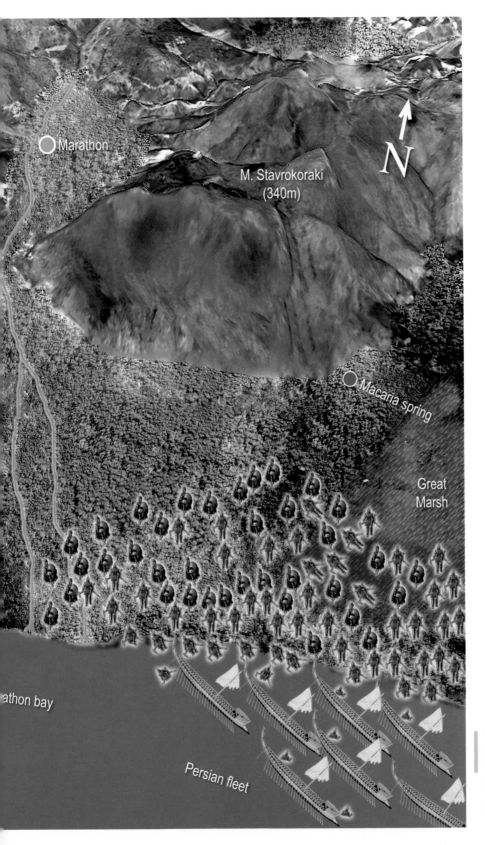

Marathon

M. Stavrokoraki
(340m)

N

Macaria spring

Great
Marsh

athon bay

Persian fleet

*Third phase
of the battle:
The pursuit of
the Persians.
The Persian
fleet departs*

Battle of Marathon scene on a black-figured lecythus, 480-480 BC (National Arcaeological Museum)

the wings of the phalanx prevailed against the enemy forces. The Athenian center slightly retreated pursued by elite Persian troops, who without realizing it were distancing themselves even more from the wings of their formation thus providing the opportunity to finish breaking up their formation to the Athenians and Plataeans .

Second phase: bilateral outflanking manoeuvre - "pliers" manoeuvre
Up to that moment, the battle was progressing according to Miltiades' plan. The two Persian wings were disbanded and the Persian center had forced the hoplites to retreat but had become isolated. Following Miltiades' orders the hoplites of the right and left wing did not pursue the deserting Persians but remained in formation just 500-600m behind enemy lines. They quickly united in the empty space left by the Persian attack and formed a strong phalanx approximately 1125m long and 8 rank deep. This phalanx was reversed compared to the initial, meaning that Callimachos was now on the left and the Plataeans on the right but this did not affect their effectiveness as the hoplites in the last ranks were just as experienced fighters as those in the front ranks.

Darius (seated in the centre) hears the news about the Persian defeat at Marathon. Depiction on a krater (Archaeological Museum of Naples)

The second phase of the battle started with an attack of the phalanx against the Persian center that was still pursuing the troops of Themistocles and Aristides. The Persians and the Sakas were surprised and forced to turn about to face the Athenians. There was probably some disorder as they regrouped to make their front equally long as the phalanx. Nevertheless, these were elite troops and maintained their numerical advantage and high morale since up to that moment they saw that victory was on their side. Thus, ferocious fighting ensued which was quickly joined by the hoplites of the Athenian center that were no longer pursued by the Persians. Probably the right wing of the Athenian phalanx, where the Plataeans were now located, had not able to prevail over the enemy, but it nevertheless maintained the cohesion of its ranks. The Athenian hoplites in the center and left wing fought intensely with coordinated force, breaking up the enemy formation and reversing their loose formation. Unable to resist the pressure on their right wing and center, the Persians retreated to the left, sweeping the left wing as well in their disorderly retreat, which was holding its position up to that moment. The formation was broken and the warriors ran towards the sea in an attempt to reach their ships as fast as possible. Miltiades' plan was a great success but the battle was not yet over.

Third phase: the pursuit

This time the hoplites were free to pursue the fleeing enemy; there were no enemy forces in the battlefield. In the confusion of disorderly retreat, many Persians lost their way in the large marsh, dragging each other down and eventually sinking and drowning (Pausanias, i.15.3). The majority of the Persian troops, however ran to board the ships across the strip of land between the large marsh and the sea. The most fierce battle scenes took place at the location called the Marathon grove (Μαραθώνειον άλσος), as Persians and Athenians fought man-to-man, the former in an attempt to reach their ships and the latter in an attempt to stop them and capture their triremes. It was then that the archon polemarch Callimachos and general Stesilaos were killed as well as Kynegeiros, the brother of poet Aeschylus, who had also taken part in the battle; his death is the only death described by Herodotus (Hist., VI.114): Kynegeiros was trying to take hold of the ship holding it by the stern when a Persian cut off his hand with an ax.

However, the Persians managed to depart and the Athenians succeeded in capturing only 7 ships. The battle had ended[140], with the Persians suffering significant losses (6400 deaths, according to Herodotus, Hist., VI.117.1) while the Athenians and Plateans lost 192troops. At this point, the herald could take off to announce the victory to the city[141] (Panagiotidis 1927: 10-11, Soulis 1970: 10-13, Despotopoulos 1971: 301-306, Lloyd 1973: 192-202, Hammond 1988: 512-513, Califf 2002: 47-58, de Souza 2004: 40-47, Hanson 2005: 107-119, Theodoratos 2007: 27-30, Ray 2009: 64, Greek Parliament 2010: 62-64).

Nevertheless, the danger had not passed. After a short stop on the Aegileia Island to load their Eretrian prisoners, the Persians headed towards cape Sounion, obviously planning to land in Phaliron and capture Athens before the Athenian army retuned. Miltiades was notified about their moves (perhaps this was the meaning of the shield signal) and leaving Aristides and the Antiochis tribe on the battlefield to guard the spoils of the battle, he ordered his troops to prepare for their return to Athens. After an 8-9-hour march, they camped in Heraklion of Kynosargos (at the beginning of Vouliagmeni Avenue, from where the ancient road to Sounion passed). When after several hours[142], the

---

140 Herodotus (Hist., VI.113) mentioned that this lasted a long time (χρόνος ἐγένετο πολλός), but given that the hoplites could not fight for long due to the weight of their armor, it is calculated at approximately three hours (Califf 2002: 54).

141 According to Plutarch (Moralia, V.625) the herald was Thersippos from Erchia and not Euclis as other claimed. Lucian however, (In Υπέρ του εν τη προσαγορεύσει πταίσματος) noted that it was Pheidippides who announced the victory with the phrase "I salute. We are victorious" (Χαίρετε. Νικῶμεν), before he collapsed and died (Lambros 1896).

142 How & Wells (1928: vi.112) supported that the arrival of the fleet and the return of the Athenians

Battle scenes between the Greeks and the Persians, while they were trying to board. Attic sarcophagus (2nd cent. BC, Arcaheological Museum of Brescia).

Persian fleet arrived in Phaliron and saw the Athenian army in formation, It did not even approach the shore; it stayed offshore for a while and then turned around and returned to Asia.

The Spartans kept their promise and after the full moon sent 2000 hoplites to Athens, who according to Herodotus (*Hist.*, VI.120), covered the distance in 3 days. They asked to go to Marathon to see the Medes[143] and after examining the battlefield they congratulated the Athenians and returned to Sparta.

4.5. Victory offerings

The Athenians did not transport their dead to Kerameikos but buried them with special honors in the Tomb (Polyandrion) or Marathon Burial Mount, an-

must be placed chronologically on the day after the battle, under the argument that after the conflict the hoplites would not be able to cover the distance between Marathon and Athens on the same day. Hammond (1968: 36-37) proved empirically that the hoplites could cover the distance in 8-9 hours. However, in an extremely interesting study, Hodge (1975) calculated that it took 35-40 hours for the Persian fleet to sail to Phaliron. Therefore, the Athenian army had ample time to return from Marathon and to make camp awaiting the arrival of the Persians.

143 They were probably Persian prisoners as it seems impossible that the dead of the battle would be unburied still (Pelekidis 1971: 306-307).

notating their names on marble steles according
to tribe while they also set a marble trophy on the
battlefield. A shrine was erected at Kerameikos,
with an epigram narrating the glorious sacrifice
of the dead (Raubitschek 1940: 58). The Plataea-
ans and slaves were buried in separate graves
while the Athenians buried the Persians in a
ditch, which has been found near the Panagia
Pesosporitissa chapel. Miltiades, the architect
of the victory was also buried in Marathon at
a later time.

Bronze Corinthian helmet. On the cheek-pieces is the incised inscription: ΜΙΛΤΙΑΔΕΣ ΑΝΕΘΕΚΕΝ ΤΟΙ ΔΙ (Miltiades dedicated it to Zeus), 490 BC. (Olympia Archaeological Museum)

According to the custom, 1/10 of the battle
spoils were dedicated to the gods. The Athenians
built their treasury in Delphi or according to another version dedicated the spoils to the existing treasury.
Phidias' bronze statue of Athena Promachos was erected
on the acropolis to commemorate the victory; similarly,
the Plataeans built the temple of Athena Areia in
their city where they installed the gilded statue of
the goddess, also by Phidias. Miltiades dedicated his
Corinthian helmet to the temple of Zeus in Olympia
(with the epigraph *ΜΙΛΤΙΑΔΕΣ ΑΝΕ[Θ]ΕΚΕΝ [Τ]ΟΙ
ΔΙ (Miltiades deposited this here)* while another warrior dedicated a Persian helmet (with the epigraph),
*ΔΙΙ ΑΘΕΝΑΙΟΝ ΜΕΔΟΝ ΛΑΒΟΝΤΕΣ (the Athenians
got this from the Medes)*. The friends of Callimachos

A Persian helmet dedicated to Zeus by the Athenians (Olympia Archaeological Museum)

dedicated the statue of Nike to the Acropolis thus keeping the promise of the
dead polemarch (Raubitschek 1940: 53-55). Pausanias (i.33.2-3), however men-

tioned a rather strange offering. It was a piece of marble
from Paros, which Datis had
brought from Asia planning
to erect it as a trophy after
his victory against the Greek
troops. From this slab of mar-

After the Battle of Marathon, the head of goddess Athena on the Athenian coins was adorned with olive wreaths, in memory of the battle. The Athenians added the waning moon beside the owl to honour goddess Artemis

Gold model chariot from the Oxus treasure (Achaemenid Period, 5th or 4th c. BC, British Museum)

ble Phidias sculpted the statue of Nemesis, which was erected in the temple of the goddess in Ramnous.

Signs of victory are depicted almost everywhere. The helmet of Athena depicted on the coins of Athens, is adorned with an olive wreath, while the tetradrachm with the waning moon that was coined after the battle symbolizes the honor due to the wild and dark Artemis. Furthermore, the demos of Athens sacrificed 500 young goats to Artemis Agrotera (the huntress), since the large number of dead Persians did not allow implementation of the vow to the goddess per se.

The earliest rendition of scenes from the battle of Marathon was painted by Polygnotos, Micon and Panaenus in the Poikile Stoa of the Athenian Agora in 460/462 BC, where apart from Callimachos, Miltiades and Kynegeiros it also depicted gods and mythical heroes who helped the Athenians. The glorious victory was also eulogized by Simonides of Ceos in the famous epigram Ἑλλήνων προμαχοῦντες Ἀθηναῖοι Μαραθῶνι χρυσοφόρων Μήδων ἐστόρεσαν δύναμιν (At Marathon the Athenians fought for the Hellenes and brought down the gilded Medes' power). In 472 BC, Aeschylus the Marathon fighter and brother of Kynegeiros received an award for his tragedy The Persians. Even

though this work refers mainly to the battle of Salamis, it condenses the historical experience (military and ideological) of the conflict between the Hellenes and the Persians. And when the tragic poet died in Gela, he requested that the following inscription be engraved on his gravestone:

> Αἰσχύλον Εὐφορίωνος Ἀθηναῖον τόδε κεῦθει
> μνῆμα καταφθίμενον πυροφόροιο Γέλας·
> ἀλκὴν δ' εὐδόκιμον Μαραθώνιον ἄλσος ἂν εἴποι
> καὶ βαθυχαιτήεις Μῆδος ἐπιστάμενος.
> (Beneath this stone lies Aeschylus, son of Euphorion,
> the Athenian,
> who perished in the wheat-bearing land of Gela;
> of his noble prowess the grove of Marathon can
> speak,
> or the long-haired Persian who knows it well.)

Aeschylus

Aristophanes

The selection of this mnemonic symbol of reference reveals that his capacity as a poet was superseded by that of citizen/warrior the extent to which the victory in Marathon had surpassed any poetic or other glory. The ideological and emotional power of the event was not threatened even by the "painless and harmless" (ἀνώδυνον καὶ οὐ φθαρτικὸν) world of comedy: in 422 BC, in the *Wasps* of Aristophanes, the chorus proudly narrates how it runs under the Persian arrows, holding the spear and the shield to fight against the Persians (verse 1081 etc.). Gradually the word "Μαραθωνομάχης" (Marathon fighter) acquired a collective meaning, denoting veteran fighters (Pelekidis1971: 307-308, Hammond 1988: 513-515, Greek Parliament 2010: 76-78).

4.6. Findings - Conclusions

It seems that there is as much dissent among historians regarding the events of the battle of Marathon as well as its significance. The raving and sometimes exaggerated opinions characterized the works of older times, mainly 19th century and up to the first decades of the 20th century. Since then, a trend is noted for more realistic approaches and assessments and even occasional

negative opinions. Although, it appears that no historian has doubted, at least up until now, that indeed the Athenians and the Plataeans defeated the army that had been unbeaten up to that point, many argue there was no special consequence to the westward Persian expansion (e.g. Maurice 1932: 24). Darius started preparing his next campaign almost immediately but death came first (486 BC). His son Xerxes assumed the responsibility of implementing his plans and invaded Greece in 480 BC immediately after he suppressed the revolts in Egypt.

The significance of an event and indeed of a battle may be studied at many levels and from many angles to find whether it is of greater or lesser importance, accordingly. Thus, if the battle of Marathon is examined vis-à-vis as to its consequences on Persian policy we shall indeed discover that it had no effect on the expansionary practice of the empire: it temporarily suspended it but it did not end it. For the Persians it was a military failure of lesser importance since most of the campaign goals had been achieved: the Aegean islands had been conquered, Naxos and Eretria had been punished. The losses sustained were not particularly significant in relation to the military potential of the empire, the fleet was almost intact and defeat could be easily attributed to the absence of cavalry. Therefore, Marathon was nothing more than an unfortunate moment. Naturally, from the viewpoint of the Greeks (and perhaps from an overall perspective) things were different if for no other reason other than the Persian army's fame as being undefeated had been invalidated and indeed in an unequal battle. Whether overrated by the Athenians or not, Marathon still constituted a victory.

Outfold representation of a Gigadomachy, of an attic black-figure lekythos. From the Tumulus of Athenians, 490 BC. Marathon Archaeological Museum.

4.6.1. The differences between the opponents

Two opposing armies clashed in Marathon with significant differences as to the composition of the forces their morale, tactics and political/social organization. Quantitatively, both in terms of the size of their army and the abundance of resources to support it, the Persians had undeniable superiority, and in fact to such an extent that the Athenian defeat was considered certain.

However, morale plays a significant role in every conflict, meaning all manifestations of human resources aiming to fully utilize all resources during war in order to defeat the enemy. Morale is associated with the following aspects: the quality of the troops and their equipment (training, performance improvement), administration, logistics and supply (good operation of forces), strategy and tactics (warfare principles and battle methodology, optimal utilization of forces at a specific place and time) and morale (strength and dynamism of the troops). The Athenians were superior with respect to the above. The Persians were good warriors as well and had an organized army with a command that had proven effective up to that point, but lacked in strategy, tactics and morale. The Athenians had uniform troops and equipment, with similar training and common ideological aspirations and their armor was appropriate for their fighting tactics. Their command was extremely effective since the strategy and tactics implemented ensured victory. Lastly, their morale was the decisive factor in their success; if the Persians were fighting following the orders of the Great King, the Greeks were fighting to maintain their national and political freedom observing the laws of their city (Gerogiannis 1956: 30-32).

Swords, slingshots and spear heads found in Marathon battlefield

The particular differences between the two opponents may be summarized as follows:

Number of óghters: the Persian forces outnumbered the Greeks.

Equipment: the Persians used missile weapons (mainly bows) which were

unsuitable for close quarters combat, for which they were not trained. The Hellenes counted on their heavy defensive armor (shield, helmet, cuirass, greaves) and their melee weapons (spear, sword) which could be utilized optimally in the warfare tactics of a hoplite phalanx.

Tactical dogma: neither the armor nor the composition of the Persian army (the majority were conquered nations) allowed for close quarters combat. The Persian dogma was defensive and proven correct and extremely effective in their wars in Asia. To the contrary, the dogma of the Greek army was attacking and based on absolute cohesion and cooperation of hoplites, which required dedication to the ideals of the city and the commitment to defend them (Soulis 1972: 10-13).

4.6.2. Application of war principles in the battle of Marathon

Marathon has been justly labeled "the victory of one general (Munro 1899: 196). Indeed, Miltiades was the first in history to apply the basic principles of war. These can be analyzed as follows:

Attack: Attacking is the decisive phase of war, where the final goal is to crush the enemy forces. By deciding to attack first, Miltiades ensured the initiative for the action and restricting the enemy's freedom, probably overturning their plans.

Economies of scale - concentration of forces: Assuming an attacking initiative implies superiority of force against each specific target. Realizing this prerequisite, Miltiades did not attack the Persians uniformly along the entire length of the front, but used different blows for each section according to the weak and strong points of the enemy formation. Thus, he strengthened the impact force at the two wings, which attacked the corresponding Persian wings and decreased the impact force at the center, which had a temporary defensive role. In this case, he was the first to abandon the uniform distribution of forces and to adopt irregular distribution applying the economies of scale principle (at the center) and concentration of force (at the two wings).

Unity of command: after Cleisthenes' reform, the Athenian army was commanded by 10 generals. At war times, the generals formed a type of War Council and command was rotated between the generals, each commanding the army in turn for a day. In the battle of Marathon, the four generals deferred their command to Miltiades, in order to have unity of command.

Surprise: Surprise was achieved with two actions and developed in phases. The running attack of the Hellenes was the first surprise for the Persians, which

was probably amplified by the fact that the attackers had neither cavalry nor archers. The unexpected outflanking manoeuver, which in essence enveloped them between the two sections of the hoplite phalanx, heightened the surprise, which finally resulted in their defeat.

Manoeuver: The uneven distribution of forces at the center and wings of the Athenian formation allowed the famous manoeuver, which was later called "bilateral outflanking manoeuver or pliers manoeuver" and "enemy weakening manoeuver". This manoeuver did not only bring victory but protected the safety of the hoplites who would have been defeated if an even formation had been applied (Tsampazis 1956: 125-126, Soulis 1972: 21-22, Gedeon: 9)

Miltiades' tactic, which was based on the principle of density and on the principle of flexibility and manoeuverability, was of mixed nature, combining the attacking and defensive principles, naturally promoting offense at the expense of defense. Therefore, it was justly considered the first revolution in war tactics. The Miltiades' manoeuver has been also used in subsequent battles: it was used by Hannibal against the Romans in the battle of Cannae (216 BC), by the Prussian field marshal von Blücher in Waterloo (1815), by Moltke in Sedan

The Greeks pursuing the Persians afte the Battle of Marathon (a work by Stelios Nigdiopoulos)

(1870), by Hindenburg in Tannenberg against the Czar's army (1914), in the greatest victory of World War I and by Eisenhower in the battle of France after the landing in Normandy (1944). The famous German hammer and anvil manoeuver used in WW II, is also inspired by Miltiades' manoeuver. The German generals used it in 1939 in Poland, in 1940 during the invasion of France and in 1941 in their attack against the Soviet Un-

Athenian hoplite fighting a Persian footman. Representation from a 5th cent. red-figured amphora

ion, where in three Marathon-type battles Hitler's army reached the gates of Moscow (Giannopoulos 2006: 52-54).

In summary, the factors that contributed to the victory in Marathon, from a military standpoint, are attributed directly or indirectly to the great Athenian general. Miltiades' personality and authority as well as his persuasive abilities, ensured the unity and effectiveness of command and the discipline of hoplites. His acumen is responsible for the selection of the battle place and time, conception of the strategic plan, the tactical formations and correct use of the terrain (Gyalistras 1960: 9-10). Finally, one of the most significant conclusions of the battle is that it demonstrated the superiority of Greek armor and warfare tactics and mainly the viability of the phalanx against the warfare tactics of the Persians (Giarenis 2008α: 227), that were successful in defeating the strong armies of the Lydians, Babylonians, Egyptians and Assyrians. Thanks to the battle of Marathon, the Hellenes who would later face the army of Xerxes realized their competitive advantage over their enemy(How 1923: 125).

4.6.3. The political significance of the battle

From a political significance standpoint Marathon was also the battle of a politician (Munro 1899: 196). In terms of key figures involved, there was conflict between the political beliefs and goals of Miltiades and Hippias. Just 15 years after the fall of tyranny and before stabilizing, the Athenian democracy was

once again faced with the threat of a tyrant. For the Athenians, victory did not only mean keeping their freedom but steadfastness of their democratic regime. Just like the Ionian revolt, the battle of Marathon was both political and national in nature. The same democratic forces that had rejected tyranny and had fought against the army of Hippias were now rejecting an entire empire (Lloyd 1973: 156, Califf 2002: 46, de Souza et al. 2004: 46).

Justifiably, the victory of the Athenians was considered a victory against the internal and external enemies of the city. As such, it had a catalytic effect on the acceleration of democratic procedures. The powers of the archon polemarch were drastically restricted and almost disappeared in the end, while the powers of the democratic instrument of 10 generals, who were now elected by the ekklesia of the demos, by all citizens, were strengthened further. It is not accidental that the Athenians formed the ideological backbone of their city

Retrieved parts from Marathon Trophy

around Marathon. If Salamis provided the spark for radical and substantive expansion of the body of citizens by allowing complete participation of the *thetes* in government, Marathon was the critical event that prepared and led to this expansion (Greek Parliament 2010: 44-45).

From this point of view, the battle of Marathon may be indeed considered as one of the most important battles in the western world (Casson 1920: 43), not for destroying a threat but for rescuing the cultural apex of Athens, the development of free institutions and the fundamental principles that govern European civilization (Creasy 1851: 57; Ray 2009: 68).

Epilogue

The battle of Marathon occupied center stage in the ideological and religious life of ancient Athens. Essentially, it is the starting point of worshiping heroes (see Paus., i.32.4: σέβονται δὲ οἱ Μαραθώνιοι τούτους τε οἵ παρὰ τὴν μάχην ἀπέθανον ἥρωας ὀνομάζοντες), which of course refers to all citizens and mainly the Athenian epheboi who went to the Tomb, laid wreaths and made sacrifices to honor the dead. Furthermore during the celebrations to honor Artemis Agrotera, apart from the sacrifice of 500 young goats, there were games where the epheboi would participate and march in procession to the temple of the goddess in Agres.

After the battle, the worship of Pan was established in the city. According to the legend, when Pheidippides was on his way to Sparta to ask for help he saw the goat-legged god on Mount Parthenio above Tegea. Pan told him to ask the Athenians why they did not honor him even though he had helped them and would help them in the future (Herodotus *Hist.*, VI.105, Pausanias. i.28.4). The Athenians believed Pheidippides tale and built a shrine to Pan under the Acropolis, where every year they held a torch race and sacrifices in his honor. And in the altar of Pan built in the Pan Cave (Πάνειον ἄντρον) also known as "Lychnospilia" on Mount Parnitha, the god's statue bore the following epigram attributed to Simonides:

Τὸν τραγόπουν ἐμὲ Πᾶνα, τὸν Ἀρκάδα τὸν κατὰ Μήδων
τὸν μετ᾽ Ἀθηναίων, στήσατο Μιλτιάδης
(Me, the Arcadian Pan, with cloven hooves,
who helped Athens against the Medes, erected by Miltiades).

It is clear that the Athenians believed that the Persians, upon seeing the running charge of the hoplites were overcome with sheer panic induced by the god[144] (Lloyd 1881: 392).

But it was not just the myth regarding the introduction of the Pan worship in Athens that was associated with the battle of Marathon. Pausanias (i.32.4)

---

144 According to Polyaenus (Stratagems in War (Στρατηγήματα), I.2), Pan was the general of the god Dionysus. The phalanx and its formation in wings (in Greek κέρατα is attributed as horns, hence Pan is usually depicted with horns) and the use of stratagems during war were all his conceptions.

narrates that every night in the valley around the Tomb one could hear horses neighing and weapons clashing. Pausanias also mentioned that a farmer appeared during the battle who slaughtered many enemies with his plough. Once the battle had ended, the Athenians tried to find him, but to no avail. So, they addressed the oracle and the god ordered them to honor the hero Echetlaeus (or Echetlos). Echetlos is depicted in the Poikile Stoa among the gods and mythical heroes who assisted the Athenians. In the same depiction, the dog of a hoplite that followed his master in battle and "fought" the Persians alongside him (Claudius Aelianus, Da Natura Animalium, VII.38) is also included. According to Plutarch, (*Theseus* 35.5) when the battle started many saw the specter of Theseus leading the hoplites to battle. Herodotus also talks about the apparition of a warrior (*Hist.*, VI.117.2-3). The Athenian Epizelos was fighting bravely when he suddenly was deprived of his eyesight without being injured. Prior to losing his sight, he saw a tall hoplite with a long beard, which covered his shield. The mysterious warrior passed him and killed a warrior who was standing next to Epizelos (Pelekides 1971: 308; Greek Parliament 2010: 76-80).

Most myths were forgotten through the centuries. One however, proved to be extremely long-lasting and was decisive in furthering the symbolism of the battle of Marathon. The story of the runner who arrived in Athens, announced the victory and fell dead, inspired the organizers of the first modern Olympic Games (Athens 1896) to create the marathon race, whose first winner was Spyros Louis (Lambros 1896). As an Olympic sport, the marathon was a reference to the victory of the Athenians but was obviously associated with peace. In 1963, this association acquired its final character as the Greek Committee for International Détente and Peace established the marathon march that started from the Marathon Tomb and ended in Pnyx, aiming to make a statement for world peace and nuclear disarmament. The first marathon march (April 1963), in which a representative of the British anti-war philosopher Bertrand Russell participated, drew the attention of Europe as it took place despite prohibitions and measure by the government. The photograph of Gregorios Lambrakis who managed to reach the Tomb and raise the black banner with the sign of peace and the word HELLAS, became the emblem of peace and democratic struggles. Once again Marathon and the Tomb of fallen heroes were associated with democracy and the demand for its establishment.

Apart from the myths mentioned above, the battle itself acquired symbolic dimensions in European contemporary thought. The conflict between Greeks and Persians, which together with the Ionian revolt were perceived as a conflict between freedom and autocracy, between democracy and despotism,

The Burial Mount

would gradually and with reference to the work of Herodotus, transform into a conflict between Europe and Asia (Giarenis 2008a: 234-235). This ideological framework would partially determine the European perception of the eastern world and would be promoted avidly from the 18th century onwards.[145] This symbolic antithesis would be further intensified on the eve of the Greek Revolution both by the Modern Greek Enlightenment scholars and by the European philhellenic movement. The revolutionary proclamations and battle songs projected the Greeks as ancestors of the glorious Marathon fighters, stressing their duty to fight for their faith and country.[146] Within this context and given that the battle of Marathon symbolizes the beginning of wars that deterred the Persian expansion to the West, the Athenian victory is considered

145 It is noteworthy that two villages were named Marathon during the time of the French revolution, when the Athenian democracy was a favorite point of reference for the revolutionaries (Vidal-Naquet 1999: 251).

146 See the proclamation of Alexander Ypsilantis (Jassy encampment 24.2.1821): *"Ας καλέσωμεν λοιπόν εκ νέου, ω Ανδρείοι και μεγαλόψυχοι Έλληνες, την ελευθερίαν εις την κλασικήν γην της Ελλάδος! Ας συγκροτήσωμεν μάχην μεταξύ του Μαραθώνος και των Θερμοπυλών! Ας πολεμήσωμεν εις τους τάφους των Πατέρων μας, οι οποίοι, διά να μας αφήσωσιν ελευθέρους, επολέμησαν και απέθανον εκεί!"* (Brave and noble Hellenes let us again call freedom to the classic soil of Hellas! Let us make battle between Marathon and Thermopylae! Let us fight by the graves of our Fathers, who fought and died there in order to give us freedom!).

the prerequisite for the existence of modern European civilization. And this is the reason for which many European 19th and early 20th century scholars regard it as one of the most important battles in world history. Indicatively, British historian E.S. Creasy (1812-1878) classified the battle first in his book on the fifteen decisive battles of the world, and the battle of Waterloo last (Creasy 1851), while British historian and strategist J.F.C. Fuller (1878-1966) stated that it signaled the birth of Europe (Gedeon: 8-9).

Overall, the history of Persian wars as narrated by Herodotus, constituted the core of an ideological notion that would decisively influence the stance of Greeks against the Persians (and by extension of Europe against Asia) - and vice versa. It is not a reference to the antithesis scheme "civilization vs barbarism", which is open to much discussion and has proven extremely resilient to time however out of context, but to the involvement of the Medes in the Trojan war. Even in the first paragraphs of the work of Herodotus, the destruction of Troy is projected as the beginning of the animosity between the Hellenes and the Persians (*Hist.*, I.5); he who started the wrongdoing (ἤρξατο χειρῶν ἀδίκων) was Alexander, son of Priam, who triggered the first war when he kidnapped Helen.[147] In this context, Xerxes' visit to the Troy acropolis (Priam's Pergamon), the sacrifice of one thousand oxen in honor of Iliad Athena and the libations to dead heroes were nothing more than a benediction ceremony for the planned revenge. In a sense, Xerxes was delivering a promise to his distant (mythical) ancestors that he would punish those culpable for their destruction (Georges 1994: 58-65).

Herodotus wrote his history in 450-445 BC. A few years later, the Peloponnesian War started in 431 BC, which would decisively divide the Hellenic world. How would the story of Herodotus sound to the Athenians after that tragic war between Greek cities? Perhaps more like a distant comforting myth of a world that was still cohesive and harmonious. It is however certain that advocates of Panhellenism, professing the need for a new unity of the Hellenic world to implement its geopolitical dreams, could find several arguments in the works of the Halicarnassus born historian. Perhaps the most important would be the campaign to Asia, which Aristagoras proposed to Cleomenes (*Hist.*, V.49). The

---

147 Herodotus' reference to the Trojan affair exceeds the simple cause and effect scheme. As has been noted, the historian from Halicarnassus is also influenced by Homer as to the way he presented historical facts. Thus, the main subject of his story is the war (and not for example the social composition or political status of Hellenic city-states), with an emphasis on the heroic deeds of leading individuals. Even though the text is written in prose his narrative assumptions are purely epic - and thus the long digressions and continuous presence of 'admiration': the Olympians continue their intervention in the Persian wars as they did during the Trojan wars, on the battlefield they appear as heroes and semi-gods, the hoplites see the gods fighting alongside them or meet them during a mission (Murray 1988: 462). Naturally, these narrative techniques do not negate the historicity of events but provide a certain ideological (and mythical) background.

relevant excerpt is considered to reflect the panhellenistic dreams, which had been sprouting in the Greek world since 480 BC, were disastrously suspended during the Peloponnesian War and were reborn after the battle of Cunaxa (401 BC) and the descent of the Myriads finding their fuller expression and crystallization in Isocrates' Panegyricus in 380 BC - exactly one century after Salamis (Cawkwell 2005: 6-8, 76-77). In his famous rhetoric speech, Isocrates wanted to bridge the gap between Athens and Sparta, remembering each city's contribution to the Persian wars. Thus, the Athenian hoplites appear as having undertaken the task to defend Greece in Marathon but at the same time, the Spartan sacrifice in Thermopylae is left out while the battle of Plataea is projected as the height of Greek unity vis-à-vis the Persian danger. Rearticulating the animosity between the Athenians and Spartans as competition among friends, Isocrates will encourage both uniting and again serving and defending the freedom of Greece (Polakos 2002: 205).

Philip II of Macedon

Alexander the Great

In Philip II of Macedon, Isocrates identified a leader who could be in charge of the united Greeks in their great campaign against the Persians. In the end, it would be Alexander the Great, son of Philip who would implement the vision of the Athenian orator and the goals of PanHellenism. The unprecedented campaign against the Persians from which a new great Hellenic world was born as noted poetically by K. P. Cavafy, was due punishment for their attacks against Greece and the destruction of temples. However, the narration of Herodotus gives one more dimension to the events. According to it, Alexander I the Philhellene had informed the Athenians with respect to the forces of Xerxes (480BC) and in Plataea he had informed them of Mardonius' intent to attack, while after the defeat of the Persians it was he who delivered the final blow to the remnants of the Persian army (Daskalakis 1960: 299-343). Therefore, Alexander III, called the Great was now coming to finish the work of his ancestor.

Just as the Persians promoted their mythical decent from the Trojans, Alexander proudly claimed descent from Achilles; when he crossed the Hellespont in 334 BC, he stopped in Troy to pay homage to his ancestor. The circle seems to close somewhere here with the overwhelming victory of the Macedonian phalanx in Gaugamela in 331 BC.

Curiously however, the mythical circles open again unexpectedly through history. In 1462, Mohamed II crossed Troy nine years after the fall of Constantinople. After walking in the ruins of the once powerful Ilion, he shook his head saying: "God left it up to me to take revenge for the destruction of this city and its residents after so many years. I tamed their enemies, besieged their cities and gave their riches a prey to the Myssoi. Because they were Hellenes and Macedonians and Thessalians and Peloponnesians those who had once besieged it and after so many years their ancestors paid to me the debt for the offense they committed then, as many times and later against us the Asians" (Vidal-Naquet 1999: 35-36). It is possible that the so called "Persian syndrome' of Turkey was founded on this abhorrence (Lygero 2010). Therefore, the revolutionary proclamation c Ypsilantis addressed to the descendants of the Marc thon fighters, was nothing more than the expecte response.

The battle of Marathon was primarily a battl for freedom, democracy and preservation of peace a condition precedent for progress, prosperity an democratic integration. Its outcome was of decisiv importance for the future conflicts between the He lenes and the Persians, as it proved in practice th effectiveness of the hoplite phalanx against grea armies which however did not have the weaponry nor its war tactics, while at the same time it boosted the moral of the Hellenes by invalidating the notion that the Persian army was unbeatable. Thus, this first victory constituted a milestone that signaled the end of the archaic and the beginning of the classical era. Greek civilization reached its apex during this era and the achievements in philosophy, political thought, the arts and literature became the basis of western civilization. This was the main reason

The famous tombstone stele of hoplite Ariston (520-510 BC, National Archaeological Museum)

why the battle of Marathon had such a long lasting and steady influence on European thought and European history and is essentially associated with the birth of Europe, not as a geographical region but as a body of ideas, perceptions and attitudes. Its main symbolism, the victory of democracy over tyranny

and freedom over despotism remain strong, engraved in memory and crystal-lized inter alia in the marathon run, enhanced with the promotion of the ideal of peace. Even though 2,500 years have passed from the day the Athenians and Plataeans defeated the strongest army of their time, the significance of that day and of that victory is still pertinent, now more than ever.

Marathon and the European identity

"Without Marathon European identity would be different. For years now, s scholars disagree as to whether European identity owes more to the ancient Greeks or the ancient Romans, where the heritage of the latter was preserved through the Roman Catholic Church. The fact that European identity stems from many sources is "identification" wisdom. If history is considered evolu-tionary, the Romans would not be the Romans as we know them, had they not adopted the Greek cultural heritage.

And if there was no Christianity, its seed could not grow on Greek soil (as many messianic religions from the Near East and Judaism, which blossomed and then died). Man-centered classic antiquity was a civilization open to the message of Christ. And where would Renaissance and the Enlightenment find inspiration for renewal of the world if not from the classic sciences and art?

Had the Athenians lost the battle of Marathon and had the Persians captured Athens converting it into a satrapy for decades, the classical era would not exist, we would have to think along the lines of a hypothetical, unreal histori-cal developments in another era, in order to acheive the same result, namely western European civilization. An era in which, somehow the same impulse for science and arts, democracy and free people would be present. Objections stem from the argument that industrialization would not have started without the momentum of the "enlightened" sciences (including certain educational mathematical books of the classical era that have been rediscovered). The return to the classical heritage of knowledge, the philosophical heritage as a means to free people from the medieval bonds proved to be the accelerators for a European revolution that would have not taken place otherwise.

And lastly: The evolution of ancient Greek democracy was a unique excep-tion. Such flourishing, such an explosion of human creativity and freedom of thought in such a small period remains unique in history. Observing such a phenomenon, either as readers of the classical works or by gazing up at the Acropolis, one finds oneself faced with a miracle the roots of which are re-vealed only through a careful study of the special circumstances in the period

preceding the Greek classical era. Hence, it is extremely difficult to imagine where European civilization would be today if its roots were not in classical Greece and without the victory of the Athenians in Marathon 2,500 years ago (de la Croix 2010:33)."

Nemesis

The Persians, who from mid 5th century BC did not abandon their ambitions, interfering in Greece in in a variety of ways always maintaining their aspirations for the Greek region, had to restrict their ambitions because they strictly opposed the shipping, commercial and cultural exchanges between the Greeks of Magna Graecia.

The conflict between the Greeks and the Persians, which culminated in Marathon and continued with confrontations in Thermopylae, Salamis and Plataea, would end two centuries later with Alexander III, known as Alexander the Great.

Herodotus supported Alexander I and enhanced the image of the Argead kings of Macedonia who had founded the Macedonian state in 803 BC. As we know, Alexander I, a young prince at the time, killed the Persian envoys in 512 BC and revealed their plans to Pausanias in the battle of Plataea.

Philip's predecessors and Philip himself organized the Macedonian state and succeeded in uniting the Greeks, so Alexander the Great could bring NEMESIS and the destruction of the Persian state, because those who suffer from the Persian Syndrome and undermine the future of civilized people have the same ending, because human values and faith in freedom and democracy will triumph in the end.

The battle of Marathon was a decisive battle and signaled the birth of Europe. Marathon became the symbol of Athenian glory, front fighter of Greece and the superiority of Athenian hoplites against Asian mercenary warriors. The Persians were no longer the undefeated rulers of the East.

Appendix

I. The American Congress Honors
The 2500th anniversary of
The Battle of Marathon

111th CONGRESS - 2nd SESSION

H. RES. 1704
HONORING THE 2500TH ANNIVERSARY OF THE BATTLE OF MARATHON

IN THE HOUSE OF REPRESENTATIVES
SEPTEMBER 29, 2010
MR. MCGOVERN (FOR HIMSELF AND MR. SARBANES) SUBMITTED THE FOLLOWING
RESOLUTION; WHICH WAS REFERRED TO THE COMMITTEE ON FOREIGN AFFAIRS

RESOLUTION
Honoring the 2500th anniversary of the Battle of Marathon

Whereas in 490 BC, Athenian warriors defeated foreign invaders and won against overwhelming odds in one of the most significant battles in human history;

Whereas the Athenian victory helped continue the development of a new form of government called "democracy";

Whereas according to legend, a messenger named Phidippides ran from the battlefield of Marathon, Greece, to Athens 26 miles away to carry news of the victory and it is said, that upon delivering the news to the citizens of Athens, Phidippides died from exhaustion;

Whereas Phidippides' run inspired the spiritual origin of what has become the sport of marathoning;

Whereas the first official marathon race was introduced in the first modern Olympics in 1896 held in Athens, Greece;

Whereas officials from the Boston Athletic Association brought the long distance Olympic running event to Boston, Massascheusetts, where it has been run annually since 1897;

Whereas a ceremony took place in Marathon, Greece, in 2007 at the Tomb of the Athenians, the burial cite of the Greek warriors who gave their lives defending their country;

Whereas this ceremony created the symbolic Flame of Marathon that embodies the strength of the human spirit, fair competition, and peace;

Whereas Hopkinton, Massachusetts, and Marathon, Greece, have a twin-city relationship, the Flame of Marathon traveled from Marathon, Greece, and was presented to the Town of Hopkinton in 2008;

Whereas the Flame of Marathon has burned continuously in Hopkinton, Massachusetts, since its arrival in the United States;

Whereas the Flame of Marathon reminds us of the sacrifice of the United States Armed Forces and their families, the defenders of democracy;

Whereas the 35th Marine Corps Marathon is receiving the Flame of Marathon as part of its celebration of the 2500th anniversary of the Battle of Marathon;

Whereas the Flame of Marathon will be displayed at events leading to and including the Marine Corps Marathon in view of 30,000 runners who embody the marathon spirit as they run through Washington, DC: Now, therefore, be it

Resolved: That the House of Representatives joins with the Greek Embassy in Washington, DC, the people of Hopkinton, Massachusetts, the people of Marathon, Greece, and the hundreds of thousands of runners participating in marathons throughout the United States, in celebrating the 2500th anniversary of the Battle of Marathon, Greece, **one of the most significant battles in human history.**

House Vote On Passage: H. Res. 1704 [111th]: Honoring the 2500th anniversary of the Battle of Marathon

Number: House Vote #618 in 2010 [primary source: house.gov]
Date: Dec 8, 2010 2:56PM
Result: Passed
Bill: H. Res. 1704 [111th]: Honoring the 2500th anniversary of the Battle of Marathon

Totals		Democrats	Republicans	Independents
Aye:	359 (83%)	235	124	0
No:	44 (10%)	2	42	0
Present:	5 (1%)	4	1	0
Not Voting:	25 (6%)	13	12	0
Required:	2/3 of 408 votes (=272 votes)			

(Vacancies in Congress will affect vote totals.)

More information: Aye versus Yea Explained

All Votes — Aye / No Vote / Nay

Vote Details

Vote [Sort]	District [Sort]	Representative [Sort by Name] [Sort by Party]
Alabama		
Aye	AL-1	Bonner, Jo [R]
Aye	AL-2	Bright, Bobby [D]
Aye	AL-3	Rogers, Michael [R]
Aye	AL-4	Aderholt, Robert [R]
Not Voting	AL-5	Griffith, Parker [R]
Aye	AL-6	Bachus, Spencer [R]
Aye	AL-7	Davis, Artur [D]
Alaska		
No	AK-0	Young, Donald [R]
Arizona		
Not Voting	AZ-1	Kirkpatrick, Ann [D]
Aye	AZ-2	Franks, Trent [R]
Aye	AZ-3	Shadegg, John [R]
Aye	AZ-4	Pastor, Edward [D]
Aye	AZ-5	Mitchell, Harry [D]
No	AZ-6	Flake, Jeff [R]
Aye	AZ-7	Grijalva, Raul [D]
Aye	AZ-8	Giffords, Gabrielle [D]
Arkansas		
Not Voting	AR-1	Berry, Robert [D]
Aye	AR-2	Snyder, Victor [D]
Aye	AR-3	Boozman, John [R]
Aye	AR-4	Ross, Mike [D]
California		
Aye	CA-1	Thompson, C. [D]
No	CA-2	Herger, Walter [R]
Aye	CA-3	Lungren, Daniel [R]
Aye	CA-4	McClintock, Tom [R]
Aye	CA-5	Matsui, Doris [D]
Aye	CA-6	Woolsey, Lynn [D]
Aye	CA-7	Miller, George [D]
Aye	CA-9	Lee, Barbara [D]
Aye	CA-10	Garamendi, John [D]
Aye	CA-11	McNerney, Jerry [D]
Aye	CA-12	Speier, Jackie [D]
Aye	CA-13	Stark, Fortney [D]
Aye	CA-14	Eshoo, Anna [D]
Aye	CA-15	Honda, Michael [D]
Aye	CA-16	Lofgren, Zoe [D]

Cartogram

Standard Projection

Cartograms give an equal area in an image to an equal number of votes by distorting the image. Senate vote cartograms are shown with each state stretched or shrunk so that the states each take up an equal area because each state has two votes. For House votes, it is each congressional district which is stretched or shrunk.

Aye	CA-17	Farr, Sam [D]
Aye	CA-18	Cardoza, Dennis [D]
Not Voting	CA-19	Radanovich, George [R]
Aye	CA-20	Costa, Jim [D]
No	CA-21	Nunes, Devin [R]
Aye	CA-22	McCarthy, Kevin [R]
Aye	CA-23	Capps, Lois [D]
Aye	CA-24	Gallegly, Elton [R]
Aye	CA-25	McKeon, Howard [R]
Aye	CA-26	Dreier, David [R]
Aye	CA-27	Sherman, Brad [D]
Aye	CA-28	Berman, Howard [D]
Aye	CA-29	Schiff, Adam [D]
Aye	CA-30	Waxman, Henry [D]
Aye	CA-31	Becerra, Xavier [D]
Not Voting	CA-32	Chu, Judy [D]
Aye	CA-33	Watson, Diane [D]
Aye	CA-34	Roybal-Allard, Lucille [D]
Aye	CA-35	Waters, Maxine [D]
Aye	CA-36	Harman, Jane [D]
Aye	CA-37	Richardson, Laura [D]
Aye	CA-38	Napolitano, Grace [D]
Aye	CA-39	Sanchez, Linda [D]
Aye	CA-40	Royce, Edward [R]
Aye	CA-41	Lewis, Jerry [R]
Aye	CA-42	Miller, Gary [R]
Aye	CA-43	Baca, Joe [D]
Aye	CA-44	Calvert, Ken [R]
Aye	CA-45	Bono Mack, Mary [R]
Aye	CA-46	Rohrabacher, Dana [R]
Aye	CA-47	Sanchez, Loretta [D]
No	CA-48	Campbell, John [R]
Aye	CA-49	Issa, Darrell [R]
Not Voting	CA-50	Bilbray, Brian [R]
Aye	CA-51	Filner, Bob [D]
Aye	CA-52	Hunter, Duncan [R]
Aye	CA-53	Davis, Susan [D]

Colorado

Aye	CO-1	DeGette, Diana [D]
Aye	CO-2	Polis, Jared [D]
Aye	CO-3	Salazar, John [D]
Aye	CO-4	Markey, Betsy [D]
Aye	CO-5	Lamborn, Doug [R]
Aye	CO-6	Coffman, Mike [R]
Aye	CO-7	Perlmutter, Ed [D]

Connecticut

Aye	CT-1	Larson, John [D]
Aye	CT-2	Courtney, Joe [D]
Aye	CT-3	DeLauro, Rosa [D]
Aye	CT-4	Himes, James [D]
Aye	CT-5	Murphy, Christopher [D]

Delaware

Aye	DE-0	Castle, Michael [R]

Florida

No	FL-1	Miller, Jeff [R]
Aye	FL-2	Boyd, Allen [D]
Aye	FL-3	Brown, Corrine [D]
Aye	FL-4	Crenshaw, Ander [R]
No	FL-5	Brown-Waite, Virginia [R]
Aye	FL-6	Stearns, Clifford [R]
No	FL-7	Mica, John [R]
Aye	FL-8	Grayson, Alan [D]
Aye	FL-9	Bilirakis, Gus [R]
Aye	FL-10	Young, C. W. [R]
Aye	FL-11	Castor, Kathy [D]
Aye	FL-12	Putnam, Adam [R]
Aye	FL-13	Buchanan, Vern [R]
Aye	FL-14	Mack, Connie [R]
Aye	FL-15	Posey, Bill [R]
No	FL-16	Rooney, Thomas [R]

Aye	FL-17	Meek, Kendrick [D]
Aye	FL-18	Ros-Lehtinen, Ileana [R]
Aye	FL-19	Deutch, Ted [D]
Aye	FL-20	Wasserman Schultz, Debbie [D]
Aye	FL-21	Diaz-Balart, Lincoln [R]
Aye	FL-22	Klein, Ron [D]
Aye	FL-23	Hastings, Alcee [D]
Aye	FL-24	Kosmas, Suzanne [D]
Aye	FL-25	Diaz-Balart, Mario [R]

Georgia

Aye	GA-1	Kingston, Jack [R]
Aye	GA-2	Bishop, Sanford [D]
No	GA-3	Westmoreland, Lynn [R]
Aye	GA-4	Johnson, Henry [D]
Aye	GA-5	Lewis, John [D]
Aye	GA-6	Price, Tom [R]
Aye	GA-7	Linder, John [R]
Present	GA-8	Marshall, James [D]
No	GA-9	Graves, Tom [R]
No	GA-10	Broun, Paul [R]
No	GA-11	Gingrey, John [R]
Aye	GA-12	Barrow, John [D]
Aye	GA-13	Scott, David [D]

Hawaii

Aye	HI-1	Djou, Charles [R]
Aye	HI-2	Hirono, Mazie [D]

Idaho

Aye	ID-1	Minnick, Walter [D]
No	ID-2	Simpson, Michael [R]

Illinois

Aye	IL-1	Rush, Bobby [D]
Aye	IL-2	Jackson, Jesse [D]
Aye	IL-3	Lipinski, Daniel [D]
Aye	IL-4	Gutierrez, Luis [D]
Aye	IL-5	Quigley, Mike [D]
Aye	IL-6	Roskam, Peter [R]
Aye	IL-7	Davis, Danny [D]
Aye	IL-8	Bean, Melissa [D]
Aye	IL-9	Schakowsky, Janice [D]
Aye	IL-11	Halvorson, Deborah [D]
Aye	IL-12	Costello, Jerry [D]
Aye	IL-13	Biggert, Judy [R]
Aye	IL-14	Foster, Bill [D]
No	IL-15	Johnson, Timothy [R]
Aye	IL-16	Manzullo, Donald [R]
Aye	IL-17	Hare, Phil [D]
No	IL-18	Schock, Aaron [R]
No	IL-19	Shimkus, John [R]

Indiana

Aye	IN-1	Visclosky, Peter [D]
Aye	IN-2	Donnelly, Joe [D]
No	IN-3	Stutzman, Marlin [R]
Aye	IN-4	Buyer, Stephen [R]
Aye	IN-5	Burton, Dan [R]
Aye	IN-6	Pence, Mike [R]
Aye	IN-7	Carson, André [D]
Not Voting	IN-8	Ellsworth, Brad [D]
Not Voting	IN-9	Hill, Baron [D]

Iowa

Aye	IA-1	Braley, Bruce [D]
Aye	IA-2	Loebsack, David [D]
Aye	IA-3	Boswell, Leonard [D]
Aye	IA-4	Latham, Thomas [R]
No	IA-5	King, Steve [R]

Kansas

Aye	KS-1	Moran, Jerry [R]
Aye	KS-2	Jenkins, Lynn [R]
Not Voting	KS-3	Moore, Dennis [D]
Not Voting	KS-4	Tiahrt, Todd [R]

Kentucky

Aye	KY-1	Whitfield, Edward [R]
Aye	KY-2	Guthrie, Brett [R]
Aye	KY-3	Yarmuth, John [D]
No	KY-4	Davis, Geoff [R]
Aye	KY-5	Rogers, Harold [R]
Aye	KY-6	Chandler, Ben [D]

Louisiana

Aye	LA-1	Scalise, Steve [R]
Aye	LA-2	Cao, Anh [R]
Aye	LA-3	Melancon, Charles [D]
Aye	LA-4	Fleming, John [R]
Aye	LA-5	Alexander, Rodney [R]
No	LA-6	Cassidy, Bill [R]
Aye	LA-7	Boustany, Charles [R]

Maine

Not Voting	ME-1	Pingree, Chellie [D]
Aye	ME-2	Michaud, Michael [D]

Maryland

Aye	MD-1	Kratovil, Frank [D]
Aye	MD-2	Ruppersberger, C.A. [D]
Aye	MD-3	Sarbanes, John [D]
Aye	MD-4	Edwards, Donna [D]
Aye	MD-5	Hoyer, Steny [D]
No	MD-6	Bartlett, Roscoe [R]
Aye	MD-7	Cummings, Elijah [D]
Aye	MD-8	Van Hollen, Christopher [D]

Massachusetts

Aye	MA-1	Olver, John [D]
Aye	MA-2	Neal, Richard [D]
Aye	MA-3	McGovern, James [D]
Aye	MA-4	Frank, Barney [D]
Aye	MA-5	Tsongas, Niki [D]
Aye	MA-6	Tierney, John [D]
Aye	MA-7	Markey, Edward [D]
Aye	MA-8	Capuano, Michael [D]
Aye	MA-9	Lynch, Stephen [D]
Not Voting	MA-10	Delahunt, William [D]

Michigan

Aye	MI-1	Stupak, Bart [D]
Not Voting	MI-2	Hoekstra, Peter [R]
Aye	MI-3	Ehlers, Vernon [R]
Aye	MI-4	Camp, David [R]
Aye	MI-5	Kildee, Dale [D]
Aye	MI-6	Upton, Frederick [R]
Aye	MI-7	Schauer, Mark [D]
No	MI-8	Rogers, Michael [R]
Aye	MI-9	Peters, Gary [D]
No	MI-10	Miller, Candice [R]
Aye	MI-11	McCotter, Thaddeus [R]
Aye	MI-12	Levin, Sander [D]
Not Voting	MI-13	Kilpatrick, Carolyn [D]
Not Voting	MI-14	Conyers, John [D]
Aye	MI-15	Dingell, John [D]

Minnesota

Aye	MN-1	Walz, Timothy [D]
Aye	MN-2	Kline, John [R]
Aye	MN-3	Paulsen, Erik [R]
Aye	MN-4	McCollum, Betty [D]
Aye	MN-5	Ellison, Keith [D]
Aye	MN-6	Bachmann, Michele [R]
Aye	MN-7	Peterson, Collin [D]
Aye	MN-8	Oberstar, James [D]

Mississippi

Aye	MS-1	Childers, Travis [D]
Aye	MS-2	Thompson, Bennie [D]
Aye	MS-3	Harper, Gregg [R]
No	MS-4	Taylor, Gene [D]

Missouri

Aye	MO-1	Clay, William [D]
Aye	MO-2	Akin, W. [R]
Aye	MO-3	Carnahan, Russ [D]
Aye	MO-4	Skelton, Ike [D]
Aye	MO-5	Cleaver, Emanuel [D]
No	MO-6	Graves, Samuel [R]
Not Voting	MO-7	Blunt, Roy [R]
No	MO-8	Emerson, Jo Ann [R]
Aye	MO-9	Luetkemeyer, Blaine [R]

Montana

No	MT-0	Rehberg, Dennis [R]

Nebraska

No	NE-1	Fortenberry, Jeffrey [R]
No	NE-2	Terry, Lee [R]
No	NE-3	Smith, Adrian [R]

Nevada

Aye	NV-1	Berkley, Shelley [D]
No	NV-2	Heller, Dean [R]
Aye	NV-3	Titus, Dina [D]

New Hampshire

Aye	NH-1	Shea-Porter, Carol [D]
Aye	NH-2	Hodes, Paul [D]

New Jersey

Aye	NJ-1	Andrews, Robert [D]
Aye	NJ-2	LoBiondo, Frank [R]
Aye	NJ-3	Adler, John [D]
Aye	NJ-4	Smith, Christopher [R]
Not Voting	NJ-5	Garrett, Scott [R]
Aye	NJ-6	Pallone, Frank [D]
Aye	NJ-7	Lance, Leonard [R]
Aye	NJ-8	Pascrell, William [D]
Aye	NJ-9	Rothman, Steven [D]
Aye	NJ-10	Payne, Donald [D]
Aye	NJ-11	Frelinghuysen, Rodney [R]
Aye	NJ-12	Holt, Rush [D]
Aye	NJ-13	Sires, Albio [D]

New Mexico

Aye	NM-1	Heinrich, Martin [D]
Aye	NM-2	Teague, Harry [D]
Aye	NM-3	Lujan, Ben [D]

New York

Aye	NY-1	Bishop, Timothy [D]
Aye	NY-2	Israel, Steve [D]
Aye	NY-3	King, Peter [R]
Aye	NY-4	McCarthy, Carolyn [D]
Aye	NY-5	Ackerman, Gary [D]
Aye	NY-6	Meeks, Gregory [D]
Aye	NY-7	Crowley, Joseph [D]
Aye	NY-8	Nadler, Jerrold [D]
Aye	NY-9	Weiner, Anthony [D]
Aye	NY-10	Towns, Edolphus [D]
Aye	NY-11	Clarke, Yvette [D]
Aye	NY-12	Velazquez, Nydia [D]
Aye	NY-13	McMahon, Michael [D]
Aye	NY-14	Maloney, Carolyn [D]
Aye	NY-15	Rangel, Charles [D]
Aye	NY-16	Serrano, José [D]
Aye	NY-17	Engel, Eliot [D]
Aye	NY-18	Lowey, Nita [D]
Present	NY-19	Hall, John [D]
Present	NY-20	Murphy, Scott [D]
Aye	NY-21	Tonko, Paul [D]
Aye	NY-22	Hinchey, Maurice [D]
Present	NY-23	Owens, William [D]
Aye	NY-24	Arcuri, Michael [D]
Aye	NY-25	Maffei, Daniel [D]
No	NY-26	Lee, Christopher [R]
Aye	NY-27	Higgins, Brian [D]
Aye	NY-28	Slaughter, Louise [D]
Aye	NY-29	Reed, Tom [R]

North Carolina

Aye	NC-1	Butterfield, George [D]

Aye	NC-2	Etheridge, Bob [D]
No	NC-3	Jones, Walter [R]
Aye	NC-4	Price, David [D]
Aye	NC-5	Foxx, Virginia [R]
Aye	NC-6	Coble, Howard [R]
Aye	NC-7	McIntyre, Mike [D]
Aye	NC-8	Kissell, Larry [D]
Aye	NC-9	Myrick, Sue [R]
Aye	NC-10	McHenry, Patrick [R]
Aye	NC-11	Shuler, Heath [D]
Aye	NC-12	Watt, Melvin [D]
Aye	NC-13	Miller, R. [D]

North Dakota

Aye	ND-0	Pomeroy, Earl [D]

Ohio

Aye	OH-1	Driehaus, Steve [D]
Aye	OH-2	Schmidt, Jean [R]
Aye	OH-3	Turner, Michael [R]
No	OH-4	Jordan, Jim [R]
Aye	OH-5	Latta, Robert [R]
Aye	OH-6	Wilson, Charles [D]
Aye	OH-7	Austria, Steve [R]
Aye	OH-8	Boehner, John [R]
Aye	OH-9	Kaptur, Marcy [D]
Aye	OH-10	Kucinich, Dennis [D]
Aye	OH-11	Fudge, Marcia [D]
Aye	OH-12	Tiberi, Patrick [R]
Aye	OH-13	Sutton, Betty [D]
Aye	OH-14	LaTourette, Steven [R]
Aye	OH-15	Kilroy, Mary Jo [D]
Aye	OH-16	Boccieri, John [D]
Aye	OH-17	Ryan, Timothy [D]
Aye	OH-18	Space, Zachary [D]

Oklahoma

Aye	OK-1	Sullivan, John [R]
Aye	OK-2	Boren, Dan [D]
Aye	OK-3	Lucas, Frank [R]
Aye	OK-4	Cole, Tom [R]
Not Voting	OK-5	Fallin, Mary [R]

Oregon

Aye	OR-1	Wu, David [D]
Aye	OR-2	Walden, Greg [R]
Aye	OR-3	Blumenauer, Earl [D]
Aye	OR-4	DeFazio, Peter [D]
Aye	OR-5	Schrader, Kurt [D]

Pennsylvania

Aye	PA-1	Brady, Robert [D]
Aye	PA-2	Fattah, Chaka [D]
Aye	PA-3	Dahlkemper, Kathleen [D]
Aye	PA-4	Altmire, Jason [D]
Aye	PA-5	Thompson, Glenn [R]
Aye	PA-6	Gerlach, Jim [R]
Aye	PA-7	Sestak, Joe [D]
Aye	PA-8	Murphy, Patrick [D]
Aye	PA-9	Shuster, William [R]
Aye	PA-10	Carney, Christopher [D]
Aye	PA-11	Kanjorski, Paul [D]
Aye	PA-12	Critz, Mark [D]
Aye	PA-13	Schwartz, Allyson [D]
Aye	PA-14	Doyle, Michael [D]
Aye	PA-15	Dent, Charles [R]
Aye	PA-16	Pitts, Joseph [R]
Aye	PA-17	Holden, Tim [D]
Aye	PA-18	Murphy, Tim [R]
Aye	PA-19	Platts, Todd [R]

Rhode Island

Aye	RI-1	Kennedy, Patrick [D]
Aye	RI-2	Langevin, James [D]

South Carolina

Aye	SC-1	Brown, Henry [R]
Aye	SC-2	Wilson, Addison [R]
Aye	SC-3	Barrett, James [R]
Aye	SC-4	Inglis, Bob [R]
Aye	SC-5	Spratt, John [D]
Aye	SC-6	Clyburn, James [D]

South Dakota

Aye	SD-0	Herseth Sandlin, Stephanie [D]

Tennessee

No	TN-1	Roe, Phil [R]
Aye	TN-2	Duncan, John [R]
Aye	TN-3	Wamp, Zach [R]
Aye	TN-4	Davis, Lincoln [D]
Aye	TN-5	Cooper, Jim [D]
Not Voting	TN-6	Gordon, Barton [D]
Aye	TN-7	Blackburn, Marsha [R]
Aye	TN-8	Tanner, John [D]
Not Voting	TN-9	Cohen, Steve [D]

Texas

Present	TX-1	Gohmert, Louis [R]
Aye	TX-2	Poe, Ted [R]
Aye	TX-3	Johnson, Samuel [R]
Aye	TX-4	Hall, Ralph [R]
Aye	TX-5	Hensarling, Jeb [R]
No	TX-6	Barton, Joe [R]
Aye	TX-7	Culberson, John [R]
Aye	TX-8	Brady, Kevin [R]
Aye	TX-9	Green, Al [D]
Aye	TX-10	McCaul, Michael [R]
No	TX-11	Conaway, K. [R]
Not Voting	TX-12	Granger, Kay [R]
Aye	TX-13	Thornberry, William [R]
No	TX-14	Paul, Ronald [R]
Aye	TX-15	Hinojosa, Rubén [D]
Aye	TX-16	Reyes, Silvestre [D]
Aye	TX-17	Edwards, Thomas [D]
Aye	TX-18	Jackson-Lee, Sheila [D]
Aye	TX-19	Neugebauer, Randy [R]
Aye	TX-20	Gonzalez, Charles [D]
Aye	TX-21	Smith, Lamar [R]
Aye	TX-22	Olson, Pete [R]
Aye	TX-23	Rodriguez, Ciro [D]
Not Voting	TX-24	Marchant, Kenny [R]
Aye	TX-25	Doggett, Lloyd [D]
Aye	TX-26	Burgess, Michael [R]
Aye	TX-27	Ortiz, Solomon [D]
Aye	TX-28	Cuellar, Henry [D]
Aye	TX-29	Green, Raymond [D]
Aye	TX-30	Johnson, Eddie [D]
Aye	TX-31	Carter, John [R]
Aye	TX-32	Sessions, Peter [R]

Utah

Aye	UT-1	Bishop, Rob [R]
Aye	UT-2	Matheson, Jim [D]
No	UT-3	Chaffetz, Jason [R]

Vermont

Aye	VT-0	Welch, Peter [D]

Virginia

Aye	VA-1	Wittman, Rob [R]
Aye	VA-2	Nye, Glenn [D]
Aye	VA-3	Scott, Robert [D]
Aye	VA-4	Forbes, J. [R]
Aye	VA-5	Perriello, Thomas [D]
Aye	VA-6	Goodlatte, Robert [R]
No	VA-7	Cantor, Eric [R]
Aye	VA-8	Moran, James [D]
Aye	VA-9	Boucher, Frederick [D]
Aye	VA-10	Wolf, Frank [R]
Aye	VA-11	Connolly, Gerald [D]

Washington

Aye	WA-1	Inslee, Jay [D]
Aye	WA-2	Larsen, Rick [D]
Aye	WA-3	Baird, Brian [D]
Aye	WA-4	Hastings, Doc [R]
Not Voting	WA-5	McMorris Rodgers, Cathy [R]
Aye	WA-6	Dicks, Norman [D]
Aye	WA-7	McDermott, James [D]
Aye	WA-8	Reichert, Dave [R]
Aye	WA-9	Smith, Adam [D]

West Virginia

Not Voting	WV-1	Mollohan, Alan [D]
Not Voting	WV-2	Capito, Shelley [R]
Aye	WV-3	Rahall, Nick [D]

Wisconsin

Aye	WI-1	Ryan, Paul [R]
Aye	WI-2	Baldwin, Tammy [D]
No	WI-3	Kind, Ronald [D]
Aye	WI-4	Moore, Gwen [D]
No	WI-5	Sensenbrenner, F. [R]
Aye	WI-6	Petri, Thomas [R]
Aye	WI-7	Obey, David [D]
Aye	WI-8	Kagen, Steve [D]

Wyoming

No	WY-0	Lummis, Cynthia [R]

II. Herodotus, *The Histories*, VI, 94-120
(English translation by **A. D. Godley**
Cambridge: Harvard University Press)

94

1 Ἀθηναίοισι μὲν δὴ πόλεμος συνῆπτο πρὸς Αἰγινήτας. ὁ δὲ Πέρσης τὸ ἑωυτοῦ ἐποίεε, ὥστε ἀναμιμνήσκοντός τε αἰεὶ τοῦ θεράποντος μεμνῆσθαί μιν τῶν Ἀθηναίων, καὶ Πεισιστρατιδέων προσκατημένων καὶ διαβαλλόντων Ἀθηναίους, ἅμα δὲ βουλόμενος ὁ Δαρεῖος ταύτης ἐχόμενος τῆς προφάσιος καταστρέφεσθαι τῆς Ἑλλάδος τοὺς μὴ δόντας αὐτῷ γῆν τε καὶ ὕδωρ. 2 Μαρδόνιον μὲν δὴ φλαύρως πρήξαντα τῷ στόλῳ παραλύει τῆς στρατηγίης, ἄλλους δὲ στρατηγοὺς ἀποδέξας ἀπέστειλε ἐπὶ τε Ἐρέτριαν καὶ Ἀθήνας, Δᾶτίν τε ἐόντα Μῆδον γένος καὶ Ἀρταφρένεα τὸν Ἀρταφρένεος παῖδα, ἀδελφιδέον ἑωυτοῦ· ἐντειλάμενος δὲ ἀπέπεμπε ἐξανδραποδίσαντας Ἀθήνας καὶ Ἐρέτριαν ἀνάγειν ἑωυτῷ ἐς ὄψιν τὰ ἀνδράποδα.

95

1 ὡς δὲ οἱ στρατηγοὶ οὗτοι οἱ ἀποδεχθέντες πορευόμενοι παρὰ βασιλέος ἀπίκοντο τῆς Κιλικίης ἐς τὸ Ἀλήιον πεδίον, ἅμα ἀγόμενοι πεζὸν στρατὸν πολλόν τε καὶ εὖ ἐσκευασμένον, ἐνθαῦτα στρατοπεδευομένοισι ἐπῆλθε μὲν ὁ ναυτικὸς πᾶς στρατὸς ὁ ἐπιταχθεὶς ἑκάστοισι, παρεγένοντο δὲ καὶ αἱ ἱππαγωγοὶ νέες, τὰς τῷ προτέρῳ ἔτεϊ προεῖπε τοῖσι ἑωυτοῦ δασμοφόροισι Δαρεῖος ἑτοιμάζειν. 2 ἐσβαλόμενοι δὲ τοὺς ἵππους ἐς ταύτας καὶ τὸν πεζὸν στρατὸν ἐσβιβάσαντες ἐς τὰς νέας, ἔπλεον ἑξακοσίῃσι τριήρεσι ἐς τὴν Ἰωνίην. ἐνθεῦτεν δὲ οὐ παρὰ τὴν ἤπειρον

94

Thus Athens and Aegina grappled together in war. The Persian was going about his own business, for his servant was constantly reminding him to remember the Athenians, and the Pisistratidae were at his elbow maligning the Athenians; moreover, Darius desired to take this pretext for subduing all the men of Hellas who had not given him earth and water. He dismissed from command Mardonius, who had fared so badly on his expedition, and appointed other generals to lead his armies against Athens and Eretria, Datis, a Mede by birth, and his own nephew Artaphrenes son of Artaphrenes; the order he gave them at their departure was to enslave Athens and Eretria and bring the slaves into his presence.

95

When these appointed generals on their way from the king reached the Aleian plain in Cilicia, bringing with them a great and well-furnished army, they camped there and were overtaken by all the fleet that was assigned to each; there also arrived the transports for horses, which in the previous year Darius had bidden his tributary subjects to make ready. Having loaded the horses into these, and embarked the land army in the ships, they sailed to Ionia with six hundred triremes. From there they held their course not by the mainland and straight towards the Hellespont and

εἶχον τὰς νέας ἰθὺ τοῦ τε Ἑλλησπόντου καὶ
τῆς Θρηίκης, ἀλλ᾽ ἐκ Σάμου ὁρμώμενοι
παρά τε Ἰκάριον καὶ διὰ νήσων τὸν πλόον
ἐποιεῦντο, ὡς μὲν ἐμοὶ δοκέειν, δείσαντες
μάλιστα τὸν περίπλοον τοῦ Ἄθω, ὅτι τῷ
προτέρῳ ἔτεϊ ποιεύμενοι ταύτῃ τὴν κομιδὴν
μεγάλως προσέπταισαν· πρὸς δὲ καὶ ἡ
Νάξος σφέας ἠνάγκαζε πρότερον οὐκ
ἁλοῦσα.

96

1 ἐπεὶ δὲ ἐκ τοῦ Ἰκαρίου πελάγεος προσ-
φερόμενοι προσέμιξαν τῇ Νάξῳ, ἐπὶ ταύτην
γὰρ δὴ πρώτην ἐπεῖχον στρατεύεσθαι οἱ
Πέρσαι μεμνημένοι τῶν πρότερον οἱ Νάξιοι
πρὸς τὰ ὄρεα οἴχοντο φεύγοντες οὐδὲ
ὑπέμειναν, οἱ δὲ Πέρσαι ἀνδραποδισάμενοι
τοὺς κατέλαβον αὐτῶν, ἐνέπρησαν καὶ τὰ
ἱρὰ καὶ τὴν πόλιν. ταῦτα δὲ ποιήσαντες
ἐπὶ τὰς ἄλλας νήσους ἀνήγοντο.

97

1 ἐν ᾧ δὲ οὗτοι ταῦτα ἐποίευν, οἱ Δήλιοι
ἐκλιπόντες καὶ αὐτοὶ τὴν Δῆλον οἴχοντο
φεύγοντες ἐς Τῆνον. τῆς δὲ στρατιῆς κα-
ταπλεούσης ὁ Δᾶτις προπλώσας οὐκ ἔα
τὰς νέας πρὸς τὴν Δῆλον προσορμίζεσθαι,
ἀλλὰ πέρην ἐν τῇ Ῥηναίῃ· αὐτὸς δὲ
πυθόμενος ἵνα ἦσαν οἱ Δήλιοι, πέμπων
κήρυκα ἠγόρευέ σφι τάδε. 2 "ἄνδρες
ἱροί, τί φεύγοντες οἴχεσθε, οὐκ ἐπιτήδεα
καταγνόντες κατ᾽ ἐμεῦ; ἐγὼ γὰρ καὶ αὐτὸς
ἐπὶ τοσοῦτό γε φρονέω καί μοι ἐκ βασιλέος
ὧδε ἐπέσταλται, ἐν τῇ χώρῃ οἱ δύο θεοὶ
ἐγένοντο, ταύτην μηδὲν σίνεσθαι, μήτε
αὐτὴν τὴν χώρην μήτε τοὺς οἰκήτορας
αὐτῆς. νῦν ὦν καὶ ἄπιτε ἐπὶ τὰ ὑμέτερα
αὐτῶν καὶ τὴν νῆσον νέμεσθε". ταῦτα μὲν
ἐπεκηρυκεύσατο τοῖσι Δηλίοισι, μετὰ δὲ
λιβανωτοῦ τριηκόσια τάλαντα κατανήσας
ἐπὶ τοῦ βωμοῦ ἐθυμίησε.

Thrace, but setting forth from Samos they
sailed by the Icarian sea and from island
to island; this, to my thinking, was because
they feared above all the voyage around
Athos, seeing that in the previous year they
had come to great disaster by holding their
course that way; moreover, Naxos was still
unconquered and constrained them.

96

When they approached Naxos from the
Icarian sea and came to land (for it was
Naxos which the Persians intended to attack first), the Naxians, remembering what
had happened before, fled away to the
mountains instead of waiting for them.
The Persians enslaved all of them that
they caught, and burnt their temples and
their city. After doing this, they set sail for
the other islands.

97

While they did this, the Delians also left
Delos and fled away to Tenos. As his expedition was sailing landwards, Datis went
on ahead and bade his fleet anchor not off
Delos, but across the water off Rhenaea.
Learning where the Delians were, he sent
a herald to them with this proclamation:
«Holy men, why have you fled away, and
so misjudged my intent? It is my own desire,
and the king's command to me, to do no
harm to the land where the two gods were
born, neither to the land itself nor to its
inhabitants. So return now to your homes
and dwell on your island.» He made this
proclamation to the Delians, and then piled
up three hundred talents of frankincense
on the altar and burnt it.

98

1 Δᾶτις μὲν δὴ ταῦτα ποιήσας ἔπλεε ἅμα τῷ στρατῷ ἐπὶ τὴν Ἐρέτριαν πρῶτα, ἅμα ἀγόμενος καὶ Ἴωνας καὶ Αἰολέας. μετὰ δὲ τοῦτον ἐνθεῦτεν ἐξαναχθέντα Δῆλος ἐκινήθη, ὡς ἔλεγον Δήλιοι, καὶ πρῶτα καὶ ὕστατα μέχρι ἐμεῦ σεισθεῖσα. καὶ τοῦτο μέν κου τέρας ἀνθρώποισι τῶν μελλόντων ἔσεσθαι κακῶν ἔφαινε ὁ θεός. 2 ἐπὶ γὰρ Δαρείου τοῦ Ὑστάσπεος καὶ Ξέρξεω τοῦ Δαρείου καὶ Ἀρτοξέρξεω τοῦ Ξέρξεω, τριῶν τουτέων ἐπεξῆς γενεέων, ἐγένετο πλέω κακὰ τῇ Ἑλλάδι ἢ ἐπὶ εἴκοσι ἄλλας γενεὰς τὰς πρὸ Δαρείου γενομένας, τὰ μὲν ἀπὸ τῶν Περσέων αὐτῇ γενόμενα, τὰ δὲ ἀπ' αὐτῶν τῶν κορυφαίων περὶ τῆς ἀρχῆς πολεμεόντων. 3 οὕτω οὐδὲν ἦν ἀεικὲς κινηθῆναι Δῆλον τὸ πρὶν ἐοῦσαν ἀκίνητον. καὶ ἐν χρησμῷ ἦν γεγραμμένον περὶ αὐτῆς ὧδε.
κινήσω καὶ Δῆλον ἀκίνητόν περ ἐοῦσαν. δύναται δὲ κατὰ Ἑλλάδα γλῶσσαν ταῦτα τὰ οὐνόματα, Δαρεῖος ἐρξίης, Ξέρξης ἀρήιος, Ἀρτοξέρξης μέγας ἀρήιος. τούτους μὲν δὴ τοὺς βασιλέας ὧδε ἂν ὀρθῶς κατὰ γλῶσσαν τὴν σφετέρην Ἕλληνες καλέοιεν.

99

1 οἱ δὲ βάρβαροι ὡς ἀπήειραν ἐκ τῆς Δήλου, προσῖσχον πρὸς τὰς νήσους, ἐνθεῦτεν δὲ στρατιήν τε παρελάμβανον καὶ ὁμήρους τῶν νησιωτέων παῖδας ἐλάμβανον. 2 ὡς δὲ περιπλέοντες τὰς νήσους προσέσχον καὶ ἐς Κάρυστον, οὐ γὰρ δή σφι οἱ Καρύστιοι οὔτε ὁμήρους ἐδίδοσαν οὔτε ἔφασαν ἐπὶ πόλιας ἀστυγείτονας στρατεύεσθαι, λέγοντες Ἐρέτριάν τε καὶ Ἀθήνας, ἐνθαῦτα τούτους ἐπολιόρκεόν τε καὶ τὴν γῆν σφεων ἔκειρον, ἐς ὃ καὶ οἱ Καρύστιοι παρέστησαν ἐς τῶν Περσέων τὴν γνώμην.

98

After doing this, Datis sailed with his army against Eretria first, taking with him Ionians and Aeolians; and after he had put out from there, Delos was shaken by an earthquake, the first and last, as the Delians say, before my time. This portent was sent by heaven, as I suppose, to be an omen of the ills that were coming on the world. For in three generations, that is, in the time of Darius son of Hystaspes and Xerxes son of Darius and Artaxerxes son of Xerxes, more ills happened to Hellas than in twenty generations before Darius; some coming from the Persians, some from the wars for preeminence among the chief of the nations themselves. Thus it was no marvel that there should be an earthquake in Delos when there had been none before. Also there was an oracle concerning Delos, where it was written: «I will» shake Delos, though unshaken before. In the Greek language these names have the following meanings: Darius is the Doer, Xerxes the Warrior, Artaxerxes the Great Warrior. The Greeks would rightly call the kings thus in their language.

99

Launching out to sea from Delos, the foreigners put in at the islands and gathered an army from there, taking the sons of the islanders for hostages. When in their voyage about the islands they put in at Carystos, the Carystians gave them no hostages and refused to join them against neighboring cities, meaning Eretria and Athens; the Persians besieged them and laid waste their land, until the Carystians too came over to their side.

100

1 Ἐρετριέες δὲ πυνθανόμενοι τὴν στρατιὴν τὴν Περσικὴν ἐπὶ σφέας ἐπιπλέουσαν Ἀθηναίων ἐδεήθησαν σφίσι βοηθοὺς γενέσθαι. Ἀθηναῖοι δὲ οὐκ ἀπείπαντο τὴν ἐπικουρίην, ἀλλὰ τοὺς τετρακισχιλίους τοὺς κληρουχέοντας τῶν ἱπποβοτέων Χαλκιδέων τὴν χώρην, τούτους σφι διδοῦσι τιμωρούς. τῶν δὲ Ἐρετριέων ἦν ἄρα οὐδὲν ὑγιὲς βούλευμα, οἳ μετεπέμποντο μὲν Ἀθηναίους, ἐφρόνεον δὲ διφασίας ἰδέας. 2 οἱ μὲν γὰρ αὐτῶν ἐβουλεύοντο ἐκλιπεῖν τὴν πόλιν ἐς τὰ ἄκρα τῆς Εὐβοίης, ἄλλοι δὲ αὐτῶν ἴδια κέρδεα προσδεκόμενοι παρὰ τοῦ Πέρσεω οἴσεσθαι προδοσίην ἐσκευάζοντο. 3 μαθὼν δὲ τούτων ἑκάτερα ὡς εἶχε Αἰσχίνης ὁ Νόθωνος, ἐὼν τῶν Ἐρετριέων τὰ πρῶτα, φράξει τοῖσι ἥκουσι Ἀθηναίων πάντα τὰ παρεόντα σφι πρήγματα, προσεδέετό τε ἀπαλλάσσεσθαι σφέας ἐς τὴν σφετέρην, ἵνα μὴ προσαπόλωνται. οἱ δὲ Ἀθηναῖοι ταῦτα Αἰσχίνῃ συμβουλεύσαντι πείθονται.

101

1 καὶ οὗτοι μὲν διαβάντες ἐς Ὠρωπὸν ἔσωζον σφέας αὐτούς· οἱ δὲ Πέρσαι πλέοντες κατέσχον τὰς νέας τῆς Ἐρετρικῆς χώρης κατὰ Τέμενος καὶ Χοιρέας καὶ Αἰγίλεα, κατασχόντες δὲ ταῦτα τὰ χωρία αὐτίκα ἵππους τε ἐξεβάλλοντο καὶ παρεσκευάζοντο ὡς προσοισόμενοι τοῖσι ἐχθροῖσι. 2 οἱ δὲ Ἐρετριέες ἐπεξελθεῖν μὲν καὶ μαχέσασθαι οὐκ ἐποιεῦντο βουλήν, εἴ κως δὲ διαφυλάξαιεν τὰ τείχεα, τούτου σφι πέρι ἔμελε, ἐπείτε ἐνίκα μὴ ἐκλιπεῖν τὴν πόλιν. προσβολῆς δὲ γινομένης καρτερῆς πρὸς τὸ τεῖχος ἔπιπτον ἐπὶ ἓξ ἡμέρας πολλοὶ μὲν ἀμφοτέρων· τῇ δὲ ἑβδόμῃ Εὔφορβός τε ὁ Ἀλκιμάχου καὶ Φίλαγρος ὁ Κυνέου ἄνδρες τῶν ἀστῶν δόκιμοι προδιδοῦσι τοῖσι Πέρσῃσι. 3 οἱ δὲ ἐσελθόντες ἐς τὴν πόλιν τοῦτο μὲν τὰ ἱρὰ

100

When the Eretrians learned that the Persian expedition was sailing to attack them, they asked for help from the Athenians. The Athenians did not refuse the aid, but gave them for defenders the four thousand tenant farmers who held the land of the Chalcidian horse-breeders. But it seems that all the plans of the Eretrians were unsound; they sent to the Athenians for aid, but their counsels were divided. Some of them planned to leave the city and make for the heights of Euboea; others plotted treason in hope of winning advantages from the Persians. When Aeschines son of Nothon, a leading man in Eretria, learned of both designs, he told the Athenians who had come how matters stood, and asked them to depart to their own country so they would not perish like the rest. The Athenians followed Aeschines' advice.

101

So they saved themselves by crossing over to Oropus; the Persians sailed holding their course for Temenos and Choereae and Aegilea, all in Eretrian territory. Landing at these places, they immediately unloaded their horses and made preparation to attack their enemies. The Eretrians had no intention of coming out and fighting; all their care was to guard their walls if they could, since it was the prevailing counsel not to leave the city. The walls were strongly attacked, and for six days many fell on both sides; but on the seventh two Eretrians of repute, Euphorbus son of Alcimachus and Philagrus son of Cineas, betrayed the city to the Persians. They entered the city and plundered and burnt the temples, in revenge for the temples

συλήσαντες ἐνέπρησαν, ἀποτινύμενοι τῶν ἐν Σάρδισι κατακαυθέντων ἱρῶν, τοῦτο δὲ τοὺς ἀνθρώπους ἠνδραποδίσαντο κατὰ τὰς Δαρείου ἐντολάς.

102

1 χειρωσάμενοι δὲ τὴν Ἐρέτριαν καὶ ἐπισχόντες ὀλίγας ἡμέρας ἔπλεον ἐς γῆν τὴν Ἀττικήν, κατέργοντές τε πολλὸν καὶ δοκέοντες ταὐτὰ τοὺς Ἀθηναίους ποιήσειν τά καὶ τοὺς Ἐρετριέας ἐποίησαν. καὶ ἦν γὰρ ὁ Μαραθὼν ἐπιτηδεότατον χωρίον τῆς Ἀττικῆς ἐνιππεῦσαι καὶ ἀγχοτάτω τῆς Ἐρετρίης, ἐς τοῦτό σφι κατηγέετο Ἱππίης ὁ Πεισιστράτου.

103

1 Ἀθηναῖοι δὲ ὡς ἐπύθοντο ταῦτα, ἐβοήθεον καὶ αὐτοὶ ἐς τὸν Μαραθῶνα. ἦγον δὲ σφέας στρατηγοὶ δέκα, τῶν ὁ δέκατος ἦν Μιλτιάδης· τοῦ τὸν πατέρα Κίμωνα τὸν Στησαγόρεω κατέλαβε φυγεῖν ἐξ Ἀθηνέων Πεισίστρατον τὸν Ἱπποκράτεος. 2 καὶ αὐτῷ φεύγοντι Ὀλυμπιάδα ἀνελέσθαι τεθρίππῳ συνέβη, καὶ ταύτην μὲν τὴν νίκην ἀνελόμενόν μιν τὠυτὸ ἐξενείκασθαι τῷ ὁμομητρίῳ ἀδελφεῷ Μιλτιάδῃ· μετὰ δὲ τῇ ὑστέρῃ Ὀλυμπιάδι τῇσι αὐτῇσι ἵπποισι νικῶν παραδιδοῖ Πεισιστράτῳ ἀνακηρυχθῆναι, καὶ τὴν νίκην παρεὶς τούτῳ κατῆλθε ἐπὶ τὰ ἑωυτοῦ ὑπόσπονδος. 3 καί μιν ἀνελόμενον τῇσι αὐτῇσι ἵπποισι ἄλλην Ὀλυμπιάδα κατέλαβε ἀποθανεῖν ὑπὸ τῶν Πεισιστράτου παίδων, οὐκέτι περιεόντος αὐτοῦ Πεισιστράτου· κτείνουσι δὲ οὗτοί μιν κατὰ τὸ πρυτανήιον νυκτὸς ὑπείσαντες ἄνδρας. τέθαπται δὲ Κίμων πρὸ τοῦ ἄστεος, πέρην τῆς διὰ Κοίλης καλεομένης ὁδοῦ· καταντίον δ᾽ αὐτοῦ αἱ ἵπποι τεθάφαται αὗται αἱ τρεῖς Ὀλυμπιάδας ἀνελόμεναι. 4 ἐποίησαν δὲ καὶ ἄλλαι ἵπποι ἤδη τὠυτὸ τοῦτο Εὐαγόρεω Λάκωνος, πλέω δὲ τουτέων οὐδαμαί. ὁ μὲν

that were burnt at Sardis; moreover, they enslaved the townspeople, according to Darius' command.

102

After subduing Eretria, the Persians waited a few days and then sailed away to the land of Attica, pressing ahead in expectation of doing to the Athenians exactly what they had done to the Eretrians. Marathon 1 was the place in Attica most suitable for riding horses and closest to Eretria, so Hippias son of Pisistratus led them there.

103

When the Athenians learned this, they too marched out to Marathon, with ten generals leading them. The tenth was Miltiades, and it had befallen his father Cimon son of Stesagoras to be banished from Athens by Pisistratus son of Hippocrates. While in exile he happened to take the Olympic prize in the four-horse chariot, and by taking this victory he won the same prize as his half-brother Miltiades. At the next Olympic games he won with the same horses but permitted Pisistratus to be proclaimed victor, and by resigning the victory to him he came back from exile to his own property under truce. After taking yet another Olympic prize with the same horses, he happened to be murdered by Pisistratus' sons, since Pisistratus was no longer living. They murdered him by placing men in ambush at night near the town-hall. Cimon was buried in front of the city, across the road called «Through the Hollow», and buried opposite him are the mares who won the three Olympic prizes. The mares of Evagoras the Laconian did the same as these, but none others. Ste-

δὴ πρεσβύτερος τῶν παίδων τῷ Κίμωνι
Στησαγόρης ἦν τηνικαῦτα παρὰ τῷ πάτρῳ
Μιλτιάδῃ τρεφόμενος ἐν τῇ Χερσονήσῳ,
ὁ δὲ νεώτερος παρ᾽ αὐτῷ Κίμωνι ἐν
Ἀθήνῃσι, οὔνομα ἔχων ἀπὸ τοῦ οἰκιστέω
τῆς Χερσονήσου Μιλτιάδεω Μιλτιάδης.

104

1 οὗτος δὴ ὢν τότε ὁ Μιλτιάδης ἥκων ἐκ
τῆς Χερσονήσου καὶ ἐκπεφευγὼς διπλόον
θάνατον ἐστρατήγεε Ἀθηναίων. ἅμα μὲν
γὰρ οἱ Φοίνικες αὐτὸν οἱ ἐπιδιώξαντες
μέχρι Ἴμβρου περὶ πολλοῦ ἐποιεῦντο λαβεῖν
τε καὶ ἀναγαγεῖν παρὰ βασιλέα· 2 ἅμα δὲ
ἐκφυγόντα τε τούτους καὶ ἀπικόμενον ἐς
τὴν ἑωυτοῦ δοκέοντά τε εἶναι ἐν σωτηρίῃ
ἤδη, τὸ ἐνθεῦτέν μιν οἱ ἐχθροὶ ὑποδεξάμενοι
ὑπὸ δικαστήριον αὐτὸν ἀγαγόντες ἐδίωξαν
τυραννίδος τῆς ἐν Χερσονήσῳ. ἀποφυγὼν
δὲ καὶ τούτους στρατηγὸς οὕτω Ἀθηναίων
ἀπεδέχθη, αἱρεθεὶς ὑπὸ τοῦ δήμου.

105

1 καὶ πρῶτα μὲν ἐόντες ἔτι ἐν τῷ ἄστεϊ
οἱ στρατηγοὶ ἀποπέμπουσι ἐς Σπάρτην
κήρυκα Φειδιππίδην Ἀθηναῖον μὲν ἄνδρα,
ἄλλως δὲ ἡμεροδρόμην τε καὶ τοῦτο
μελετῶντα· τῷ δή, ὡς αὐτός τε ἔλεγε
Φειδιππίδης καὶ Ἀθηναίοισι ἀπήγγελλε,
περὶ τὸ Παρθένιον ὄρος τὸ ὑπὲρ Τεγέης ὁ
Πὰν περιπίπτει· 2 βώσαντα δὲ τὸ οὔνομα
τοῦ Φειδιππίδεω τὸν Πᾶνα Ἀθηναίοισι
κελεῦσαι ἀπαγγεῖλαι, δι᾽ ὅ τι ἑωυτοῦ
οὐδεμίαν ἐπιμελείην ποιεῦνται ἐόντος
εὐνόου Ἀθηναίοισι καὶ πολλαχῇ γενομένου
σφι ἤδη χρησίμου, τὰ δ᾽ ἔτι καὶ ἐσομένου.
3 καὶ ταῦτα μὲν Ἀθηναῖοι, καταστάντων
σφι εὖ ἤδη τῶν πρηγμάτων, πιστεύσαντες
εἶναι ἀληθέα ἱδρύσαντο ὑπὸ τῇ ἀκροπόλι
Πανὸς ἱρόν, καὶ αὐτὸν ἀπὸ ταύτης τῆς
ἀγγελίης θυσίῃσι ἐπετείοισι καὶ λαμπάδι
ἱλάσκονται.

sagoras, the elder of Cimon's sons, was then being brought up with his uncle Miltiades in the Chersonese. The younger was with Cimon at Athens, and he took the name Miltiades from Miltiades the founder of the Chersonese.

104

It was this Miltiades who was now the Athenian general, after coming from the Chersonese and escaping a two-fold death. The Phoenicians pursued him as far as Imbros, considering it of great importance to catch him and bring him to the king. He escaped from them, but when he reached his own country and thought he was safe, then his enemies met him. They brought him to court and prosecuted him for tyranny in the Chersonese, but he was acquitted and appointed Athenian general, chosen by the people.

105

While still in the city, the generals first sent to Sparta the herald Philippides, an Athenian and a long-distance runner who made that his calling. As Philippides himself said when he brought the message to the Athenians, when he was in the Parthenian mountain above Tegea he encountered Pan. Pan called out Philippides' name and bade him ask the Athenians why they paid him no attention, though he was of goodwill to the Athenians, had often been of service to them, and would be in the future. The Athenians believed that these things were true, and when they became prosperous they established a sacred precinct of Pan beneath the Acropolis. Ever since that message they propitiate him with annual sacrifices and a torch-race.

106

1 τότε δὲ πεμφθεὶς ὑπὸ τῶν στρατηγῶν ὁ Φειδιππίδης οὗτος, ὅτε πέρ οἱ ἔφη καὶ τὸν Πᾶνα φανῆναι, δευτεραῖος ἐκ τοῦ Ἀθηναίων ἄστεος ἦν ἐν Σπάρτῃ, ἀπικόμενος δὲ ἐπὶ τοὺς ἄρχοντας ἔλεγε 2 "ὦ Λακεδαιμόνιοι, Ἀθηναῖοι ὑμέων δέονται σφίσι βοηθῆσαι καὶ μὴ περιιδεῖν πόλιν ἀρχαιοτάτην ἐν τοῖσιῬΈλλησι δουλοσύνῃ περιπεσοῦσαν πρὸς ἀνδρῶν βαρβάρων· καὶ γὰρ νῦν Ἐρέτριά τε ἠνδραπόδισται καὶ πόλι λογίμῳ ἡῬΈλλὰς γέγονε ἀσθενεστέρη". 3 ὃ μὲν δὴ σφι τὰ ἐντεταλμένα ἀπήγγελλε, τοῖσι δὲ ἕαδε μὲν βοηθέειν Ἀθηναίοισι, ἀδύνατα δέ σφι ἦν τὸ παραυτίκα ποιέειν ταῦτα, οὐ βουλομένοισι λύειν τὸν νόμον· ἦν γὰρ ἱσταμένου τοῦ μηνὸς εἰνάτη, εἰνάτῃ δὲ οὐκ ἐξελεύσεσθαι ἔφασαν μὴ οὐ πλήρεος ἐόντος τοῦ κύκλου.

107

1 οὗτοι μέν νυν τὴν πανσέληνον ἔμενον. τοῖσι δὲ βαρβάροισι κατηγέετο Ἱππίης ὁ Πεισιστράτου ἐς τὸν Μαραθῶνα, τῆς παροιχομένης νυκτὸς ὄψιν ἰδὼν τοιήνδε· ἐδόκεε ὁ Ἱππίης τῇ μητρὶ τῇ ἑωυτοῦ συνευνηθῆναι. 2 συνεβάλετο ὦν ἐκ τοῦ ὀνείρου κατελθὼν ἐς τὰς Ἀθήνας καὶ ἀνασωσάμενος τὴν ἀρχὴν τελευτήσειν ἐν τῇ ἑωυτοῦ γηραιός. ἐκ μὲν δὴ τῆς ὄψιος συνεβάλετο ταῦτα, τότε δὲ κατηγεόμενος τοῦτο μὲν τὰ ἀνδράποδα τὰ ἐξῬΈρετρίης ἀπέβησε ἐς τὴν νῆσον τὴν Στυρέων, καλεομένην δὲ Αἰγλείην, τοῦτο δὲ καταγομένας ἐς τὸν Μαραθῶνα τὰς νέας ὅρμιζε οὗτος, ἐκβάντας τε ἐς γῆν τοὺς βαρβάρους διέτασσε. 3 καὶ οἱ ταῦτα διέποντι ἐπῆλθε πταρεῖν τε καὶ βῆξαι μεζόνως ἢ ὡς ἐώθεε· οἷα δέ οἱ πρεσβυτέρῳ ἐόντι τῶν ὀδόντων οἱ πλεῦνες ἐσείοντο· τούτων ὦν ἕνα τῶν ὀδόντων ἐκβάλλει ὑπὸ βίης βήξας· ἐκπεσόντος δὲ ἐς τὴν ψάμμον

106

This Philippides was in Sparta on the day after leaving the city of Athens, that time when he was sent by the generals and said that Pan had appeared to him. He came to the magistrates and said, «Lacedae-monians, the Athenians ask you to come to their aid and not allow the most ancient city among the Hellenes to fall into slavery at the hands of the foreigners. Even now Eretria has been enslaved, and Hellas has become weaker by an important city.» He told them what he had been ordered to say, and they resolved to send help to the Athenians, but they could not do this immediately, for they were unwilling to break the law. It was the ninth day of the rising month, and they said that on the ninth they could not go out to war until the moon's circle was full.

107

So they waited for the full moon, while the foreigners were guided to Marathon by Hippias son of Pisistratus. The previous night Hippias had a dream in which he slept with his mother. He supposed from the dream that he would return from exile to Athens, recover his rule, and end his days an old man in his own country. Thus he reckoned from the dream. Then as guide he unloaded the slaves from Eretria onto the island of the Styrians called Aegilia, and brought to anchor the ships that had put ashore at Marathon, then marshalled the foreigners who had disembarked onto land. As he was tending to this, he happened to sneeze and cough more violently than usual. Since he was an elderly man, most of his teeth were loose, and he lost one of them by the force of his cough. It fell into the sand and he expended much effort in looking for it, but the tooth could

αὐτοῦ ἐποιέετο σπουδὴν πολλὴν ἐξευρεῖν. 4 ὡς δὲ οὐκ ἐφαίνετό οἱ ὁ ὀδών, ἀναστενάξας εἶπε πρὸς τοὺς παραστάτας "ἡ γῆ ἥδε οὐκ ἡμετέρη ἐστί, οὐδέ μιν δυνησόμεθα ὑποχειρίην ποιήσασθαι· ὁκόσον δέ τι μοι μέρος μετῆν, ὁ ὀδὼν μετέχει".

not be found. He groaned aloud and said to those standing by him: «This land is not ours and we will not be able to subdue it. My tooth holds whatever share of it was mine.»

108

1 Ἱππίης μὲν δὴ ταύτῃ τὴν ὄψιν συνεβάλετο ἐξεληλυθέναι. Ἀθηναίοισι δὲ τεταγμένοισι ἐν τεμένεϊ Ἡρακλέος ἐπῆλθον βοηθέοντες Πλαταιέες πανδημεί. καὶ γὰρ καὶ ἐδεδώκεσαν σφέας αὐτοὺς τοῖσι Ἀθηναίοισι οἱ Πλαταιέες, καὶ πόνους ὑπὲρ αὐτῶν οἱ Ἀθηναῖοι συχνοὺς ἤδη ἀναραιρέατο· ἔδοσαν δὲ ὧδε. 2 πιεζεύμενοι ὑπὸ Θηβαίων οἱ Πλαταιέες ἐδίδοσαν πρῶτα παρατυχοῦσι Κλεομένεΐ τε τῷ Ἀναξανδρίδεω καὶ Λακεδαιμονίοισι σφέας αὐτούς. οἳ δὲ οὐ δεκόμενοι ἔλεγόν σφι τάδε. "ἡμεῖς μὲν ἑκαστέρω τε οἰκέομεν, καὶ ὑμῖν τοιήδε τις γίνοιτ᾽ ἂν ἐπικουρίη ψυχρή· φθαίητε γὰρ ἂν πολλάκις ἐξανδραποδισθέντες ἤ τινα πυθέσθαι ἡμέων. 3 συμβουλεύομεν δὲ ὑμῖν δοῦναι ὑμέας αὐτοὺς Ἀθηναίοισι, πλησιοχώροισί τε ἀνδράσι καὶ τιμωρέειν ἐοῦσι οὐ κακοῖσι". ταῦτα συνεβούλευον οἱ Λακεδαιμόνιοι οὐ κατὰ τὴν εὐνοίην οὕτω τῶν Πλαταιέων ὡς βουλόμενοι τοὺς Ἀθηναίους ἔχειν πόνους συνεστεῶτας Βοιωτοῖσι. 4 Λακεδαιμόνιοι μέν νυν Πλαταιεῦσι ταῦτα συνεβούλευον, οἳ δὲ οὐκ ἠπίστησαν, ἀλλ᾽ Ἀθηναίων ἱρὰ ποιεύντων τοῖσι δυώδεκα θεοῖσι ἱκέται ἱζόμενοι ἐπὶ τὸν βωμὸν ἐδίδοσαν σφέας αὐτούς. Θηβαῖοι δὲ πυθόμενοι ταῦτα ἐστρατεύοντο ἐπὶ τοὺς Πλαταιέας, Ἀθηναῖοι δέ σφι ἐβοήθεον. 5 μελλόντων δὲ συνάπτειν μάχην Κορίνθιοι οὐ περιεῖδον, παρατυχόντες δὲ καὶ καταλλάξαντες ἐπιτρεψάντων ἀμφοτέρων οὔρισαν τὴν χώρην ἐπὶ τοῖσιδε, ἐὰν Θηβαίους Βοιωτῶν τοὺς μὴ βουλομένους ἐς Βοιωτοὺς τελέειν. Κορίνθιοι μὲν δὴ ταῦτα

108

Hippias supposed that the dream had in this way come true. As the Athenians were marshalled in the precinct of Hercules, the Plataeans came to help them in full force. The Plataeans had put themselves under the protection of the Athenians, and the Athenians had undergone many labors on their behalf. This is how they did it: when the Plataeans were pressed by the Thebans, they first tried to put themselves under the protection of Cleomenes son of Anaxandrides and the Lacedaemonians, who happened to be there. But they did not accept them, saying, «We live too far away, and our help would be cold comfort to you. You could be enslaved many times over before any of us heard about it. We advise you to put yourselves under the protection of the Athenians, since they are your neighbors and not bad men at giving help.» The Lacedaemonians gave this advice not so much out of goodwill toward the Plataeans as wishing to cause trouble for the Athenians with the Boeotians. So the Lacedaemonians gave this advice to the Plataeans, who did not disobey it. When the Athenians were making sacrifices to the twelve gods, they sat at the altar as suppliants and put themselves under protection. When the Thebans heard this, they marched against the Plataeans, but the Athenians came to their aid. As they were about to join battle, the Corinthians, who happened to be there, prevented them and brought about a reconciliation. Since

γνόντες ἀπαλλάσσοντο, Ἀθηναίοισι δὲ ἀπιοῦσι ἐπεθήκαντο Βοιωτοί, ἐπιθέμενοι δὲ ἐσσώθησαν τῇ μάχῃ. 6 ὑπερβάντες δὲ οἱ Ἀθηναῖοι τοὺς οἱ Κορίνθιοι ἔθηκαν Πλαταιεῦσι εἶναι οὔρους, τούτους ὑπερβάντες τὸν Ἀσωπὸν αὐτὸν ἐποιήσαντο οὖρον Θηβαίοισι πρὸς Πλαταιέας εἶναι καὶ Ὑσιάς. ἔδοσαν μὲν δὴ οἱ Πλαταιέες σφέας αὐτοὺς Ἀθηναίοισι τρόπῳ τῷ εἰρημένῳ, ἧκον δὲ τότε ἐς Μαραθῶνα βοηθέοντες.

both sides desired them to arbitrate, they fixed the boundaries of the country on condition that the Thebans leave alone those Boeotians who were unwilling to be enrolled as Boeotian. After rendering this decision, the Corinthians departed. The Boeotians attacked the Athenians as they were leaving but were defeated in battle. The Athenians went beyond the boundaries the Corinthians had made for the Plataeans, fixing the Asopus river as the boundary for the Thebans in the direction of Plataea and Hysiae. So the Plataeans had put themselves under the protection of the Athenians in the aforesaid manner, and now came to help at Marathon.

109

1 τοῖσι δὲ Ἀθηναίων στρατηγοῖσι ἐγίνοντο δίχα αἱ γνῶμαι, τῶν μὲν οὐκ ἐώντων συμβαλεῖν (ὀλίγους γὰρ εἶναι στρατιῇ τῇ Μήδων συμβάλλειν) τῶν δὲ καὶ Μιλτιάδεω κελευόντων. 2 ὡς δὲ δίχα τε ἐγίνοντο καὶ ἐνίκα ἡ χείρων τῶν γνωμέων, ἐνθαῦτα, ἦν γὰρ ἑνδέκατος ψηφιδοφόρος ὁ τῷ κυάμῳ λαχὼν Ἀθηναίων πολεμαρχέειν (τὸ Παλαιὸν γὰρ Ἀθηναῖοι ὁμόψηφον τὸν πολέμαρχον ἐποιεῦντο τοῖσι στρατηγοῖσι), ἦν δὲ τότε πολέμαρχος Καλλίμαχος Ἀφιδναῖος· πρὸς τοῦτον ἐλθὼν Μιλτιάδης ἔλεγε τάδε. 3 "ἐν σοὶ νῦν Καλλίμαχε ἐστὶ ἢ καταδουλῶσαι Ἀθήνας ἢ ἐλευθέρας ποιήσαντα μνημόσυνα λιπέσθαι ἐς τὸν ἅπαντα ἀνθρώπων βίον οἷα οὐδὲ Ἁρμόδιός τε καὶ Ἀριστογείτων λείπουσι. νῦν γὰρ δὴ ἐξ οὗ ἐγένοντο Ἀθηναῖοι ἐς κίνδυνον ἥκουσι μέγιστον, καὶ ἢν μέν γε ὑποκύψωσι τοῖσι Μήδοισι, δέδοκται τὰ πείσονται παραδεδομένοι Ἱππίῃ, ἢν δὲ περιγένηται αὕτη ἡ πόλις, οἵη τε ἐστὶ πρώτη τῶν Ἑλληνίδων πολίων γενέσθαι. 4 κῶς ὦν δὴ ταῦτα οἷά τε ἐστὶ γενέσθαι, καὶ κῶς ἐς σέ τοι τούτων ἀνήκει τῶν πρηγμάτων τὸ

109

The Athenian generals were of divided opinion, some advocating not fighting because they were too few to attack the army of the Medes; others, including Miltiades, advocating fighting. Thus they were at odds, and the inferior plan prevailed. An eleventh man had a vote, chosen by lot to be polemarch of Athens, and by ancient custom the Athenians had made his vote of equal weight with the generals. Callimachus of Aphidnae was polemarch at this time. Miltiades approached him and said, «Callimachus, it is now in your hands to enslave Athens or make her free, and thereby leave behind for all posterity a memorial such as not even Harmodius and Aristogeiton left. Now the Athenians have come to their greatest danger since they first came into being, and, if we surrender, it is clear what we will suffer when handed over to Hippias. But if the city prevails, it will take first place among Hellenic cities. I will tell you how this can happen, and how the deciding voice on these matters has devolved upon you. The ten gener-

κῦρος ἔχειν, νῦν ἔρχομαι φράσων. ἡμέων τῶν στρατηγῶν ἐόντων δέκα δίχα γίνονται αἱ γνῶμαι, τῶν μὲν κελευόντων τῶν δὲ οὒ συμβάλλειν. 5 ἢν μέν νυν μὴ συμβάλωμεν, ἔλπομαι τινὰ στάσιν μεγάλην διασείσειν ἐμπεσοῦσαν τὰ Ἀθηναίων φρονήματα ὥστε μηδίσαι· ἢν δὲ συμβάλωμεν πρίν τι καὶ σαθρὸν Ἀθηναίων μετεξετέροισι ἐγγενέσθαι, θεῶν τὰ ἴσα νεμόντων οἷοί τε εἰμὲν περιγενέσθαι τῇ συμβολῇ. 6 ταῦτα ὦν πάντα ἐς σὲ νῦν τείνει καὶ ἐκ σέο ἤρτηται. ἢν γὰρ σὺ γνώμῃ τῇ ἐμῇ προσθῇ, ἔστι τοι πατρίς τε ἐλευθέρη καὶ πόλις πρώτη τῶν ἐν τῇ Ἑλλάδι· ἢν δὲ τὴν τῶν ἀποσπευδόντων τὴν συμβολὴν ἕλῃ, ὑπάρξει τοι τῶν ἐγὼ κατέλεξα ἀγαθῶν τὰ ἐναντία".

als are of divided opinion, some urging to attack, others urging not to. If we do not attack now, I expect that great strife will fall upon and shake the spirit of the Athenians, leading them to medize. But if we attack now, before anything unsound corrupts the Athenians, we can win the battle, if the gods are fair.
All this concerns and depends on you in this way: if you vote with me, your country will be free and your city the first in Hellas. But if you side with those eager to avoid battle, you will have the opposite to all the good things I enumerated.»

110

1 ταῦτα λέγων ὁ Μιλτιάδης προσκτᾶται τὸν Καλλίμαχον· προσγενομένης δὲ τοῦ πολεμάρχου τῆς γνώμης ἐκεκύρωτο συμβάλλειν. μετὰ δὲ οἱ στρατηγοὶ τῶν ἡ γνώμη ἔφερε συμβάλλειν, ὡς ἑκάστου αὐτῶν ἐγίνετο πρυτανηίη τῆς ἡμέρης, Μιλτιάδῃ παρεδίδοσαν· ὁ δὲ δεκόμενος οὔτι κω συμβολὴν ἐποιέετο, πρίν γε δὴ αὐτοῦ πρυτανηίη ἐγένετο.

110

By saying this Miltiades won over Callimachus. The polemarch's vote was counted in, and the decision to attack was resolved upon. Thereafter the generals who had voted to fight turned the presidency over to Miltiades as each one's day came in turn. He accepted the office but did not make an attack until it was his own day to preside.

111

1 ὡς δὲ ἐς ἐκεῖνον περιῆλθε, ἐνθαῦτα δὴ ἐτάσσοντο ὧδε οἱ Ἀθηναῖοι ὡς συμβαλέοντες· τοῦ μὲν δεξιοῦ κέρεος ἡγέετο ὁ πολέμαρχος Καλλίμαχος· ὁ γὰρ νόμος τότε εἶχε οὕτω τοῖσι Ἀθηναίοισι, τὸν πολέμαρχον ἔχειν κέρας τὸ δεξιόν· ἡγεομένου δὲ τούτου ἐξεδέκοντο ὡς ἀριθμέοντο αἱ φυλαὶ ἐχόμεναι ἀλλήλεων, τελευταῖοι δὲ ἐτάσσοντο ἔχοντες τὸ εὐώνυμον κέρας Πλαταιέες. 2 ἀπὸ ταύτης [γὰρ] σφι τῆς μάχης, Ἀθηναίων θυσίας ἀναγόντων ἐς τὰς πανηγύριας τὰς ἐν τῇσι πεντετηρίσι γινομένας, κατεύχεται ὁ κῆρυξ ὁ Ἀθηναῖος ἅμα τε

111

When the presidency came round to him, he arrayed the Athenians for battle, with the polemarch Callimachus commanding the right wing, since it was then the Athenian custom for the polemarch to hold the right wing. He led, and the other tribes were numbered out in succession next to each other. The Plataeans were marshalled last, holding the left wing. Ever since that battle, when the Athenians are conducting sacrifices at the festivals every fourth year, the Athenian herald prays for good things for the Athenians and Plataeans together. As the Athenians were marshalled

Ἀθηναίοισι λέγων γίνεσθαι τὰ ἀγαθὰ καὶ Πλαταιεῦσι. 3 τότε δὲ τασσομένων τῶν Ἀθηναίων ἐν τῷ Μαραθῶνι ἐγίνετο τοιόνδε τι· τὸ στρατόπεδον ἐξισούμενον τῷ Μηδικῷ στρατοπέδῳ, τὸ μὲν αὐτοῦ μέσον ἐγίνετο ἐπὶ τάξιας ὀλίγας, καὶ ταύτῃ ἦν ἀσθενέστατον τὸ στρατόπεδον, τὸ δὲ κέρας ἑκάτερον ἔρρωτο πλήθεϊ.

112

1 ὡς δέ σφι διετέτακτο καὶ τὰ σφάγια ἐγίνετο καλά, ἐνθαῦτα ὡς ἀπείθησαν οἱ Ἀθηναῖοι δρόμῳ ἵεντο ἐς τοὺς βαρβάρους. ἦσαν δὲ στάδιοι οὐκ ἐλάσσονες τὸ μεταίχμιον αὐτῶν ἢ ὀκτώ. 2 οἱ δὲ Πέρσαι ὁρέοντες δρόμῳ ἐπιόντας παρεσκευάζοντο ὡς δεξόμενοι, μανίην τε τοῖσι Ἀθηναίοισι ἐπέφερον καὶ πάγχυ ὀλεθρίην, ὁρέοντες αὐτοὺς ὀλίγους καὶ τούτους δρόμῳ ἐπειγομένους, οὔτε ἵππου ὑπαρχούσης σφι οὔτε τοξευμάτων. 3 ταῦτα μέν νυν οἱ βάρβαροι κατείκαζον· Ἀθηναῖοι δὲ ἐπείτε ἀθρόοι προσέμιξαν τοῖσι βαρβάροισι, ἐμάχοντο ἀξίως λόγου. πρῶτοι μὲν γὰρ Ἑλλήνων πάντων τῶν ἡμεῖς ἴδμεν δρόμῳ ἐς πολεμίους ἐχρήσαντο, πρῶτοι δὲ ἀνέσχοντο ἐσθῆτά τε Μηδικὴν ὁρέοντες καὶ τοὺς ἄνδρας ταύτην ἐσθημένους· τέως δὲ ἦν τοῖσι Ἕλλησι καὶ τὸ οὔνομα τὸ Μήδων φόβος ἀκοῦσαι.

113

1 μαχομένων δὲ ἐν τῷ Μαραθῶνι χρόνος ἐγίνετο πολλός, καὶ τὸ μὲν μέσον τοῦ στρατοπέδου ἐνίκων οἱ βάρβαροι, τῇ Πέρσαι τε αὐτοὶ καὶ Σάκαι ἐτετάχατο· κατὰ τοῦτο μὲν δὴ ἐνίκων οἱ βάρβαροι καὶ ῥήξαντες ἐδίωκον ἐς τὴν μεσόγαιαν, τὸ δὲ κέρας ἑκάτερον ἐνίκων Ἀθηναῖοί τε καὶ Πλαταιέες· 2 νικῶντες δὲ τὸ μὲν τετραμμένον τῶν βαρβάρων φεύγειν ἔων, τοῖσι δὲ τὸ μέσον ῥήξασι αὐτῶν συναγαγόντες τὰ κέρεα ἀμφότερα

at Marathon, it happened that their line of battle was as long as the line of the Medes. The center, where the line was weakest, was only a few ranks deep, but each wing was strong in numbers.

112

When they had been set in order and the sacrifices were favorable, the Athenians were sent forth and charged the foreigners at a run. The space between the armies was no less than eight stadia. The Persians saw them running to attack and prepared to receive them, thinking the Athenians absolutely crazy, since they saw how few of them there were and that they ran up so fast without either cavalry or archers. So the foreigners imagined, but when the Athenians all together fell upon the foreigners they fought in a way worthy of record. These are the first Hellenes whom we know of to use running against the enemy. They are also the first to endure looking at Median dress and men wearing it, for up until then just hearing the name of the Medes caused the Hellenes to panic.

113

They fought a long time at Marathon. In the center of the line the foreigners prevailed, where the Persians and Sacae were arrayed. The foreigners prevailed there and broke through in pursuit inland, but on each wing the Athenians and Plataeans prevailed. In victory they let the routed foreigners flee, and brought the wings together to fight those who had broken through the center. The Athenians prevailed, then followed the fleeing Persians

ἐμάχοντο, καὶ ἐνίκων Ἀθηναῖοι. φεύγουσι δὲ τοῖσι Πέρσῃσι εἵποντο κόπτοντες, ἐς ὃ ἐς τὴν θάλασσαν ἀπικόμενοι πῦρ τε αἴτεον καὶ ἐπελαμβάνοντο τῶν νεῶν.

and struck them down. When they reached the sea they demanded fire and laid hold of the Persian ships.

114

1 καὶ τοῦτο μὲν ἐν τούτῳ τῷ πόνῳ ὁ πολέμαρχος διαφθείρεται, ἀνὴρ γενόμενος ἀγαθός, ἀπὸ δ᾽ ἔθανε τῶν στρατηγῶν Στησίλεως ὁ Θρασύλεω· τοῦτο δὲ Κυνέγειρος ὁ Εὐφορίωνος ἐνθαῦτα ἐπιλαμβανόμενος τῶν ἀφλάστων νεός, τὴν χεῖρα ἀποκοπεὶς πελέκεϊ πίπτει, τοῦτο δὲ ἄλλοι Ἀθηναίων πολλοί τε καὶ ὀνομαστοί.

114

In this labor Callimachus the polemarch was slain, a brave man, and of the generals Stesilaus son of Thrasylaus died. Cynegirus son of Euphorion fell there, his hand cut off with an ax as he grabbed a ship's figurehead. Many other famous Athenians also fell there.

115

1 ἑπτὰ μὲν δὴ τῶν νεῶν ἐπεκράτησαν τρόπῳ τοιῷδε Ἀθηναῖοι· τῇσι δὲ λοιπῇσι οἱ βάρβαροι ἐξανακρουσάμενοι, καὶ ἀναλαβόντες ἐκ τῆς νήσου ἐν τῇ ἔλιπον τὰ ἐξ Ἐρετρίης ἀνδράποδα, περιέπλεον Σούνιον βουλόμενοι φθῆναι τοὺς Ἀθηναίους ἀπικόμενοι ἐς τὸ ἄστυ. αἰτίην δὲ ἔσχε ἐν Ἀθηναίοισι ἐξ Ἀλκμεωνιδέων μηχανῆς αὐτοὺς ταῦτα ἐπινοηθῆναι· τούτους γὰρ συνθεμένους τοῖσι Πέρσῃσι ἀναδέξαι ἀσπίδα ἐοῦσι ἤδη ἐν τῇσι νηυσί.

115

In this way the Athenians overpowered seven ships. The foreigners pushed off with the rest, picked up the Eretrian slaves from the island where they had left them, and sailed around Sunium hoping to reach the city before the Athenians. There was an accusation at Athens that they devised this by a plan of the Alcmeonidae, who were said to have arranged to hold up a shield as a signal once the Persians were in their ships.

116

1 οὗτοι μὲν δὴ περιέπλεον Σούνιον· Ἀθηναῖοι δὲ ὡς ποδῶν εἶχον τάχιστα ἐβοήθεον ἐς τὸ ἄστυ, καὶ ἔφθησάν τε ἀπικόμενοι πρὶν ἢ τοὺς βαρβάρους ἥκειν, καὶ ἐστρατοπεδεύσαντο ἀπιγμένοι ἐξ Ἡρακλείου τοῦ ἐν Μαραθῶνι ἐν ἄλλῳ Ἡρακλείῳ τῷ ἐν Κυνοσάργεϊ. οἱ δὲ βάρβαροι τῇσι νηυσὶ ὑπεραιωρηθέντες Φαλήρου, τοῦτο γὰρ ἦν ἐπίνειον τότε τῶν Ἀθηναίων, ὑπὲρ τούτου ἀνακωχεύσαντες τὰς νέας ἀπέπλεον ὀπίσω ἐς τὴν Ἀσίην.

116

They sailed around Sunium, but the Athenians marched back to defend the city as fast as their feet could carry them and got there ahead of the foreigners. Coming from the sacred precinct of Hercules in Marathon, they pitched camp in the sacred precinct of Hercules in Cynosarges. The foreigners lay at anchor off Phalerum, the Athenian naval port at that time. After riding anchor there, they sailed their ships back to Asia.

117

1 ἐν ταύτῃ τῇ ἐν Μαραθῶνι μάχῃ ἀπέθανον τῶν βαρβάρων κατὰ ἑξακισχιλίους καὶ τετρακοσίους ἄνδρας, Ἀθηναίων δὲ ἑκατὸν καὶ ἐνενήκοντα καὶ δύο. ἔπεσον μὲν ἀμφοτέρων τοσοῦτοι. 2 συνήνεικε δὲ αὐτόθι θῶμα γενέσθαι τοιόνδε, Ἀθηναῖον ἄνδρα Ἐπίζηλον τὸν Κουφαγόρεω ἐν τῇ συστάσι μαχόμενόν τε καὶ ἄνδρα γινόμενον ἀγαθὸν τῶν ὀμμάτων στερηθῆναι οὔτε πληγέντα οὐδὲν τοῦ σώματος οὔτε βληθέντα, καὶ τὸ λοιπὸν τῆς ζόης διατελέειν ἀπὸ τούτου τοῦ χρόνου ἐόντα τυφλόν. 3 λέγειν δὲ αὐτὸν περὶ τοῦ πάθεος ἤκουσα τοιόνδε τινὰ λόγον, ἄνδρα οἱ δοκέειν ὁπλίτην ἀντιστῆναι μέγαν, τοῦ τὸ γένειον τὴν ἀσπίδα πᾶσαν σκιάζειν· τὸ δὲ φάσμα τοῦτο ἑωυτὸν μὲν παρεξελθεῖν, τὸν δὲ ἑωυτοῦ παραστάτην ἀποκτεῖναι. ταῦτα μὲν δὴ Ἐπίζηλον ἐπυθόμην λέγειν.

118

1 Δᾶτις δὲ πορευόμενος ἅμα τῷ στρατῷ ἐς τὴν Ἀσίην, ἐπείτε ἐγένετο ἐν Μυκόνῳ, εἶδε ὄψιν ἐν τῷ ὕπνῳ. καὶ ἥτις μὲν ἦν ἡ ὄψις, οὐ λέγεται· ὁ δέ, ὡς ἡμέρη τάχιστα ἐπέλαμψε, ζήτησιν ἐποιέετο τῶν νεῶν, εὑρὼν δὲ ἐν νηὶ Φοινίσσῃ ἄγαλμα Ἀπόλλωνος κεχρυσωμένον ἐπυνθάνετο ὁκόθεν σεσυλημένον εἴη, πυθόμενος δὲ ἐξ οὗ ἦν ἱροῦ, ἔπλεε τῇ ἑωυτοῦ νηὶ ἐς Δῆλον· 2 καὶ ἀπίκατο γὰρ τηνικαῦτα οἱ Δήλιοι ὀπίσω ἐς τὴν νῆσον, κατατίθεταί τε ἐς τὸ ἱρὸν τὸ ἄγαλμα καὶ ἐντέλλεται τοῖσι Δηλίοισι ἀπαγαγεῖν τὸ ἄγαλμα ἐς Δήλιον τὸ Θηβαίων· τὸ δ᾽ ἔστι ἐπὶ θαλάσσῃ Χαλκίδος καταντίον. 3 Δᾶτις μὲν δὴ ταῦτα ἐντειλάμενος ἀπέπλεε, τὸν δὲ ἀνδριάντα τοῦτον Δήλιοι οὐκ ἀπήγαγον, ἀλλά μιν δι᾽ ἐτέων εἴκοσι Θηβαῖοι αὐτοὶ ἐκ θεοπροπίου ἐκομίσαντο ἐπὶ Δήλιον.

117

In the battle at Marathon about six thousand four hundred men of the foreigners were killed, and one hundred and ninety-two Athenians; that many fell on each side. The following marvel happened there: an Athenian, Epizelus son of Couphagoras, was fighting as a brave man in the battle when he was deprived of his sight, though struck or hit nowhere on his body, and from that time on he spent the rest of his life in blindness. I have heard that he tells this story about his misfortune: he saw opposing him a tall armed man, whose beard overshadowed his shield, but the phantom passed him by and killed the man next to him. I learned by inquiry that this is the story Epizelus tells.

118

Datis journeyed with his army to Asia, and when he arrived at Myconos he saw a vision in his sleep. What that vision was is not told, but as soon as day broke Datis made a search of his ships. He found in a Phoenician ship a gilded image of Apollo, and asked where this plunder had been taken. Learning from what temple it had come, he sailed in his own ship to Delos. The Delians had now returned to their island, and Datis set the image in the temple, instructing the Delians to carry it away to Theban Delium, on the coast opposite Chalcis. Datis gave this order and sailed away, but the Delians never carried that statue away; twenty years later the Thebans brought it to Delium by command of an oracle.

119

1 τοὺς δὲ τῶν Ἐρετριέων ἀνδραποδισμένους
Δᾶτίς τε καὶ Ἀρταφρένης, ὡς προσέσχον
πρὸς τὴν Ἀσίην πλέοντες, ἀνήγαγον ἐς
Σοῦσα. βασιλεὺς δὲ Δαρεῖος, πρὶν μὲν
αἰχμαλώτους γενέσθαι τοὺς Ἐρετριέας,
ἐνεῖχέ σφι δεινὸν χόλον, οἷα ἀρξάντων
ἀδικίης προτέρων τῶν Ἐρετριέων· 2 ἐπείτε
δὲ εἶδε σφέας ἀπαχθέντας παρ᾽ ἑωυτὸν
καὶ ἑωυτῷ ὑποχειρίους ἐόντας, ἐποίησε
κακὸν ἄλλο οὐδέν, ἀλλὰ σφέας τῆς Κισσίης
χώρης κατοίκισε ἐν σταθμῷ ἑωυτοῦ τῷ
οὔνομα ἐστὶ Ἀρδέρικκα, ἀπὸ μὲν Σούσων
δέκα καὶ διηκοσίους σταδίους ἀπέχοντι,
τεσσεράκοντα δὲ ἀπὸ τοῦ φρέατος τὸ
παρέχεται τριφασίας ἰδέας· καὶ γὰρ
ἄσφαλτον καὶ ἅλας καὶ ἔλαιον ἀρύσσονται
ἐξ αὐτοῦ τρόπῳ τοιῷδε· 3 ἀντλέεται μὲν
κηλωνηίῳ, ἀντὶ δὲ γαυλοῦ ἥμισυ ἀσκοῦ οἱ
προσδέδεται· ὑποτύψας δὲ τούτῳ ἀντλέει
καὶ ἔπειτα ἐγχέει ἐς δεξαμενήν· ἐκ δὲ ταύτης
ἐς ἄλλο διαχεόμενον τρέπεται τριφασίας
ὁδούς. καὶ ἡ μὲν ἄσφαλτος καὶ οἱ ἅλες
πήγνυνται παραυτίκα· τὸ δὲ ἔλαιον οἱ
Πέρσαι καλέουσι τοῦτο ῥαδινάκην, ἔστι
δὲ μέλαν καὶ ὀδμὴν παρεχόμενον βαρέαν.
4 ἐνθαῦτα τοὺς Ἐρετριέας κατοίκισε
βασιλεὺς Δαρεῖος, οἳ καὶ μέχρι ἐμέο
εἶχον τὴν χώρην ταύτην, φυλάσοντες
τὴν ἀρχαίην γλῶσσαν. τὰ μὲν δὴ περὶ
Ἐρετριέας ἔσχε οὕτω.

120

1 Λακεδαιμονίων δὲ ἧκον ἐς τὰς Ἀθήνας
δισχίλιοι μετὰ τὴν πανσέληνον, ἔχοντες
σπουδὴν πολλὴν καταλαβεῖν, οὕτω ὥστε
τριταῖοι ἐκ Σπάρτης ἐγένοντο ἐν τῇ Ἀττικῇ.
ὕστεροι δὲ ἀπικόμενοι τῆς συμβολῆς
ἱμείροντο ὅμως θεήσασθαι τοὺς Μήδους·
ἐλθόντες δὲ ἐς τὸν Μαραθῶνα ἐθεήσαντο.
μετὰ δὲ αἰνέοντες Ἀθηναίους καὶ τὸ ἔργον
αὐτῶν ἀπαλλάσσοντο ὀπίσω.

119

When Datis and Artaphrenes reached Asia in their voyage, they carried the enslaved Eretrians inland to Susa. Before the Eretrians were taken captive, king Darius had been terribly angry with them for doing him unprovoked wrong; but when he saw them brought before him and subject to him, he did them no harm, but settled them in a domain of his own called Ardericca in the Cissian land; this place is two hundred and ten stadia distant from Susa, and forty from the well that is of three kinds. Asphalt and salt and oil are drawn from it in the following way: a windlass is used in the drawing, with half a skin tied to it in place of a bucket; this is dipped into the well and then poured into a tank; then what is drawn is poured into another tank and goes three ways: the asphalt and the salt congeal immediately; the oil, which the Persians call rhadinace, is dark and evil-smelling. There king Darius settled the Eretrians, and they dwelt in that place until my time, keeping their ancient language. Such was the fate of the Eretrians.

120

After the full moon two thousand Lacedaemonians came to Athens, making such great haste to reach it that they were in Attica on the third day after leaving Sparta. Although they came too late for the battle, they desired to see the Medes, so they went to Marathon and saw them. Then they departed again, praising the Athenians and their achievement.

III. Biographies

Aeschylus (525/524-456/455 BC). Tragic poet often considered the "father of tragedy". He was born in Eleusis and his father Euphorion was a descendant of the aristocratic Kodridon family. His first appearance in tragic competitions was in 499/496 BC where the renowned tragic poets of the time Choerilus and Pratinas also participated. Aeschylus and his brothers Kynegeiros and Amynias fought in the Persian Wars; Kynegeirus died heroically in Marathon. His tragedy *The Persians*, which was first taught in Athens in 472 BC and received first prize in the Great Dionysia, refers to the battle of Salamis but condenses the historical experience of the clash between the Hellenic and Persian worlds. According to Suida, he was crowned 28 times in tragedy competitions; among the winning tragedies was the trilogy *Oresteia* (the only surviving trilogy). He travelled many times to Sicily, to the court of tyrant Hiero, where it is thought that he taught *The Persians* for the second time. He died in Gela in 456/455 BC. He requested an inscription to be placed on his gravestone, commemorating his participation in the Median wars. Seven of his tragedies survive: *The Persians, Prometheus Bound, Seven against Thebes, the Suppliants (Hiketides)* and the trilogy *Oresteia* (*Agamemnon, The Libation Bearers, Eumenides*).

Aristides (550 BC - 467 BC). Athenian general, nicknamed "the just". The son of Lysimachus he came from the Alopeki demos of the Antiochis tribe. A supporter of Cleisthenes and later of Miltiades, he was considered the leader of conservatives and the chief political opponent of Themistocles. He participated in the battle of Marathon as the general of his tribe and was positioned at the weak center of the Athenian phalanx, together with Themistocles. In 489 BC he was elected archon and opposed the suggestions of Themistocles on building a fleet. Because of that he was ostracized in 484/483 BC and fled to Aegina, but returned to Athens in 480 BC and placed himself under the orders of Themistocles. He fought in the battle of Salamis (480 BC) and the battle of Plataea (479 BC) as an elected general. Subsequently, he managed to ensure the participation of the Ionians in the First Athenian alliance and probably supported Kimon, son of Miltiades. We do not have details on his life after 477 BC. According to some authorities, he died in 467 BC during a journey to the Black Sea. His body was moved to Athens and buried in Phaliron.

Themistocles (527 BC - 461? BC). A general and politician, he was the founder of Athenian naval power. His father, Neocles disowned him because of his indiscretions of youth. In 493/492 BC he was elected archon and he begun the fortification of Piraeus. However, his naval plan was temporarily suspended after Miltiades rose to power in the Athenian political scene. He fought in the battle of Marathon as a general of the Leontis tribe and was positioned in the center of the Athenian phalanx, together with

Aristides. After the first Athenian victory, he managed to convince the *Ecclesia* to use part of the revenue from the Laurium silver mine to build a fleet and continued building the Long Walls. He was the architect of the victory in Salamina but his increasing influence and prestige led to his ostracism in 471 BC. He sought refuge in the court of Artaxerxes where he probably committed suicide in 461 BC.

Miltiades (540 BC - 489 BC). Athenian general and politician, a member of the noble family Philaids. His father Cimon was exiled by Peisistratus while his uncle Miltiades (his father's half-brother) was the tyrant in the Thracian Chersonese. Miltiades, the son of Cimon, was elected archon in 524 BC when the Peisistratus family attempted to appease the disgruntled aristocrats. However, the murder of his father forced him to self-exile in the Chersonese, were he rose to power following the death of his uncle and of his cousin. Together with the other tyrants of subjugated cities he participated in Darius' expedition in Thrace (513 BC) and accepted the suggestions of Scythians to destroy the floating bridges in the Danube and in the Hellespont, in order to trap the Persians in Scythia but Histiaeus, tyrant of Miletus opposed the plan. Subsequently, he was forced to abandon the Chersonese temporarily following the Scythian attacks and permanently in 492 BC during the Mardonius campaign. Upon his return to Athens, he was tried for his tyrannical rule over barbarian and Greek people, but was finally acquitted. He was the architect and the mastermind behind the victory in Marathon, while his timely arrival with the army in Phaliron negated the Persian plan for an attack against Athens. In 489 BC, he reclaimed Naxos that had been conquered by the Persians in 490 BC and he then led the expedition to Paros that was not successful. Upon returning to Athens he was again tried, accused of organizing the expedition to serve his personal interests. He was sentenced to pay a fine of 50 talents, which he could not afford and was imprisoned, dying of gangrene from a leg wound suffered during the Paros expedition.

Herodotus (485/484 BC - 421/415 BC A historian and geographer from Halicarnassus in Asia Minor. His father was Lyxes and his mother Dryo or Roio, while his uncle Panyassis was an epic poet. It is possible that Herodotus and his family were involved in the conspiracy against the tyrant Lygdamis and were exiled in Samos (around 468 or 467 BC). After their return to Halicarnassus they took active part in the overthrow of Lygdamis (455 BC). Herodotus travelled extensively in the known world (inland from Asia Minor, the Black Sea, Crimea, Scythia, Syria, Babylonia, Egypt, Cyrene, Cyprus). During his extended stay in Athens, he was closely affiliated with the Alcmaeonid family, especially Pericles while the tragic poet Sophocles was his friend. He abandoned Athens around 443 BC and together with the sophist Protagoras established the colony of Thurium in southern Italy. Very little is known about the last years of his life, while his death is placed sometime between 421 and 415 BC. Herodotus is considered the "father of History". His work, which the Alexandrian scholars separated into nine books (each book taking the name of one the nine Muses), presented the history of the confrontation between the Greeks and the Persians, from 560 BC to

478 BC. Even though his work focuses on the Persian wars, his narration includes long digressions with extensive historical information, geographical descriptions, myths, customs, genealogical information, etc. Thus, the Histories of Herodotus provided a unique source of information not restricted to historical facts but to the mindset of the current period.

Kynaigeirus or Kynegeirus (? - 490 BC). Son of Euphorion and brother of the tragic poet Aeschylus with whom they fought in the battle of Marathon. As the Persians were being pursued by the Athenians, he tried to prevent an enemy ship from sailing when a Persian cut off his hands with an ax. For this gallant deed, the Athenians pronounced him a hero.

Callimachos. The Athenian polemarch in Marathon. He was born in Aphidnae. He supported Miltiades' suggestion regarding the strategy against the Persians and followed his plan. He died heroically in Marathon and was honored by the Athenians as a hero.

Darius I (550-486 BC). Son of the Parthia satrap Hystaspes, Darius, nicknamed "the Great", was one of the most important kings of the Achaemenid dynasty. He established his rule through a series of revolts and confrontations, while his marriage to Atossa, daughter of Cyrus strengthened his position in the dynasty. In the immense empire created by Cyrus, he followed a reform policy, restructuring the satrapy system and expanding them to twenty, while he imposed a fixed and strictly defined taxation system. At the same time, he improved and expanded the road network to facilitate trade within his empire. A characteristic example is the Royal Road 1,500 miles long, connecting the Aegean with Susa, which was used by his heralds. He adopted the monetary system of Lydia, and parallel circulation of gold and silver coins of a uniform price; the gold coins of Persia are called "daric". He tried to expand the empire to the West, conquering Thrace and Macedonia first. A few years after the defeat of his army in Marathon, and while he was busy trying to crush a revolt in Egypt Darius died in 486 BC, before he had the time to attack Greece a second time.

Datis and Artaphernes. Heading the Persian army in Marathon, the two noblemen enjoyed the trust of Darius. Datis was a Mede and an experienced general while the Persian Artaphernes was the king's nephew and son of Artaphernes, satrap of Sardis. The Sardis satrapy had jurisdiction over the Ionian cities and it was Artaphernes senior who dealt with the Ionian Revolt and warned the Greeks of the consequences they would suffer if they did not take Hippias back. Naturally, the Persians supported Hippias since he was serving their interests as did the Ionian tyrants that preceded him. They were not particularly interested in the political regime of a city, as long it accepted Persian dominance. Typically, following the Ionian Revolt, Artaphernes deposed - and often executed - the revolting tyrants and promoted democratic regimes in many Ionian cities.

Alexander I of Macedon. Alexander I, nicknamed "Philhellene"*, was the king of Macedonia from 495 BC to 454 BC. He was the son of king Amyntas I. At an early age he showed his anger during a symposium his father organized in honor of the Persian envoys of Bakabadus. Since the Persians misbehaved and disrespected the women of the Macedonian House, he killed them (512 BC). However, when he came to the throne after the death of his father, he was forced to recognize the Persian dominance and followed Xerxes in his campaign against the Greek city-states. Nevertheless, he was friendly towards his compatriots during the battle at Thermopylae, the battle of Plataea; as the survivors of the Persian army were fleeing Macedonia, he himself completed their destruction. After the end of the Persian wars, Alexander I expanded the Macedonian state to the west by subjugating mountainous Lyncestae (Florina area today), Orestae and Elmiotae (the area west of Kozani today) reaching towards Pydna and Thermi (Thermaikos). Apart from the nickname "Philhellene", for his friendly feelings towards the other Greeks the Athenians made him official Ambassador and the Argives proclaimed him a descendant of the Temenus family. He also adorned Delphi and Olympia with exquisite offerings. He ruled for 34 years. In 454 BC he was succeeded by his son Perdiccas II. It should be noted that during the 71st Olympiad (496 BC), Alexander I visited Greece for the first time. According to Herodotus, Alexander I participated in the *stadion*, in the cross country race. Many Greeks who were contesting the championship demanded his exclusion. Alexander I competed in the *stadion* race. His victory was relative because he finished together with another athlete. His name was never listed on the stele of Olympians because one had to win in many events to be considered an Olympian and that was not the case with Alexander I.

* The term "Philhellene" in antiquity did not have the same meaning as it does today; at the time it signified Greek descent. In antiquity, the word "philhellene" was used to characterize a prominent Greek who was fond of Greece, promoted Greek ideas and offered his services to the entire Greek nation. In other words, a philhellene was a Greek who did not restrict his actions and his thought to the narrow local environment of the city or a state where he was born or lived, but opened his horizons to pan-Hellenic thought, talked and acted not as a citizen of a particular Greek city-state but as a Greek who belonged to all of Greece. The fact that ancient writers, whether they were philosophers, historians or orators used the term "philhellene" consistenly to signify Greek descent, dispels any doubt as to the meaning of the term.(Daskalakis 1960: 343).

Bibliography

Ancient Texts
Aeschylus, *Persians*
Apollodorus, *Bibliotheca*
Aristotle, *Athenian Constitution*
Aristotle, *Poetics*
Aristotle, *Politics*
Aristophanes, *Wasps*
Diodorus Siculus, *Bibliotheca Historica*
Euripides, *Hercules furens* (Euripides *Fabulae*, εκδ. G. Murray, Oxford: Clarendon 1913)
Herodotus, *Histories*
Thucydides, *History*
Claudius Aelianus, *De natura animalium*
Lycurgus, *Against Leocrates*
Pausanias, *Description of Greece. Attica.*
Plutarch, *Theseus*
Plutarch, *Lycurgus*
Polybius, *The Histories*
Polyaenus, *Stratagems in War*
Strabo, *Geographica*
Xenophon, *Hellenica*
Xenophon, *Cyropaedia*
Xenophon, *Lacedaemonian Constitution.*

Secondary Sources

Adcock, F.E. 1957: *The Greek and Macedonian Art of War*, Berkeley: University of California Press

Anderson, J.K. 1970: *Military Theory and Practice in the Age of Xenophon*, Berkeley: University of California Press

Anderson, J.K. 1999: "Hoplite Weapons and Offensive arms", in Hanson 1999, p. 15-37

Andrewes, A. 1981: "The hoplite katalogos" in G.S. Shrimpton & D.J. McCargar (ed.), *Classical Contributions: Studies in honour of Malcolm Francis McGregor*, Locus Valley, NJ: Augustin, p. 1-3

Balcer, J.M. 1938: "The Greeks and the Persians: The processes of acculturation", *Historia*, 32/3, p. 257-267

Beye, Charles Rowan 1964: "Homeric Battle narrative and Catalogues", *Harvard Studies in Classical Philology* 68, p. 345-373

Blaise, Fabienne 2006: "Poetics and Politics: Tradition Re-Worked in Solon's 'Eunomia' (Poem 4)", Block & Lardinois 2006: 114-133

Blamire, A. 1959: "Herodotus and Histiaeus", *Classical Quarterly*, 9/2, p. 142-154

Block, Josine H. & Lardinois, P.M.H. (ed.) 2006: *Solon of Athens. New Historical and Philological Perspectives*, Boston/Leiden: Brill

Boegehold, Alan L. & Scafuro, Adele C. 1994: *Athenian Identity and Civic Ideology*, Baltimore: Johns Hopkins University Press

Brosius, Maria 2006: *The Persians. An Introduction*, London/New York: Routledge

Brunt, P.A. 1953: "The Hellenic League against Persia", *Historia* 2/2, p. 135-163

Bugh, G.R. 1988: *The horsemen of Athens*, Princeton, NJ: Princeton University Press

Burn, A. R. 1984: *Persia and the Greeks: The defense of the West*, Stanfrod, California: Stanford University Press

Bury, J.B. 1896: "The battle of Marathon", *Classical Review* 10/2, 95-98

CAH 1988: J. Boardman et al., *The Cambridge Ancient History*, τ. 4. Persia, Greece and the Western Mediterranean, Cambridge: Cambridge University Press

Califf, David J. 2002: *Marathon*, Philadeplhia: Chelsea House

Cartledge, Paul 1977: "Hoplites and Heroes: Sparta's Contribution to the Technique of Ancient Warfare", *Journal of Hellenic Studies* 97, p. 11-27

Catledge, Paul 2002: *Sparta and Lakonia: A Regional History 1300-362 BC*, London/New York: Routledge

Cartledge, Paul 2003a: *The Spartans. The world of the Warrior-Heroes of Ancient Greece*, Woodstock, NY: Overlook Press

Cartledge, Paul 2003b: *Spartan Reflections*, Berkeley: University of California Press

Caspari, M.O.B. 1911: "Stray notes on the Persian Wars", *Journal of Hellenic Studies* 31, p. 100-109

Casson, S. 1920: "Cornelius Nepos. Some further notes", *Journal of Hellenic Studies* 40, p. 43-46

Cawkwell, G.L. 1995: "Early Greek Tyranny and the People", *Classical Quarterly*, 45/1, p. 73-86

Cawkwell, G.L. 2005: *The Greek Wars: The failure of Persia*, Oxford: Oxford University Press

Chaniotis, A. 2005: *War in the Hellenistic World*, Oxford: Blackwell

Chrimes, K.M.T. 1999: *Ancient Sparta. A Re-examination of the Evidence*, Manchester: Manchester University Press (1st ed. 1949)

Coleman, J.E. & Walz, C. 1997: *Greeks and Barbarians: Essays on the Interactions between Greeks and Non-Greeks in Antiquity and the Consequences for Eurocentrism*, Bethesda, Md: CDL Press

Conolly, P., *Greece and Rome at war*, trans. in Greek, Athens: Sideris n.d.

Connor, W.R. 1988: "Early Greek Land Warfare as Symbolic Expression", *Past and Present* 119, p. 3-29

Connor, W.R. 1994: "The problem of Athenian civic identity", in Boegehold & Scafuro 1994: 34-44

Creasy, Edward Shepherd 1851: *The Fifteen Decisive Battles of the World. From Marathon to Waterloo*, τ. 1, London: Bentley

David, E. 1978: "The Spartan Syssitia and Plato's *Laws*", *American Journal of Philology* 99, p. 486-495

de Sanctis, G. 1931: "Aristagora di Mileto", *Rivista di filologia e di istruzione classica* 39, p. 48-72

de Souza, P. 2003: *The Greek and Persian Wars 499-386 BC*, Oxford/New York: Routledge

de Souza et al. 2004: P. de Souza – W. Heckel – L. Llewelly-Jones, *The Greeks at War, from Athens to Alexander*, Oxford: Osprey

de Ste. Croix, G.E.M. 2004: *Athenian Democratic Origins and other essays*, ed. D. Harvey – R. Parker, Oxford/New York: Oxford University Press

Donlan, W. 1970: "Archilochus, Strabo, and the Lelantine War", *TAPA* 101, p. 131-142

Donlan, W. & Thompson, J. 1976: "The Charge at Marathon: Herodotus 6.112", *Classical Journal* 71, p. 339-343

Drew, A.J. 2003: *A Wiccan Bible. Exploring the mysteries of the craft from birth to summerland*, Franklin Lakes, NJ: New Page Books

Ducrey, P. 1986: *Warfare in Ancient Greece*, trans. by J. Lloyd, New York: Schocken Books

Evans, J.A.S. 1963: "Histiaeus and Aristagoras: Notes on the Ionian Revolt", *American Journal of Philology*, 84/2, p. 113-128

Evans, J.A.S. 1984: "Herodotus and Marathon", *Florilegium* 6, p. 1-27

Evans, J.A.S. 1993: "Herodotus and the battle of Marathon", *Historia* 52/3, p. 279-307

Evans, Nancy 2010: *Civic Rites. Democracy and Religion in Ancient Athens*, Berkeley: University of California Press

Ferrill, A. 1985: *The Origins of War from the Stone Age to Alexander the Great*, London: Thames & Hudson

Fields, Nic 2007: *Ancient Greek Warship 500-322 BC*, Oxford: Osprey

Finley, M.I. 1964: *The World of Odysseus*, London: Chatto & Windus

Finley, M.I. 1983: *Politics in the Ancient World*, Cambridge/New York: Cambridge University Press

Fol, A. & Hammond, N.G.L. 1988: "Persia in Europe, apart from Greece", in *CAH* 1988: 234-253

Forrest, W.G. 1957: "Colonization and the Rise of Delphi", *Historia* 6, p. 160-175

Forsdyke, Sara 2006: "Labor and Economy in Solonian Athens: Breaking the Impasse between Archaeology and History", in Block & Lardinois 2006: 334-347

Frost, F.J. 1994: "Aspects of early Athenian citizenship", in Boegehold & Scafuro 1994: 45-56

Frye, Richard N. 1963: *The Heritage of Persia*, Cleveland: World Publications

Fuller, J.F.C. 1993: *Decisive Battles of the Western World*, London: Spa Books

Gaebel, R.E. 2002: *Cavalry operations in the ancient Greek world*, Norman: University of Oklhoma Press

Gardner, P. 1911: "The coinage of the Ionian Revolt", *Journal of Hellenic Studies* 31, p. 151-160

Garnsey, P. 1988: *Famine and food supply in the Greco-Roman World*, Cambridge/New York: Cambridge University Press

Georges, Pericles 1994: *Barbarian Asia and the Greek Experience. From the Archaic Period to the Age of Xenophon*, Baltimore/London: Johns Hopkins University Press

Goldhill, Simon 1988: "Battle narrative and politics in Aeschylus' *Persae*", *JHS* 108, p. 189-193

Gomme, A.W. 1945: *A Historical Commentary on Thucydides*, τ. 2, Oxford: Clarendon

Gomme, A. 1952: "Herodotus and Marathon", *Phoenix* 6, p. 77-83

Goodspeed, George S. 1899: "The Persian empire from Darius to Artaxerxes", *Biblical World*, 14/4, p. 251-257

Gouschin, V. 1999: "Pisistratus' leadership in A.P. 13.4 and the establishment of tyranny of 561/60 BC", *Classical Quarterly*, 49/1, p. 14-23

Graham, A.J. 1983: *Colony and Mother City in Ancient Greece*, Chicago: Ares (1st ed. 1964)

Graves, Robert 1990a-b: *The Greek Myths*, τ. 1-2, London: Penguin (1st ed. 1955)

Green, Peter 1996: *The Greco-Persian Wars*, Berkley/Los Angeles: University of California Press

Greswell, Edward 1862: *Origines kalendariae hellenicae; or the history of the primitive calendar among the Greeks, before and after the legislation of Solon*, Oxford: Oxford University Press

Grote, George 2002: *A History of Greece: from the time of Solon to 403 BC*, ed. J.M. Mitchell – M.O.B. Caspari, introduction Paul Cartledge, London/New York: Routledge

Grundy, G.B. 1901: *The Great Persian War and its Preliminaries*, London: Murray

Hammond, N.G.L. 1968: "The campaign and the battle of Marathon", *Journal of Hellenic Studies* 88, p. 13-57

Hammond, N.G.L. 1988: "The expedition of Datis and Artaphernis", in *CAH* 1988: 491-517

Hansen, M.H. 1986: *Demography and Democracy. The number of Athenian citizens in the fourth century*, Herning, Denmark: Systime

Hanson, V.D. 1983: *Warfare and Agriculture in Classical Greece*, Pisa: Giardini

Hanson, V.D. 1999 (ed.): *Hoplites. The Classical Greek Battle Experience*, London/New York: Routledge

Hanson, V.D. 2000: "Hoplite Battle as Ancient Greek Warfare: When, Where, and Why?", in H. van Wees (ed.), *War and Violence in Classical Greece*, London: Duckworth

Hignett, C. 1963: *Xerxes' Invasion of Greece*, Oxford: Clarendon

Hodge, A. Trevor & Losada, Luis A. 1970: "The time of the shield signal at Marathon", *American Journal of Archaeology*, 74/1, p. 31-36

Hodge, A. Trevor 1975: "Marathon: The Persian's voyage", *TAPA* 105, p. 155-173

Holladay, A.J. 1982: "Hoplites and Heresies", *Journal of Hellenic Studies* 102, p. 94-103

How, W.W. 1923: "Arms, tactics, an strategy in the Persian War", *Journal of Hellenic Studies* 43, p. 117-132

How & Wells 1928: W.W. How & J. Wells, *A commentary on Herodotus, with introduction and appendixes*, Oxford: Clarendon

Huart, Clément 1972: *Ancient Persia and Iranian Civilization*, London: Routledge & Kegan Paul

Hudson, Harris Gary 1937: "The shield signal at Marathon", *American Historical Review*, 42/3, p. 443-459

Hunt, Peter 2008: "Military forces", in Sabin et al. 2008: 108-146

Jackson, A.H. 1999: "Hoplites and the Gods: The Dedication of Captures Arms and Armours", in Hanson 1999, p. 228-249

Jeffery, L.H. 1988: "Greece before the Persian invasion", in *CAH* 1988: 347-367

Keanevey, A. 1988: "The attack on Naxos: a 'forgotten cause' of the Ionian Revolt", *Classical Quarterly*, 38/1, p. 76-81

Krentz, Peter 2002: "Fighting by the Rules: The Invention of Hoplite Agôn", *Hesperia*, 71/1, p. 23-39

Latacz, J. 1977: *Kampfparänese, Kampfdarstellung und Kampfwirklichkeitin der Ilias, bei Kallinos und Tyrtaios*, Munich: Beck

Lazenby, J. F. 1964: "The strategy of the Greeks and the opening campaign of the Persian War", *Hermes* 92, p. 264-284

Lazenby, J. F. 1993: *The defense of Greece 490-479 BC*, Warminster: Aris & Phillips

Lewis, D.M. 1988: "The Tyranny of the Pisistratidai", in *CAH* 1988: 287-302

Lewis, D.M. 2004: "Cleisthenis and Attica", in Rhodes 2004: 287-308

Lloyd, Alan 1973: *Marathon. The Story of Civilizations on Collision Course*, London: Souvenir Press

Lloyd, W. Watkiss 1881: "The battle of Marathon: 490 BC", *Journal of Hellenic Studies* 2, p. 380-395

Loreaux, Nicole 1986: *The invention of Athens: The Funeral Oration in the Classical City*, Cambridge, MA: Harvard University Press

Loreaux, Nicole 2000: *Born of the Earth. Myth and Politics in Athens*, trans. by Selina Stewart, Ithaca, NY/London: Cornell University Press

Lorimer, H.L. 1947: "The Hoplite Phalanx with Special Reference to the Poems of Archilochus and Tyrtaeus", *Annual of the British School at Athens* 42, p. 76-138

MacDowell, M.D. 1978: *The Law in classical Athens*, London: Thames & Hudson

McLeon, W. 1970: "The bowshot at Marathon", *Journal of Hellenic Studies* 90, p. 197-198

Manville, P.B. 1977: "Aristagoras and Histiaios: the leadership struggle in the Ionian Revolt", *Classical Quarterly*, 27/1, p. 80-91

Maurice, F. 1932: "The campaign of Marathon", *Journal of Hellenic Studies* 52, p. 13-24

Meritt, Benjamin D. 1961: *The Athenian Year*, Berkeley: University of California Press

Mill, John Stuart 1846: "*A History of Greece*. By George Grote", *Edinburgh Review* 54, p. 343-377 (= *Collected Works of John Stuart Mill*, ed. J. M. Robson – εισαγωγή F.E. Sparshott, Toronto: University of Toronto Press 1978, τ. 11. Essays on Philosophy and the Classics, p. 272-305)

Michell, H. 1964: *Sparta: Το κρυπτόν της πολιτείας των Λακεδαιμονίων*, Cambridge: Cambridge University Press

Mommsen, August 1864: *Heortologie. Antiquarische Untersuchungen über die Städtischen Festen der Athener*, Leipzig: Teubner

Montagu, J.D 2000: *Battles of the Greek and Roman Worlds*, London: Greenhill

Morris, Ian 1987: *Burial and Ancient Society: the Rise of the Greek City-State*, Cambridge: Cambridge University Press

Morrison, J.S. & Williams, R.T. 1968: *Greek Oared Ships 900-322 BC*, London: Cambridge

Mossé, Claude 2004: "How a political myth takes shape: Solon, 'Founding Father' of Athenian democracy", in Rhodes 2004: 242-259

Munro, J.A.R. 1899: "Some observations on the Persian Wars", *Journal of Hellenic Studies* 19, p. 185-197

Munro, J.A.R. 1939: "The ancestral laws of Cleisthenis", *Classical Quarterly*, 33/2, p. 84-97

Murray, Oswyn 1988: "The Ionian Revolt", in *CAH* 1988: 461-490

Myres, J.L. 1953: *Herodotus: Father of History*, Oxford: Clarendon

Noussia, Maria 2006: "Strategies of persuasion in Solon's Elegies", Block & Lardinois 2006: 134-156

Ober, J. 1996: *The Athenian Revolution. Essays on Ancient Greek Democracy and Political Theory*, Princeton: Princeton University Press

Ober, J. 2004: "The Athenian revolution of 508/7 BC: violence, authority, and the origins of democ-

racy", in Rhodes 2004: 260-286

Osborne, Robin 1996: *Greece in the making: 1200-479 BC*, London: Routledge

Ostwald, M. 1988: "The reforms of the Athenian State by Cleisthenis", in *CAH* 1988: 303-346

Parker, Victor 2007: "Tyrants and Lawgivers", in Shapiro 2007: 13-39

Pelekidis, Ch. P. 1962: *Histoire de l'éphébie attique des origines à 31 avant J. Christ*, Paris: E. de Boc-card

Pritchett, W.K. 1975: *The Greek State at War*, τ. 2, Berkeley: University of California Press

Pritchett, W.K. 1985: *The Greek State at War*, τ. 4, Berkeley: University of California Press

Pritchett, W.K. 1991: *The Greek State at War*, τ. 5, Berkeley: University of California Press

Prost, F. 1999: "Les Combatants de Marathon: Idéologie et société hoplitiques à Athènes au Ve s.", in F. Prost (ed.), *Armées et sociétés de la Grèce classique*, Paris: Errance

Raubitschek, A.E. 1940: "Two monuments erected after the victory of Marathon", *American Journal of Archaeology* 44/1, p. 53-59

Raubitschek, A.E. 1963: "Book Review. *Solone* by Agostino Masaracchia", *Classical Philology*, 58/2, p. 137-140

Ray, Fred Eugene, Jr. 2009: *Land Battles in 5th century BC Greece*, Jefferson, North Carolina/London: McFarland

Reynolds, P.K. Baillie 1929: "The shield signal at the battle of Marathon", *Journal of Hellenic Studies* 49, p. 100-105

Rhodes, P.J. (ed.) 2004: *Athenian Democracy*, Edinburgh: Edinburgh University Press

Ridley, R.T. 1979: "The hoplite as citizen: Athenian military institutions in their social context", *Classique* 48, p. 508-548

Rostovtzeff, M. 1963: *Greece*, trans. J.D. Duff, New York: Oxford University Press

Runciman, W.G. 1998: "Greek Hoplites, Warrior Culture, and Indirect Bias", *Journal of Royal Anthropological Institute*, 4/4, p. 731-751

Sabin, Philip et al. 2008: *The Cambridge History of Greek and Roman Warfare*, τ. 1. Greece, the Hellenistic world and the rise of Rome, Cambridge: Cambridge University Press

Sage, Michael M. 1996: *Warfare in Ancient Greece. A Sourcebook*, London/New York: Routledge

Salmon, J. 1977: "Political hoplites?", *Journal of Hellenic Studies* 97, p. 84-101

Samuel, Alan E. 1972: *Greek and Roman Chronology. Calendars and Years in Classical Antiquity*, München: Beck

Schachermeyr, F. 1951: "Marathon und die persische politik", *Historische Zeitschrift* 172/1, p. 1-35

Sekunda, N. 1986: *Warriors of Ancient Greece*, Oxford: Osprey

Sekunda, N. 1992: *The Persian Army 560-330 BC*, Oxford: Osprey

Sekunda, N. 2000: *Greek Hoplite 480-323 BC*, Oxford: Osprey

Shapiro, H.A. (ed.) 2007: *The Cambridge Companion to Archaic Greece*, Cambridge: Cambridge University Press

Shrimton, Gordon 1980: "The Persian Cavalry at Marathon", *Phoenix* 34/1, p. 20-37

Siewert, P. 1982: *Die Trittyen Attikas und die Heeresform des Kleisthenes*, München: Beck

Sky & Telescope 2004: "Astronomers unravel Marathon mystery", http://www.skyandtelescope.com/about/pressreleases/3309276.html (retrieved 13.08.2010)

Smith, Sir William 1870: *Dictionary of Greek and Roman Biography and Mythology*, 3τ., Boston: Little & Brown

Snodgrass, A.M. 1965: "The Hoplite Reform and History", *Journal of Hellenic Studies* 85, p. 110-122

Snodgrass, A.M. 1967: *Arms and Armours of the Greeks*, Ithaca, NY: Cornell University Press

Snodgrass, A.M. 1993: "The 'Hoplite Reform' revisited", *Dialogues d'histoire ancienne* 19, p. 47-61

Stanton, G.R. 1984: "The tribal reform of Kleisthenis the Alkmeonid", *Chiron* 14, p. 1-41

Starr, C.G. 1962: "Why did the Greeks defeat the Persians?" *Parola del Passato* 17, p. 321-332

Stehle, Eva 2006: "Solon's Self-Reflexive Politcal Persona and its Audience", Block & Lardinois 2006: 79-113

Toulmin, Stephen 2001: *Return to Reason*, Cambridge, MA: Harvard University Press

Tozzi, Pierluigi 1978: *La rivolta ionica*, Pisa: Giardini

van der Veer, J.A.G. 1982: "The Battle of Marathon: A topographical survey", *Mnemosyne* 35, p. 290-321

van Effenterre, H. 1976: "Clitshène et les mesures de mobilisation", *REG* 89, p. 1-17

van Wees, Hans 1994: "The Homeric Way of War: The *Iliad* and the Hoplite Phalanx", *Greece and Rome*, 41/1, p. 1-18 και 41/2, p. 131-155

Wardman, A.E. 1959: "Tactics and the tradition of the Persian Wars", *Historia*, 8/1, p. 49-60

Wardman, A.E. 1961: "Herodotus on the cause of the Greco-Persian Wars", *American Journal of Philology*, 82/2, p. 133-150

Warry, J. 1980: *Warfare in the Classical World. War and the Ancient Civilizations of Greece and Rome*, London: Salamander Books

Whatley, N. 1964: "On the possibility of reconstructing Marathon and other ancient battles", *Journal of Hellenic Studies* 84, p. 119-139

Wheeler, Everett L. 1987: "Ephorus and the Prohibition of Missiles", *TAPA* 117, p. 157-182

White, Mary E. 1961: "Greek Colonization", *Journal of Economic History*, 21/4, p. 443-454

Whitehead, David 1981: "The Archaic Athenian ΖΕΥΓΙΤΑΙ", *Classical Quarterly*, 31/2, p. 282-286

Young, T. Cuyler, Jr. 1988a: "The early history of the Medes and the Persians and the Achaemenid empire to the death of Cambyses", in *CAH* 1988: 1-52

Young, T. Cuyler, Jr. 1988b: "The consolidation of the empire and its limits of growth under Darius and Xerxes", in *CAH* 1988: 53-110

Zimmerman, J.E. 1966: *Dictionary of Classical Mythology*, New York/London: Bantam Books (1η έκδ. 1964)

Translated in Greek

Amouretti, M.C & Ruze, F. 2004: *Les sociétés grecques et la guerre à l'époque classi*que (Paris : Hachette supérieur, 2003), trans. by G. Georgamlis, Athens: Patakis

Bengston, H. 1981: *Griechische Geschichte von den Anfängen bis in die römische Kaiserzeit* (München Beck 1976), trans. by A. Gabrilis, Athens, Melissa

Bury, J.B. & Meiggs, R. 1992: *A history of Greece to the death of Alexander the Great* (New York : St. Martin's Press 1975), Athens, Kardamitsa

Grimal, Pierre 1991: *Dictionary of Greek and Roman mythology* (Oxford : Blackwell) 1985), trans. by B. Atsalos, Thessaloniki: University Studio Press

Hanson, V.D. 2003: *The western way of war : infantry battle in classical Greece* (New York: Oxford University Press 1990), trans. by M. Bletas, Athens: K. Tournikis

Hanson, V.D. 2004: *Carnage and culture: landmark battles in the rise of Western power* (New York: Doubleday 2001), trans. by S. Konstantinea, Athens: Kaktos

Hanson, V.D. 2005: *Wars of the ancient Greeks* (Washington: Smithsonian Books 2004), trans. by G. Kousounelos, Athens: Enalios

Holland, T. 2006: *Persian fire : the first world empire and the battle for the West* (New York: Doubleday 2005), trans. by D. Stefanakis, Athens: Oceanida

Liddell Hart, B.H. 1963: *Strategy: the indirect approach*, trans. by the Department of Military Studies, Athens: Hellenic Army General Staff

MacDowell, M.D. 1999: *Spartan law* (Edinburgh: Scottish Academic Press 1986), trans. N. Konomis, Athens: Papadimas

Mossé, Claude 1989: *La Tyrannie dans la Grèce antique* (Paris: PUF 1969), trans. by A. Calogeropoulou, Athens: Asty

Mossé, Claude & Schnapp-Courbeillon, Annie 1996: *Précis d'histoire grecque: du début du deuxième millénaire et la bataille d'Actium* (Paris: Armand Colin 1990) trans. by L. Stefanou, Athens: Papadimas

Mossé, Claude 1988: *Histoire d'une démocratie: Athènes, dès origines à la conquête macédonienne* (Paris:Seuil 1971), trans. by D. Angelidou, Athens: MIET

Osborne, Robin 2000: *Greece in the making : 1200-479 BC* (London/New York: Routledge 1996),

trans. by T. Sieti, Athens: Odysseas

Schuller, W. 2001: *Griechische Geschichte* (München/Wien: Oldenbourg 1980), trans. by A. Kamara – Ch. Kokkinia, Athens: MIET

Snodgrass, A.M., 2003: *Arms and Armours of the Greeks* (Ithaca, NY: Cornell University Press 1967), trans. by V. Stamatopoulou, Thessaloniki: University Press

Vernant, J.P. 1981: *Problèmes de la guerre en Grèce ancienne* (Paris: le Grand livre du mois 1999), trans. by P. Kafetzopoulos et al., Athens: Hellenic Army General Staff

Vidal-Naquet, Pierre 1983: *Le chasseur noir: formes de penseé et formes de société dans le monde grec* (Paris: F. Maspero 1981), trans. by G. Andreadis – P. Rigopoulou, Athens: Livanis

Vidal-Naquet, Pierre 1999: *La Démocratie grecque vue d'ailleurs: essais d'historiographie ancienne et modern* (Paris: Flammarion 1996), trans. by Th. Michael, Athens: Alexandreia

Wilcken, U. 1976: *Griechische Geschichte im Rahmen der Alterumsgeschichte* (München: Oldenbourg 1962), trans. by I. Touloumakou, Athens: Papazisis

In Greek

Angelis, F. 1955. 1955: *Principles and Law from Herodotus history*, Athens: n.ed.

Adam-Magnesali, R. 1998: *Human age and the Law. Legal consequences of human age in classical Athens,* Thesis diss., Athens: Panteion University

Anagnostou, Chr. 2007: "Cimon, an Athenian politician and general in the first half of 5th cent. BC", *Military Review* (May)

Antonakopoulos, A. 1979: *Cleisthenes' reforms and its contribution to the formation of the state,* Athens/Komotini: Σάκκουλας

Barbakis, G. 2010: 2599 years after the Athenian victory at Marathon," *Focus*, 124 (June) 60-64

Belezos, D. 2006a: "Political and military organization in Athens", *Military History*, 21 (March) 4-7

Belezos, D. 2006b: "The Ionian Revolution", *Military History*, 21 (March) 8-19

Birgalias, N. 2001: "Spartan education", *E-Historica*, sp. ed. of *Elefterotypia* newsp. (14.6.2001) 28-31

Daskalakis, A. B. 1960: *Ancient Macedonia's Hellenism,* Athens: n.ed.

de la Croix, G.F. 2010: "Marathon and the European Identity", *Illustrated History* 507 (September) 33

Depastas, N. 1999: "Ancient Greek military organization and warfare", *Military Review*

Despotopoulos, A. 1971: "New strategy and tactics: Miltiades", *History of Hellenic Nation*, v. 2, Athens: Ekdotiki, p. 296-306

Garoufalis, D.N. 1997: "The Battle of Marathon, a glorious moment of the hoplite phalanx", *Military History* 13 (September)

Garoufalis, D.N. 2003: *Persian Wars: the titanic struggle that moved the ancient world,* Athens: Periskopio

Gedeon, D.: *The Battle of Marathon. September 490 BC,* Athens: Hellenic Army General Staff, n.d.

Gedeon, D. 2002: "Tactics innovations in Ancient Greece", *Military Review*, 65 (January)

Georgis, K., 1995: "Ancient Greek art of war", *Military Review* (April)

Gerogiannis, A. 1956: *Marathon 490 BC,* Athens: n.ed.

Giannikopoulos, A.B., 1990: "When did the institution of adolescence start?", *Archaeology* 35 (June) 54-73

Giannopoulos, N. 2006: "Marathon. Athens smashes Persian arrogance", *Military History*, 21 (March) 20-55

Giarenis, E. A. 2004: "War and Humanism", *Military Review* (Μάιος)

Giarenis, E. A. 2008a: *The Law of Ear and Military Penal Law. Contemporary and Ancient Greek approaches,* Athens: Legal Library

Giarenis, E. A 2008b: "Ancient Greek tactics", *Military Review* (June) 8-22

Giarenis, E. A. 2008c: "Military ideology in Classical Greece", *Military Review* (October)

Giouni, M.R., 1998: *ΑΤΙΜΟΣ ΕΣΤΩ – ΑΤΙΜΟΣ ΤΕΘΝΑΤΩ. A contribution to the study of the sentence of disgrace in Attica's Law,* Thessaloniki: University Studio Press

Giouni, M.R., 2006: *The city's Law: justice and legislation in ancient city-states*, Athens/Thessaloniki: Vanias

Gregoriadis, N. 1951: *The Art of War from Homer to Alexander the Great*, Athens: n.ed.

Gregoropoulos, K. 2009: *Ancient Greek Cavarlymen*, Athens: Periskopio

Gyalistras, P. 1960: "Marathon-Salamis. The first foundation of contemporary strategy", *Military Review* (July)

Hadjimichalis , Ch. 1972: "Ancient Greek military history", *Military Review* (May)

Hellenic Parliament 2010: *The Battle of Marathon. History and Legend*, Athens: Hellenic Parliament Foundation

Ioannides, E.K. 2010: "494 BC. The naval battle of Lade. Strategic mistakes", *Naval Review* (July)

Ioannides, I., 1976: "The real run of the Marathon herald", *Gymnastics and Sports*, 5

Kampouris, M. 2000: *Ancient Greek Warriors. Weapons – Tactics – Organization in Classical Greece*, Athens: Epikoinonies

Kanellopoulos, P. 1982: *A History of Ancient Greece*, Athens: Gialelis

Kargakos, S. I. 2004: *A History of Ancient Athens*, v. 1, Athens: Gutenberg

Kastanis, A. 2008: *Military History*, Athens: Hellenic Army Academy

Kontratou-Rassia, N. 2009: "The Battle of Marathon, minute by minute", *Elefterotypia* newsp., 3.12.2009

Kordatos, J. 1956: *A History of Ancient Greece*, Athens: 20th Century

Kormalis, A., 2010: *Fighting in the forefront of the Hellenes, the Athenians at Marathon…*, Athens: Pelasgos

Kourakis, N. 1985: *Law Enforcement: between the past and the future*, Athens/Komotini: Sakkoulas

Koutroumanis, D. 2004: "Communications and tele-communications in antiquity", *Military Review* (January)

Lambros, S.P., 1896: "The matathon race", *Hestia* newsp., 9.3.1896

Lygeros, N. 2010: "The Persian syndrome of Turkey", http://www.lygeros.org/5815-gr.html (retrieved 15.08.2010)

Mertzanis, A.J., 2010: *The Peloponnesian War*, Athens: Vergina

Nikolaou, Ch. 1987: "The Battle of Plataea (27 August 479 BC)", *Military Review* (February)

Nikolaou, Ch. 1988: "The naval battle of Salamis (September 480 BC)", *Military Review* (February)

Nikolaidou, E., 2003: *The Battle of Marathon*, Athens: Savvalas

Panagiotidis, E., 1927: "The Battle of Marathon", *Military Review* (October)

Panagopoulos, A. 1987: "Education in Dorian Crete and Sparta", *Archaeology* 25, p. 8-14

Paschalidis, J. 2006: "The psychological effect in ancient Greeks", *Military Review* (March)

Pelekidis, Ch. C., 1971: "From Marathon to Thermopylae and Paltaea", *History of Hellenic Nation*, v. 2, Athens: Ekdotiki, p. 280-296, 306-323

Petrakos, B. Ch., 1995: *Marathon*, Athens: Archaeological Society

Polakos, T. 2002: "Rhetoric and politics in Thucydides and Isocrates", in K. Voudouris (ed.), *Rhetoric, communication, politics, and Philosophy*, Athens: Ionia, p. 191-208

Sakellariou, M. 1971a: "The crystallization of Hellenic world" *History of Hellenic Nation*, v. 2, Athens: Ekdotiki, p. 16-65

Sakellariou, M. 1971b: "The flourishing of Hellenic world", ελληνισμού», *History of Hellenic Nation*, v. 2, Athens: Ekdotiki, p. 204-277

Soulis, M., 1972: "Miltiades at Marathon: a master of the art of war", *Military Review* (Februrary)

Spyropoulos, G., 2009: *The Steles of the heroes in the Battle of Marathon from Herodes Atticus' villa at Eva, Cynuria*, Athens: Kardamitsa

Spyropoulos, H., 1995: *Herodotus, Historiae*, Athens: Govostis

Steinhauer, G., 2000: *War in Ancient Greece*, Athens: Papadimas

Theodoratos, H. 2007: *The greatest battles in ancient Greek world*, Athens: Talos

Tzachos, E., 1994: "The Athenian trireme", *Military Review* (June)

Tsambazis, D., 1956: "The Battle of Marathon", *Military Review* (February)

Voutyropoulos, N., Νίκος 1996: "David's weapon", *Archaeology* 59 (June) 64-68

Zenakos, A., 2003: "The Battle of Marathon (490 BC)", *To Vima* newsp., 23.2.2003

Proceedings – Special Editions (in Greek)

Hellenic Parliament, *Argonaut campaign*. International Conference, Volos, 12-13 June 2008

Municipality of Marathon, *The Battle of Marathon 490 BC*, Proceedings of the 1st International Conference (June 2007)

The Battle of Marathon 490 BC, E-Historica, sp. ed. of *Eleftherotypia* newsp., nr. 232, 15.04.2004

Web Sources

http://users.thess.sch.gr/ipap/Ellinikos%20Politismos/maxes/marathonas.htm

http://www.army.gr/n/g/archive/history/marathon/index.shtm

http://el.wikipedia.org,

http://gov.exnet.gr/l/nomo-anatoliki-attiki/dimo-marathono/387-i-maxi-tou-marathona.pdf

http://www.athina984.gr/node/103515

http://www.tovima.gr/default.asp?pid=2&artied=149919&st=83&dt=23/2/2003#ixzz0oHiOJeDV

http://www.eie.gr/archaeologia/gr/02_DELTIA/Metroon.aspx

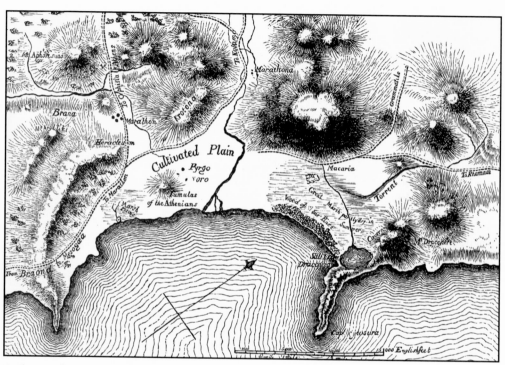

The area of Marathon according to Christopher Wordsworth's description (engraving, 19th cent.)

Index of Proper Names and Places

Some of the Reviews for the Book

I have studied your book with meticulous attention; it deserves it both for its theme and its origin. Indeed, the Battle of Marathon is not a simple, even significant, episode of the antiquity; but it has undoubtedly become a history-making event, which literally defined in a decisive way the anticipated evolution of the humanity; of the world civilization itself. Therefore, in essence, your intellectual effort discussed an event of immense historical dimensions; to treat it correctly demands, apart from the necessary mental integrity, both cultural capabilities and unusual qualities, devotion of significant free, but outside the normal duties, time, and certainly peculiar judgement and prudence. I am content because every current reader of your work can effortlessly realise the concurrence of such prerequisites. As regards its origin, it is particularly noteworthy that this book is a product of a man that has devoted his life in the ranks of the Armed Forces of our homeland; he served them with such dedication and effectiveness and success that, after completing all the career prospects, he has reached a distinguished position. As a citizen of Greece that loves his homeland, of which no other is major, I enjoy more security in the feeling that these hands, also professing exceptional spiritual-mental affluence, steer one of the most important rudders of our national defence and indeed in these so volatile times of the multidimensional both straightforward and shameless conspiracy against our territorial integrity and our national independence.

His Excellency the President of the Hellenich Republic (former)
Christos Sartzetakis

... As a university professor, I'm impressed by the discipline of this book, that is, its methodology, its technical characteristics, the illustrations, the argumentation, all those qualities that consist a work which, of course, addresses to every reader – and we should note that there is no such thing as an "average reader" (although we constantly use this term), because each reader is a single and unique personality. It is also a book with monographic claims, therefore I'd like to congratulate and thank the Chief of H.A.G.S., General Fragos, and to urge him to continue on the same path his course in the Army as well as in society in general.

Evangelos Venizelos
Minister of National Defence

...Mr. Fragoulis Fragos, with clarity, in great depth, illustrated from the very beginning, in his excellent book, what is locus communis in western civilization: the Battle of Marathon was the ark which safeguarded all the achievements and the great ideas that resulted from Athens and Athenian democracy, ideas and achievements of philosophical, political, social and artistic significance. General Fragos sees very clearly the conflict between two worlds, that happened 2500 years ago, at Marathon.

To my view, it is extremely important the fact that the author analyses the battle from a military point of view and simultaneously gives us a panoramic view of the ancient world, using an excellent analytic approach and combining the grace of the mythical explanation with the cynicism of history and the valuable gift of tradition: from the Marathon of myths he leads us to an impressive geopolitical analysis of Hellenism, and then to an even more detailed analysis of the 5th century BC, to its great advancement towards Athenian democracy. In the same time there is also, in an admirable style, the narration of the art of war...

Georgos Lianis
Member of the Hellenic Parliament, f. Minister

I liked the book for two reasons: apart from the fact that it is arranged and structured in an excellent way, it is also a useful and a beautiful book. It is poetic and moving; and it is marvellously illustrated. I happened to read it very quickly, in a rather difficult time. And it affected me in a peculiar way (which is very hard to achieve, since I am not a convenient person, due to my way of life): it structured my thoughts.

You are not obliged to read the book – because it is not an obligation, you are going to enjoy it. But you are obliged to spread it... introduce it to the schools, show it to as many persons as possible...

Liana Kanelli
Journalist, Member of the Hellenic Parliament

Based on primary sources, with ample bibliography and impressive illustrations, the book contains almost everything about Ancient Greece, reaching to the end of the conflict between the Greeks and the Persian with Alexander the Great. I would say, in certainty, that it could replace all the textbooks about Ancient Greece.

The main idea of the book, its thesis, are present in the last page, provided that one will read between the lines. It refers to the Persians, who never abandoned their designs against Greece, until Nemesis came, in the form and the military personality of Alexander the Great, the Macedonian king who destroyed the Persian empire. As General Fragos puts it, all those possessed by the "Persian syndrome" (needles to be more specific), by necessity end in destruction, because human values and the devotion to Freedom and Democracy finally triumph.

Sofia Voultepsi
Journalist, f. Member of the Hellenic Parliament

Fragoulis Fragos was born in Komotini, Thrace. Admitted in the Hellenic Military Academy, first among the 1st-Year Cadets in 1970; graduated head of his class in 1974 and was commissioned as Second Lieutenant in the Infantry. Served in the Hellenic Army Special Forces, he is still an active Parachutist. Graduate of the Hellenic Army War College and of the NATO Defence College (NADEFCOL). Accredited as Army Attaché and as Defence Attaché in the Hellenic Embassy in Ankara, Turkey, for six years. Assumed the duties of the Director of the Joint Military Intelligence Directorate, in 2004, during the Olympic Games in Athens. He served as Commanding General of Marine Force Battalion and Brigade, of Mechanised Infantry Division, of the Hellenic Army II Corps, and of the Hellenic First Army, and appointed as Hellenic Army Inspector General. In August 2009, appointed as Chief of the Hellenic Army General Staff.

He is a graduate of the Panteion University of Athens, where he also attended post-graduate courses and got two M.A. degrees. He got his Ph.D. in Geopolitics and Geostrategic at the Ionian University (Corfu). He speaks English, Turkish, and Russian.

He is married, with two children.